THE ART OF
SEEING THINGS

John Burroughs. Courtesy of the American Museum of Natural History.

THE ART OF
SEEING THINGS

Essays by John Burroughs

Edited by Charlotte Zoë Walker

Syracuse University Press

Copyright © 2001 by Syracuse University Press
Syracuse, New York 13244-5160
All Rights Reserved
First Edition 2001
01 02 03 04 05   6 5 4 3 2 1

The paper used in this publication meets the mini-
mum requirements of American National Standard
for Information Sciences—Permanence of Paper for
Printed Library Materials, ANSI Z39.48-1984. ∞™

Library of Congress Cataloging-in-Publication Data

Burroughs, John, 1837–1921
    The art of seeing things : essays / by John Burroughs ; edited by
Charlotte Zoë Walker. — 1st ed.
        p.   cm.
Includes bibliographical references.
ISBN 0-8156-2880-3 (alk. paper) — ISBN 0-8156-0678-8 (pbk. : alk.
paper)
        1. Natural history. I. Walker, Charlotte Zoë. II. Title.

QH81 .B914 2001
508—dc21

                                00-058331

Manufactured in the United States of America

To my parents,
Cmdr. Charles Henry Walker, U.S. Navy, Ret.,
and Helen Corinne Reynolds Walker,
and
to all our farming ancestors,
brought to life again in the writing of Burroughs,
and all those who carry on today
the natural ways of farming that
are so threatened in our time.

"Blessed is he whose youth was passed upon the farm."
John Burroughs, "Phases of Farm Life"

Charlotte Zoë Walker is a professor of English and Women's Studies at the State University of New York, College at Oneonta, where she developed a course called "Nature and the Self in Literature" in the early 1980s and has taught courses called "World Environmental Literature" and "Women and Nature." A fiction writer whose work is often informed by her interest in nature and the environment, she has published a novel, *Condor and Hummingbird* (1986 and 1987), and more than a dozen short stories, one of which was included in the *O. Henry Awards* for 1991. She is the editor of *Sharp Eyes: John Burroughs and American Nature Writing* (Syracuse University Press).

Contents

Contents

Illustrations

Acknowledgments

THE ESSAYS REPRINTED HERE are from the Riverby edition of the writings of John Burroughs, the first fourteen volumes of which were published in 1905, with subsequent volumes added as they appeared, so that in 1922 the Riverby edition included twenty-three volumes. (For details on the variant publications of John Burroughs's writings, see *Index to the Writings of John Burroughs* by William Perkins, published by the John Burroughs Association.) Also included here is a selection from *My Boyhood*, Burroughs's autobiography, published in 1922 by Doubleday, Page, with a memoir by Julian Burroughs.

Throughout this book, I have retained Burroughs's spelling and punctuation as representative of his time and context, making changes only when absolutely needed for clarity or when I deemed them to be actual misspellings or typos (Burroughs was not known for excellence in spelling). For instance, Burroughs tended to hyphenate words that were frequently joined together, such as *mother-bird;* most, but not all, of such hyphenations have been retained, with as much consistency as possible in an oeuvre that stretches more than sixty years. Burroughs also was rather inconsistent about paragraphing. On occasion, I have divided some very long paragraphs for the sake of readers more used to contemporary paragraphing.

Although *The Art of Seeing Things* is meant to stand on its own, it is also a companion to *Sharp Eyes: John Burroughs and American Nature Writing* (Syracuse University Press, 2000), the first major collection of scholarly essays on Burroughs, in which twenty-three distinguished scholars explore the many-faceted legacy of John Burroughs in a variety of ways: from appreciation to critical analysis, to comparison with other writers, to feminist critique. *The Art of Seeing Things* offers readers convenient access to some of the essays discussed in that collection. And readers of this volume may wish to turn to *Sharp Eyes* for discussion of some of Burroughs's writings included here.

Acknowledgments

My appreciation goes to all those who have helped me in my studies of John Burroughs, particularly the contributors to *Sharp Eyes: John Burroughs and American Nature Writing,* with special thanks to Edward Kanze, Robert Titus, and Frank Bergon for their expert advice. Thanks also to the State University of New York, College at Oneonta, the American Museum of Natural History, and the John Burroughs Association (JBA)—particularly Lisa Breslof, secretary, and Frank Knight, president. The American Museum of Natural History generously provided most of the photographs included in the book. Thanks also to the splendid staff at Syracuse University Press and to copyeditor extraordinaire Annie Barva.

Personal thanks to my husband, Roland Greefkes, for his loving support of this project; to Stan and Sue Walker for sharing their knowledge and love of nature literature; to Marian Walker Stauffer, David Méndez, Rebecca Méndez, Mark Evans, Rachel Méndez, and Ariel, Eli, Sam, and Zoë Méndez, and Cassius Oldenburg for carrying on values that John Burroughs would have been pleased to see and for making the earth a better place; finally, grateful appreciation to all our farming ancestors, from John Burroughs's time and earlier, whose lives Burroughs helps us understand a little better.

Introduction

IN THE LAST SUMMER of the twentieth century, two much-loved voices from a century earlier: as I was working on the selections for this book, reading once again through the lively abundance of John Burroughs's essays—greatly loved by readers of a century ago and now nearly forgotten—I began to be conscious of a hermit thrush in the woods near our house. Burroughs had a particular love for the haunting song of the hermit thrush and even inspired Walt Whitman to immortalize it in his poetic eulogy to Lincoln. At the end of days in which I had spent too much time indoors, I would especially enjoy my walk to the bench in the woods where I knew "my beautiful singer," as Burroughs called the hermit thrush, would soon be offering its serene, echoing song, immersed somehow in silence. In one of his essays, Burroughs mentions the hermit thrush as one of those birds of the deep woods "that only the privileged ones hear." It amazed me that I, who have never been an especially good observer, should be one of "the privileged ones" at just this time. Somehow, reading Burroughs had tuned my ear, I suppose, but it felt as if Burroughs himself had been teaching me. "You must have the bird in your heart, before you can find it in the bush," he says in "The Art of Seeing Things." As I walked up the path through the woods, I knew the hermit thrush was not waiting for me, but I had the joy of waiting for it. Whenever the song came, that voice so mysterious, solitary, and peaceful at the end of day, I felt that it was indeed a privilege to immerse myself in this project, to help this book to find its shape so that the words of "John O'Birds" might revive old friendships with his work and kindle new ones—perhaps inspire readers with the charm and wisdom of this writing from a century ago, and perhaps even encourage them to live more simply, to care for the earth, to question old assumptions, to practice the art of seeing things, or just to seek out the voice of the hermit thrush.

> The strain of the hermit thrush which floats down to me from the wooded heights above day after day at all hours, but more as the shades of night are falling—what does this pure, serene, exalted strain mean but that, in

Browning's familiar words, "God's in his heaven—All's right with the world!" ("Near Views of Wild Life," *Under the Maples,* 87)

The Art of Seeing Things celebrates the relevance and value of John Burroughs's work a century after the midpoint of his career. It celebrates also the pleasures and illuminations of renewing our acquaintance with a great literary naturalist at a time when the entire field of nature writing is experiencing its own renewal. This volume is a departure from previous anthologies of essays by Burroughs, which have reprinted mainly his most characteristic nature essays. Although his writings about nature remain at the heart of these selections, the emphasis is on perception—on the "art of seeing things." In addition, in the hope of helping to revive his stature as a significant figure in American literary history, I have attempted to broaden the general view of Burroughs through a selection of works that represent the surprising range of his writing.

During his lifetime, John Burroughs achieved a fame that seemed somehow incongruent with the simplicity of his life and the quiet nature of his work. He was born April 3, 1837, in Roxbury, New York, and died March 29, 1921, a few days before his eighty-fourth birthday. Having grown up in the Catskill Mountains of New York State—"the son of a farmer who was the son of a farmer who was again the son of a farmer," as he put it in his autobiography—Burroughs lived simply all his life. Even when he worked for the U.S. government in Washington, D.C., in the 1860s, he and his wife Ursula kept a cow on the common near the Capitol, an especially engaging fact for readers of the twenty-first century. And in his middle years, after he and Ursula moved back to New York State and built their home on the Hudson, he returned to making part of his living from fruit and vegetable crops. (By then, he was also earning a modest income from his writing.) Burroughs walked in nature with unceasing pleasure and perceptiveness, and wrote about it in informal, inviting, yet scientifically responsible essays. Somehow, his writing struck a chord with both critics and public, and his lifetime work of twenty-five books went through many printings. His writings on nature were placed in schools throughout the United States and became the model through which children learned to observe and appreciate nature; some schools were even named after him, a number of which still bear his name today.

Burroughs states in his autobiography, *My Boyhood,* that he saw himself as a lucky man: "My books are, in a way, a record of my life—that part of it that came to flower and fruit in my mind. You could reconstruct my days pretty well from these volumes. A writer who gleans his literary harvest in the fields and woods reaps mainly where he has sown himself." And, he continues, "My life has been a fortunate one; I was born under a lucky star. . . . I am pessimistic by night, but by day I am a confirmed optimist, and it is the days that have stamped my life. I have found this planet a good corner of the universe to live in and I am not in a hurry to exchange it for any other" (4–5).

No wonder that readers were and are still drawn to such a "fortunate" temperament and that they feel in his writing the encouragement of joy he addresses to his son in this opening of his autobiography. But the accomplishment of his writing and its great contribution to American nature literature are in the sunlit work itself and in the wooded, bird-attended path it helped create for other writers. Though his work has been neglected for many years, recent reassessments of Burroughs have accompanied a general revival of interest in nature writing, and his work is receiving new attention and appreciation.

Burroughs's approach to the nature essay was uniquely his own and yet far more influential than is commonly realized. The writers who extolled the great vistas of the West and the drama of wilderness explorations and adventures became the more celebrated representatives of American nature writing as the twentieth century developed. Yet Burroughs's quiet and close-to-home approach to experiencing, enjoying, and writing about nature began to gain renewed appreciation toward the end of the twentieth century. His essays are always close to human life, as well as to nature. They are artfully composed, though casual in style. The sensibility is a reliable one that the reader can trust for the carefulness of its observations and for the friendliness of its invitations to participate, appreciate, respect, and enjoy.

In the tradition of the personal essay, Burroughs builds his observations and interpretations at a comfortable pace, as if taking the reader on one of his countless walks. An observation is followed by interpretation, then by further illustration and observation, until a new light of understanding seems to come over writer and reader at the same time. Burroughs trusts the reader to have reached this enlarged understanding with him and typically does not belabor it in his conclusion. The essay will simply end—often with a graceful echo of the main topic rather than with a methodical reiteration.

In "The Spring Bird Procession," for instance, Burroughs expresses his pleasure at the spring migration of birds, but dwells particularly on the lost pleasure of the great migrations of the now extinct passenger pigeon: "In my boyhood the vast armies of the passenger pigeons were one of the most notable spring tokens. Often late in March, or early in April, the naked beechwoods would suddenly become blue with them, and vocal with their soft, childlike calls" (*Field and Study,* 1919, 3–4). He describes the last great migration of pigeons he witnessed, concluding, "The pigeons never came back. Death and destruction, in the shape of the greed and cupidity of man, were on their trail" (4). With typical forthrightness, he confesses to having killed the last passenger pigeon that he himself ever saw, "little dreaming that, so far as I was concerned, I was killing the last pigeon." He follows this confession with the rueful statement, "What man now in his old age who witnessed in youth that spring or fall festival and migration of the passenger pigeons would not hail it as one of the gladdest hours of his life if he could be permitted to witness it once more? It was such a spectacle of bounty, of joyous, copious animal life, of fertility in the air and in the wilderness, as to make the heart glad."

The essay might have ended here, but instead it goes on to describe the migrations of many other bird species and to speculate about their lives. The essay closes many pages later with the description of purple finches stealing cherry blossoms from his orchard. After his alarm that they might ruin his crop, he discovered that "they had only done a little of the much-needed thinning. Out of a cluster of six or eight blossoms they seldom took more than two or three, as if they knew precisely what they were about, and were intent on rendering me a service" (26). He does not spell out the contrast between the finches' moderation in thinning his cherry blossoms and the human "greed and cupidity" that drove the passenger pigeon to extinction, but leaves it to the reader to make the connection in his or her own understanding.

The Art of Seeing Things is ordered thematically rather than chronologically. The dates of publication are given, however, so that chronological comparison can be made. The book begins with a section on perception and the natural world. Perhaps Burroughs's greatest gift to the reader in a new century is his emphasis on the joys and gifts of an attentive eye and ear—a "heart that watches and receives," as Wordsworth put it. This theme is present in nearly all of Burroughs's work, but the first four essays of this book address themselves especially to the art of seeing things (or of hearing bird songs), as well as to the lively connection he makes between walking and perceiving. These essays especially devoted to perception are followed by several in which Burroughs's powers of perception are combined with his sense of the pleasures of the natural world: the art of seeing things demonstrated. "The Bluebird," from *Wake-Robin* (1871), is the earliest of Burroughs's essays represented here. "Speckled Trout" is a classic and much-loved Burroughs essay, conveying his love of fishing and his narrative as well as descriptive talents. "The Crow" is included for its charm and humor as well as for its perceptiveness.

The next section, "Farming and Rural Life," expresses Burroughs's life-long love of farming and of simple rural living. The lengthy "Phases of Farm Life" provides readers with a fascinating look at farming in the nine-teenth century based on Burroughs's childhood and adult experience. With "A Walk in the Fields," we are invited to experience a farmer's relationship to his fields and to the stone walls that he or those before him built there. A brief portion of a longer essay, "Our Rural Divinity," illustrates the ex-tent of Burroughs's fondness for cows, as he relates his experience of keep-ing a cow in the nation's capital.

The section "Far from Home" reveals the home-loving Burroughs as an engaging travel writer, with an excerpt from "In Green Alaska," Burroughs's record of the 1899 Harriman Expedition to Alaska. In this abbreviated se-lection from a lengthy report, I've attempted to include some of Bur-roughs's poignant comparisons of Alaska to his Hudson River Valley. This excerpt also contains an interesting moment in which Burroughs, writing for the Harriman Expedition, withholds comment but nevertheless conveys through pure description the sadness and desecration as totem poles are taken from a deserted Indian village for the purpose of display in the muse-ums represented by expedition scholars. Though Burroughs seldom ex-presses a greater sensitivity to Native American culture than was common in his time (see, however, the essay "Thoreau's Wildness" in this book for another apparently sympathetic view), this moment allows the reader a chance to consider the possibility that Burroughs is not merely reporting, but bearing witness.

The charming "A Hunt for the Nightingale" (slightly abridged) is a record of a visit to England in which Burroughs makes gentle fun of the English (some may find him a trifle jingoistic), but even more of "one crazy American" in search of a nightingale's song too late in the season. As with several other of the essays in this volume, "A Hunt for the Nightingale" re-veals the humorist in Burroughs.

In the section "Science and Field Study," we sample Burroughs's love of the scientific approach to nature, including his fascination with the ad-vances in science during his lifetime. In "The Animal and the Puzzle-Box," he compares the field naturalist's work to the laboratory animal experiments in ascendance at the time. "Reading the Book of Nature" is representative of a certain contrast in attitude in Burroughs's consciously scientific work with some of his own earlier and later writings about wildlife. That is, when he is speaking consciously about scientific reporting (as in "Reading the Book of Nature" or in the well-known "Real and Sham Natural History," which is not included here), Burroughs is assiduous to disassociate himself from anthropomorphic assumptions about animal behavior. However, in some of his own most engaging work, he indulges freely in often humorous comments about the motivations of the creatures he observes. There may be no actual conflict in these attitudes, but rather an assumption on Burroughs's part that the reader understands a certain poetic license has been taken in his essays; he gives his readers credit for understanding the differences between such stylistic enjoyments and a kind of nature writing that ignores science for the sake of popular sentimentality. Indeed, in one of these essays, Burroughs points out that the best observer of nature is both scientist and poet. (These issues, by the way, are discussed in *Sharp Eyes: John Burroughs and American Nature Writing,* in essays by Ralph Lutts, Elizabeth Donaldson, Robert Titus, and others.)

Though Burroughs was not known as an active conservationist, readers of his collected works will find many distinct moments of environmental awareness. For instance, the selection from "In Green Alaska" in this volume shows Burroughs quietly horrified by the abundance of dead salmon at a cannery. And in "Wild Life about my Cabin," he chides the hunter who will have "only a dead duck," whereas Burroughs himself will have "a live duck with whistling wings, cleaving the air northward." The section "Conservation and Environmental Concerns" specifically highlights Burroughs's awareness of environmental issues (as discussed in Frank Bergon's essay "Sensitive to the Verge of the Horizon" in *Sharp Eyes*) and includes "The Ways of Sportsmen," a passage from "A Strenuous Holiday," and his sad remembrance of the extinct passenger pigeon in "The Spring Bird Procession."

As a writer and literary scholar myself, I have taken particular pleasure in discovering Burroughs's literary accomplishment. Not only is he an engaging poet (two of his lighter poems can be found like buried treasure in essays in this book, and his more serious poem "Waiting" closes the book), but he is an astute literary critic and was himself devoted to the art of writing. In Julian Burroughs's memoir about his father, published with Burroughs's autobiography *My Boyhood,* he emphasizes his father's devotion to writing: "With what eagerness he went at his writing! For sixty years and over he found his greatest joy in his craft—as he once wrote me, 'There is no joy like it, when sap runs there is no fun like writing.'" In "An Egotistical Chapter," which closes the section "On Writers and Writing," Burroughs speaks about his craft. Only a sampling of his writing about other literary figures is included here, but it gives an inkling of how perceptively he could write about writing: a wonderfully insightful discussion of Thoreau's "wildness," a whimsical comparison of Emerson to the pine tree, and, most important, some substantial excerpts from his 1896 book on Walt Whitman.

John Burroughs's understanding and advocacy of Whitman—his warm defense of Whitman against the harsh criticism directed at him and his poetry in the nineteenth century—are moving in themselves. Even more, however, Burroughs's writing on Whitman reveals the best of his own mind. Burroughs's essays occasionally disappoint the contemporary reader by failing to rise above some of the social and racial assumptions of his time, even though he fails in this regard no more than most of the canonical writers of the nineteenth and early twentieth century. When he writes of Whitman, however, Burroughs seems to shake off the limitations of cultural conditioning as he defends the vision and the poetry of his friend and mentor. In stating what Whitman stands for and what he rejects, Burroughs expresses many of his own spiritual and egalitarian values. Through his work on Whitman, as in his writings on religion, we see how radical Burroughs actually was, not merely for his own time, but in relation to much of the twentieth century as well. Burroughs's friendship with Whitman was surely one of the most powerful and ennobling influences of his life. Their friendship is, in fact, one of the most neglected and most interesting significant literary friendships in our history.

The next section, "Religion and Philosophy of Life," includes "The Faith of a Naturalist" and "An Outlook upon Life," two essays on Burroughs's religious and philosophical views that further confirm his unorthodox philosophy—rooted in American transcendentalism and romanticism, nurtured by changes in science and by Burroughs's lifelong immersion in nature, and expressed in his unique voice. Space does not allow a larger selection of his writings on religion and philosophy, but it is important to observe that he wrote extensively on these topics, especially in his books *The Light of Day, The Breath of Life,* and *Accepting the Universe,* with scattered essays in many of his other books as well. This fascinating aspect of Burroughs's work is deserving of more attention and makes thought-provoking reading at the beginning of a new millennium, just as it did when he wrote these essays. The more personal essay "An Outlook upon Life" is an expression not only of Burroughs's philosophical outlook, but also of his "prescription" for living a good life.

The volume closes with the section on autobiography. "Wild Life about My Cabin" would at first thought seem to be better grouped with Burroughs's nature essays or with his works on simple rural living or even among his works that convey a conservationist awareness, for in it he clearly takes sides with the birds over their human predators. However, it is also an essay about Burroughs's personal life and about the yearnings that led to the building of Slabsides. Beyond that, with its intermingling of personal life and nature observation, "Wild Life about My Cabin" is an excellent example of how, as Burroughs himself remarks in *My Boyhood,* all of his writings are in some way about his life. The final prose selection in this volume is, indeed, an excerpt from that engaging autobiography, *My Boyhood.* I find it emblematic of the undeserved neglect of Burroughs's writing in the past half-century or more that this charming and historically interesting autobiography should remain out of print, whereas the autobiography of his friend John Muir is in print and available to readers. In a time when autobiographies and memoirs are being published at an unprecedented rate and taught in universities, *My Boyhood* makes a valuable contribution to the genre. This work is also interesting as an instance of what in my teaching I have called "dual autobiography," in which the voices of two family members are interwoven. The person addressed in *My Boyhood* is Burroughs's son Julian, and the published version of the book also includes Julian's own perceptive memoir about his father.

Throughout this collection, I have endeavored to bring into the foreground writings that convey Burroughs's exuberance in sharing his appreciation of the joys and beauties of life. He is everywhere eloquent in this regard, but particularly in his most autobiographical writings. In many ways a prescriptive as well as a descriptive writer, Burroughs is eager to share with his readers the joys that he has found in living simply and close to nature, and he offers an alternative to materialistic lifestyles. There are moments in his writing—as when he complains about greed, faddishness, and a frenetic devotion to money for its own sake—when he seems to be speaking to our own time as well as to his. His exuberant and hopeful message is worth taking to heart.

Part One
Perception and the Natural World

The Art of Seeing Things

I DO NOT PURPOSE to attempt to tell my reader how to see things, but only to talk about the art of seeing things, as one might talk of any other art. One might discourse about the art of poetry, or of painting, or of oratory, without any hope of making one's readers or hearers poets or painters or orators.

The science of anything may be taught or acquired by study; the art of it comes by practice or inspiration. The art of seeing things is not something that may be conveyed in rules and precepts; it is a matter vital in the eye and ear, yea, in the mind and soul, of which these are the organs. I have as little hope of being able to tell the reader how to see things as I would have in trying to tell him how to fall in love or to enjoy his dinner. Either he does or he does not, and that is about all there is of it. Some people seem born with eyes in their heads, and others with buttons or painted marbles, and no amount of science can make the one equal to the other in the art of seeing things. The great mass of mankind are, in this respect, like the rank and file of an army: they fire vaguely in the direction of the enemy, and if they hit, it is more a matter of chance than of accurate aim. But here and there is the keen-eyed observer; he is the sharpshooter; his eye selects and discriminates, his purpose goes to the mark.

Even the successful angler seems born, and not made; he appears to know instinctively the ways of trout. The secret is, no doubt, love of the sport. Love sharpens the eye, the ear, the touch; it quickens the feet, it steadies the hand, it arms against the wet and the cold. What we love to do, that we do well. To know is not all; it is only half. To love is the other half. Wordsworth's poet was contented if he might enjoy the things which others understood. This is generally the attitude of the young and of the poetic nature. The man of science, on the other hand, is contented if he may understand the things that others enjoy: that is his enjoyment. Contemplation

From *Leaf and Tendril,* 1908.

John Burroughs beneath rock ledge. Courtesy of the American Museum of Natural History.

and absorption for the one; investigation and classification for the other. We probably all have, in varying degrees, one or the other of these ways of enjoying Nature: either the sympathetic and emotional enjoyment of her which the young and the artistic and the poetic temperament have, or the enjoyment through our knowing faculties afforded by natural science, or, it may be, the two combined, as they certainly were in such a man as Tyndall.

But nothing can take the place of love. Love is the measure of life: only so far as we love do we really live. The variety of our interests, the width of our sympathies, the susceptibilities of our hearts—if these do not measure our lives, what does? As the years go by, we are all of us more or less subject to two dangers, the danger of petrifaction and the danger of putrefaction; either that we shall become hard and callous, crusted over with customs and conventions till no new ray of light or of joy can reach us, or that we shall become lax and disorganized, losing our grip upon the real and vital sources of happiness and power. Now, there is no preservative and antiseptic, nothing that keeps one's heart young, like love, like sympathy, like giving one's self with enthusiasm to some worthy thing or cause.

If I were to name the three most precious resources of life, I should say books, friends, and nature; and the greatest of these, at least the most constant and always at hand, is nature. Nature we have always with us, an inexhaustible storehouse of that which moves the heart, appeals to the mind, and fires the imagination—health to the body, a stimulus to the intellect, and joy to the soul. To the scientist Nature is a storehouse of facts, laws, processes; to the artist she is a storehouse of pictures; to the poet she is a storehouse of images, fancies, a source of inspiration; to the moralist she is a storehouse of precepts and parables; to all she may be a source of knowledge and joy.

II

There is nothing in which people differ more than in their powers of observation. Some are only half alive to what is going on around them. Others, again, are keenly alive: their intelligence, their powers of recognition, are in full force in eye and ear at all times. They see and hear everything, whether it directly concerns them or not. They never pass unseen a familiar face on the interesting street; they are never oblivious of any feature or sound or object in the earth or sky about them. Their power of attention is always on the alert, not by conscious effort, but by natural habit and disposition. Their perceptive faculties may be said to be always on duty. They turn to the outward world a more highly sensitized mind than other people. The things that pass before them are caught and individualized instantly. If they visit new countries, they see the characteristic features of the people and scenery at once. The impression is never blurred or confused. Their powers of observation suggest the sight and scent of wild animals; only, whereas it is fear that sharpens the one, it is love and curiosity that sharpens the other. The mother turkey with her brood sees the hawk when it is a mere speck against the sky; she is, in her solicitude for her young, thinking of hawks, and is on her guard against them. Fear makes keen her eye. The hunter does not see the hawk till his attention is thus called to it by the turkey, because his interests are not endangered; but he outsees the wild creatures of the plain and mountain—the elk, the antelope, and the mountain-sheep—he makes it his business to look for them, and his eyes carry farther than do theirs.

We may see coarsely and vaguely, as most people do, noting only masses and unusual appearances, or we may see finely and discriminatingly, taking in the minute and the specific. In a collection of stuffed birds, the other day, I observed that a wood thrush was mounted as in the act of song, its open beak pointing straight to the zenith. The taxidermist had not seen truly. The thrush sings with its beak but slightly elevated. Who has not seen a red squirrel or a gray squirrel running up and down the trunk of a tree? But probably very few have noticed that the position of the hind feet is the reverse in the one case from what it is in the other. In descending they are extended to the rear, the toenails hooking to the bark, checking and controlling the fall. In most pictures the feet are shown well drawn up under the body in both cases.

People who discourse pleasantly and accurately about the birds and flowers and external nature generally are not invariably good observers. In their walks do they see anything they did not come out to see? Is there any spontaneous or unpremeditated seeing? Do they make discoveries? Any bird or creature may be hunted down, any nest discovered, if you lay siege to it; but to find what you are not looking for, to catch the shy winks and gestures on every side, to see all the byplay going on around you, missing no significant note or movement, penetrating every screen with your eye-beams — that is to be an observer; that is to have "an eye practiced like a blind man's touch," — a touch that can distinguish a white horse from a black — a detective eye that reads the faintest signs. When Thoreau was at Cape Cod, he noticed that the horses there had a certain muscle in their hips inordinately developed by reason of the insecure footing in the ever-yielding sand. Thoreau's vision at times fitted things closely. During some great fete in Paris, the Empress Eugénie and Queen Victoria were both present. A reporter noticed that when the royal personages came to sit down, Eugénie looked behind her before doing so, to see that the chair was really there, but Victoria seated herself without the backward glance, knowing there must be a seat ready: there always had been, and there always would be, for her. The correspondent inferred that the incident showed the difference between born royalty and hastily made royalty. I wonder how many persons in that vast assembly made this observation; probably very few. It denoted a gift for seeing things.

If our powers of observation were quick and sure enough, no doubt we should see through most of the tricks of the sleight-of-hand man. He fools us because his hand is more dexterous than our eye. He captures our attention, and then commands us to see only what he wishes us to see.

In the field of natural history, things escape us because the actors are small, and the stage is very large and more or less veiled and obstructed. The movement is quick across a background that tends to conceal rather than expose it. In the printed page the white paper plays quite as important a part as the type and the ink; but the book of nature is on a different plan: the page rarely presents a contrast of black and white, or even black and brown, but only of similar tints, gray upon gray, green upon green, or drab upon brown.

By a close observer I do not mean a minute, cold-blooded specialist—

> a fingering slave
> One who would peep and botanize
> Upon his mother's grave—

but a man who looks closely and steadily at nature, and notes the individual features of tree and rock and field, and allows no subtle flavor of the night or day, of the place and the season, to escape him. His senses are so delicate that in his evening walks he feels the warm and the cool streaks in the air, his nose detects the most fugitive odors, his ears the most furtive sounds. As he stands musing in the April twilight, he hears that fine, elusive stir and rustle made by the angleworms reaching out from their holes for leaves and grasses; he hears the whistling wings of the woodcock as it goes swiftly by him in the dusk; he hears the call of the killdeer come down out of the March sky; he hears far above him in the early morning the squeaking cackle of the arriving blackbirds pushing north; he hears the soft, pro-longed, lulling call of the little owl in the cedars in the early spring twilight; he hears at night the roar of the distant waterfall, and the rumble of the train miles across the country when the air is "hollow"; before a storm he notes how distant objects stand out and are brought near on those brilliant days that we call "weather-breeders." When the mercury is at zero or lower, he notes how the passing trains hiss and simmer as if the rails or wheels were red-hot. He reads the subtle signs of the weather. The stars at night forecast the coming day to him; the clouds at evening and at morning are a sign. He knows there is the wet-weather diathesis and the dry-weather diathesis, or, as Goethe said, water affirmative and water negative, and he interprets the symptoms accordingly. He is keenly alive to all outward im-pressions. When he descends from the hill in the autumn twilight, he notes the cooler air of the valley like a lake about him; he notes how, at other sea-sons, the cooler air at times settles down between the mountains like a vast body of water, as shown by the level line of the fog or the frost upon the trees.

The modern man looks at nature with an eye of sympathy and love where the earlier man looked with an eye of fear and superstition. Hence he sees more closely and accurately; science has made his eye steady and clear.

To a hasty traveler through the land, the farms and country homes all seem much alike, but to the people born and reared there, what a difference! They have read the fine print that escapes the hurried eye and that is so full of meaning. Every horizon line, every curve in hill or valley, every tree and rock and spring run, every turn in the road and vista in the landscape, has its special features and makes its own impression.

Scott wrote in his journal: "Nothing is so tiresome as walking through some beautiful scene with a minute philosopher, a botanist, or a pebble gatherer, who is eternally calling your attention from the grand features of the natural picture to look at grasses and chuckie-stanes." No doubt Scott's large, generous way of looking at things kindles the imagination and touches the sentiments more than does this minute way of the specialist. The nature that Scott gives us is like the air and the water that all may absorb, while what the specialist gives us is more like some particular element or substance that only the few can appropriate. But Scott had his specialties, too, the specialties of the sportsman: he was the first to see the hare's eyes as she sat in her form, and he knew the ways of grouse and pheasants and trout. The ideal observer turns the enthusiasm of the sportsman into the channels of natural history, and brings home a finer game than ever fell to shot or bullet. He too has an eye for the fox and the rabbit and the migrating waterfowl, but he sees them with loving and not with murderous eyes.

III

So far as seeing things is an art, it is the art of keeping your eyes and ears open. The art of nature is all in the direction of concealment. The birds, the animals, all the wild creatures, for the most part try to elude your observation. The art of the bird is to hide her nest; the art of the game you are in quest of is to make itself invisible. The flower seeks to attract the bee and the moth by its color and perfume, because they are of service to it; but I presume it would hide from the excursionists and the picnickers if it could, because they extirpate it.

Power of attention and a mind sensitive to outward objects, in these lies the secret of seeing things. Can you bring all your faculties to the front, like a house with many faces at the doors and windows; or do you live retired within yourself, shut up in your own meditations? The thinker puts all the powers of his mind in reflection: the observer puts all the powers of his mind in perception; every faculty is directed outward; the whole mind sees through the eye and hears through the ear. He has an objective turn of mind as opposed to a subjective. A person with the latter turn of mind sees little. If you are occupied with your own thoughts, you may go through a museum of curiosities and observe nothing.

Of course one's powers of observation may be cultivated as well as anything else. The senses of seeing and hearing may be quickened and trained as well as the sense of touch. Blind persons come to be marvelously acute in their powers of touch. Their feet find the path and keep it. They come to know the lay of the land through this sense, and recognize the roads and surfaces they have once traveled over. Helen Keller reads your speech by putting her hand upon your lips, and is thrilled by the music of an instrument through the same sense of touch. The perceptions of schoolchildren should be trained as well as their powers of reflection and memory. A teacher in Connecticut, Miss Aiken—whose work on mind-training I commend to teachers—has hit upon a simple and ingenious method of doing this. She has a revolving black board upon which she writes various figures, numbers, words, sentences, which she exposes to the view of the class for one or two or three seconds as the case may be, and then asks them to copy or repeat what was written. In time they become astonishingly quick, especially the girls, and can take in a multitude of things at a glance. Detectives, I am told, are trained after a similar method; a man is led quickly by a show-window, for instance, and asked to name and describe the object he saw there. Life itself is of course more or less a school of this kind, but the power of concentrated attention in most persons needs stimulating. Here comes in the benefit of manual-training schools. To *do* a thing, to make something, the powers of the mind must be focused. A boy in building a boat will get something that all the books in the world cannot give him. The concrete, the definite, the discipline of real things, the educational values that lie here, are not enough appreciated.

IV

The book of nature is like a page written over or printed upon with different-sized characters and in many different languages, interlined and cross-lined, and with a great variety of marginal notes and references. There is coarse print and fine print; there are obscure signs and hieroglyphics. We all read the large type more or less appreciatively, but only the students and lovers of nature read the fine lines and the footnotes. It is a book which he reads best who goes most slowly or even tarries long by the way. He who runs may read some things. We may take in the general features of sky,

plain, and river from the express train, but only the pedestrian, the saunterer, with eyes in his head and love in his heart, turns every leaf and peruses
every line. One man sees only the migrating water-fowls and the larger
birds of the air; another sees the passing kinglets and hurrying warblers as
well. For my part, my delight is to linger long over each page of this marvelous record, and to dwell fondly upon its most obscure text.

I take pleasure in noting the minute things about me. I am interested
even in the ways of the wild bees, and in all the little dramas and tragedies
that occur in field and wood. One June day, in my walk, as I crossed a
rather dry, high-lying field, my attention was attracted by small mounds of
fresh earth all over the ground, scarcely more than a handful in each. On
looking closely, I saw that in the middle of each mound there was a hole not
quite so large as a lead-pencil. Now, I had never observed these mounds before, and my curiosity was aroused. "Here is some fine print," I said, "that I
have overlooked."

So I set to work to try to read it; I waited for a sign of life. Presently I saw
here and there a bee hovering about over the mounds. It looked like the
honeybee, only less pronounced in color and manner. One of them alighted
on one of the mounds near me, and was about to disappear in the hole in
the centre when I caught it in my hand. Though it stung me, I retained it
and looked it over, and in the process was stung several times; but the pain
was slight. I saw it was one of our native wild bees, cousin to the leafrollers,
that build their nests under stones and in decayed fence-rails. (In Packard I
found it described under the name of *Andrena*.) Then I inserted a small
weed-stalk into one of the holes, and, with a little trowel I carried, proceeded to dig out the nest. The hole was about a foot deep; at the bottom of
it I found a little semitransparent, membranous sac or cell, a little larger
than that of the honeybee; in this sac was a little pellet of yellow pollen—a
loaf of bread for the young grub when the egg should have hatched. I explored other nests and found them all the same. This discovery was not a
great addition to my sum of natural knowledge, but it was something. Now
when I see the signs in a field, I know what they mean—they indicate the
tiny earthen cradles of *Andrena*.

Near by I chanced to spy a large hole in the turf, with no mound of soil
about it. I could put the end of my little finger into it. I peered down, and
saw the gleam of two small, beadlike eyes. I knew it to be the den of the
wolf-spider. Was she waiting for some blundering insect to tumble in? I say
she, because the real ogre among the spiders is the female. The male is small
and of little consequence. A few days later I paused by this den again and

saw the members of the ogress scattered about her own door. Had some insect Jack the Giant-Killer been there, or had a still more formidable ogress, the sand-hornet, dragged her forth and carried away her limbless body to her den in the bank?

What the wolf-spider does with the earth it excavates in making its den is a mystery. There is no sign of it anywhere about. Does it force its way down by pushing the soil to one side and packing it there firmly? The entrance to the hole usually has a slight rim or hem to keep the edge from crumbling in.

As it happened, I chanced upon another interesting footnote that very day. I was on my way to a muck swamp in the woods, to see if the showy lady's-slipper was in bloom. Just on the margin of the swamp, in the deep shade of the hemlocks, my eye took note of some small, unshapely creature crawling hurriedly over the ground. I stooped down, and saw it was some large species of moth just out of its case, and in a great hurry to find a suitable place in which to hang itself up and give its wings a chance to unfold before the air dried them. I thrust a small twig in its way, which it instantly seized upon. I lifted it gently, carried it to drier ground, and fixed the stick in the fork of a tree, so that the moth hung free a few feet from the ground. Its body was distended nearly to the size of one's little finger, and surmounted by wings that were so crumpled and stubby that they seemed quite rudimentary. The creature evidently knew what it wanted, and knew the importance of haste. Instantly these rude, stubby wings began to grow. It was a slow process, but one could see the change from minute to minute. As the wings expanded, the body contracted. By some kind of pumping arrangement air was being forced from a reservoir in the one into the tubes of the other. The wings were not really growing, as they at first seemed to be, but they were unfolding and expanding under this pneumatic pressure from the body. In the course of about half an hour the process was completed, and the winged creature hung there in all its full-fledged beauty. Its color was checked black and white like a loon's back, but its name I know not. My chief interest in it, aside from the interest we feel in any new form of life, arose from the creature's extreme anxiety to reach a perch where it could unfold its wings. A little delay would doubtless have been fatal to it. I wonder how many human geniuses are hatched whose wings are blighted by some accident or untoward circumstance. Or do the wings of genius always unfold, no matter what the environment may be?

One seldom takes a walk without encountering some of this fine print on nature's page. Now it is a little yellowish-white moth that spreads itself upon the middle of a leaf as if to imitate the droppings of birds; or it is the young cicadas working up out of the ground, and in the damp, cool places building little chimneys or tubes above the surface to get more warmth and hasten their development; or it is a wood-newt gorging a tree-cricket, or a small snake gorging the newt, or a bird song with some striking peculiarity —a strange defect, or a rare excellence. Now it is a shrike impaling his victim, or blue jays mocking and teasing a hawk and dropping quickly into the branches to avoid his angry blows, or a robin hustling a cuckoo out of the tree where her nest is, or a vireo driving away a cowbird, or the partridge blustering about your feet till her young are hidden. One October morning I was walking along the road on the edge of the woods, when I came into a gentle shower of butternuts; one of them struck my hat-brim. I paused and looked about me; here one fell, there another, yonder a third. There was no wind blowing, and I wondered what was loosening the butternuts. Turning my attention to the top of the tree, I soon saw the explanation: a red squirrel was at work gathering his harvest. He would seize a nut, give it a twist, when down it would come; then he would dart to another and another. Farther along I found where he had covered the ground with chestnut burs; he could not wait for the frost and the winds; did he know that the burs would dry and open upon the ground, and that the bitter covering of the butternuts would soon fall away from the nut?

There are three things that perhaps happen near me each season that I have never yet seen: — the toad casting its skin, the snake swallowing its young, and the larvae of the moth and butterfly constructing their shrouds. It is a mooted question whether or not the snake does swallow its young, but if there is no other good reason for it, may they not retreat into their mother's stomach to feed? How else are they to be nourished? That the moth larva can weave its own cocoon and attach it to a twig seems more incredible. Yesterday, in my walk, I found a firm, silver-gray cocoon, about two inches long and shaped like an Egyptian mummy (probably *Promethea*), suspended from a branch of a bush by a narrow, stout ribbon twice as long as itself. The fastening was woven around the limb, upon which it turned as if it grew there. I would have given something to have seen the creature perform this feat, and then incase itself so snugly in the silken shroud at the end of this tether. By swinging free, its firm, compact case was in no danger from woodpeckers, as it might have been if resting directly upon a branch or tree-trunk. Near by was the cocoon of another species (*Cecropia*) that was fastened directly to the limb; but this was vague, loose, and much more involved and netlike. I have seen the downy woodpecker assaulting one of these cocoons, but its yielding surface and webby interior seemed to puzzle and baffle him.

I am interested even in the way each climbing plant or vine goes up the pole, whether from right to left, or from left to right—that is, with the hands of a clock or against them—whether it is under the law of the great cyclonic storms of the northern hemisphere, which all move against the hands of a clock, or in the contrary direction, like the cyclones in the southern hemisphere. I take pleasure in noting every little dancing whirlwind of a summer day that catches up the dust or the leaves before me, and every little funnel-shaped whirlpool in the swollen stream or river, whether or not they spin from right to left or the reverse. If I were in the southern hemisphere, I am sure I should note whether these things were under the law of its cyclones in this respect or under the law of ours. As a rule, our twining plants and toy whirlwinds copy our revolving storms and go against the hands of the clock. But there are exceptions. While the bean, the bittersweet, the morning-glory, and others go up from left to right, the hop, the wild buckwheat, and some others go up from right to left. Most of our forest trees show a tendency to wind one way or the other, the hard woods going in one direction, and the hemlocks and pines and cedars and butternuts and chestnuts in another. In different localities, or on different geological formations, I find these directions reversed. I recall one instance in the case of a hemlock six or seven inches in diameter, where this tendency to twist had come out of the grain, as it were, and shaped the outward form of the tree, causing it to make, in an ascent of about thirty feet, one complete revolution about a larger tree close to which it grew. On a smaller scale I have seen the same thing in a pine.

Persons lost in the woods or on the plains, or traveling at night, tend, I believe, toward the left. The movements of men and women, it is said, differ in this respect, one sex turning to the right and the other to the left.

I had lived in the world more than fifty years before I noticed a peculiarity about the rays of light one often sees diverging from an opening, or a series of openings, in the clouds, namely, that they are like spokes in a wheel, the hub, or centre, of which appears to be just there in the vapory masses, instead of being, as is really the case, nearly ninety-three millions of miles beyond. The beams of light that come through cracks or chinks in a wall do not converge in this way, but to the eye run parallel to one another. There is another fact: this fan-shaped display of converging rays is always immediately in front of the observer; that is, exactly between him and the sun, so that the central spoke or shaft in his front is always perpendicular. You cannot see this fan to the right or left of the sun, but only between you and it. Hence, as in the case of the rainbow, no two persons see exactly the same rays.

The eye sees what it has the means of seeing, and its means of seeing are in proportion to the love and desire behind it. The eye is informed and sharpened by the thought. My boy sees ducks on the river where and when I cannot, because at certain seasons he thinks ducks and dreams ducks. One season my neighbor asked me if the bees had injured my grapes. I said, "No; the bees never injure my grapes."

"They do mine," he replied; " they puncture the skin for the juice, and at times the clusters are covered with them."

"No," I said, "it is not the bees that puncture the skin; it is the birds."

"What birds?"

"The orioles."

"But I haven't seen any orioles," he rejoined.

"We have," I continued, "because at this season we think orioles; we have learned by experience how destructive these birds are in the vineyard, and we are on the lookout for them; our eyes and ears are ready for them."

If we think birds, we shall see birds wherever we go; if we think arrowheads, as Thoreau did, we shall pick up arrowheads in every field. Some people have an eye for four-leaved clovers; they see them as they walk hastily over the turf, for they already have them in their eyes. I once took a walk with the late Professor Eaton of Yale. He was just then specially interested in the mosses, and he found them, all kinds, everywhere. I can see him yet, every few minutes upon his knees, adjusting his eye-glasses before some rare specimen. The beauty he found in them, and pointed out to me, kindled my enthusiasm also. I once spent a summer day at the mountain home of a well-known literary woman and editor. She lamented the absence of birds about her house. I named a half-dozen or more I had heard or seen in her trees within an hour—the indigo-bird, the purple finch, the yellow-bird, the veery thrush, the red-eyed vireo, the song sparrow.

"Do you mean to say you have seen or heard all these birds while sitting here on my porch?" she inquired.

"I really have," I said.

"I do not see them or hear them," she replied, "and yet I want to very much."

"No," said I; "you only *want to want* to see and hear them."

You must have the bird in your heart before you can find it in the bush.

I was sitting in front of a farmhouse one day in company with the local

Nimrod. In a maple tree in front of us I saw the great crested flycatcher. I called the hunter's attention to it, and asked him if he had ever seen that bird before. No, he had not; it was a new bird to him. But he probably had seen it scores of times—seen it without regarding it. It was not the game he was in quest of, and his eye heeded it not.

Human and artificial sounds and objects thrust themselves upon us; they are within our sphere, so to speak: but the life of nature we must meet halfway; it is shy, withdrawn, and blends itself with a vast neutral background. We must be initiated; it is an order the secrets of which are well guarded.

Sharp Eyes

NOTING HOW one eye seconds and reinforces the other, I have often amused myself by wondering what the effect would be if one could go on opening eye after eye to the number say of a dozen or more. What would he see? Perhaps not the invisible — not the odors of flowers or the fever germs in the air — not the infinitely small of the microscope or the infinitely distant of the telescope. This would require not more eyes so much as an eye constructed with more and different lenses; but would he not see with augmented power within the natural limits of vision? At any rate, some persons seem to have opened more eyes than others, they see with such force and distinctness; their vision penetrates the tangle and obscurity where that of others fails like a spent or impotent bullet. How many eyes did Gilbert White open? How many did Henry Thoreau? How many did Audubon? How many does the hunter, matching his sight against the keen and alert sense of a deer or a moose, or a fox or a wolf? Not outward eyes, but inward. We open another eye whenever we see beyond the first general features or outlines of things — whenever we grasp the special details and characteristic markings that this mask covers. Whenever you have learned to discriminate the birds, or the plants, or the geological features of a country, it is as if new and keener eyes were added.

Of course one must not only see sharply, but read aright what he sees. The facts in the life of Nature that are transpiring about us are like written words that the observer is to arrange into sentences. Or the writing is in cipher and he must furnish the key. A female oriole was one day observed very much preoccupied under a shed where the refuse from the horse stable was thrown. She hopped about among the barn fowls, scolding them sharply when they came too near her. The stable, dark and cavernous, was just beyond. The bird, not finding what she wanted outside, boldly ventured into the stable, and was presently captured by the farmer. What did

---

From *Locusts and Wild Honey,* 1879.

she want? was the query. What, but a horsehair for her nest which was in an apple tree near by; and she was so bent on having one that I have no doubt she would have tweaked one out of the horse's tail had he been in the stable. Later in the season I examined her nest and found it sewed through and through with several long horsehairs, so that the bird persisted in her search till the hair was found.

Little dramas and tragedies and comedies, little characteristic scenes, are always being enacted in the lives of the birds, if our eyes are sharp enough to see them. Some clever observer saw this little comedy played among some English sparrows and wrote an account of it in his newspaper; it is too good not to be true: A male bird brought out his box a large, fine goose feather, which is a great find for a sparrow and much coveted. After he had deposited his prize and chattered his gratulations over it, he went away in quest of his mate. His next-door neighbor, a female bird, seeing her chance, quickly slipped in and seized the feather, — and here the wit of the bird came out, for instead of carrying it into her own box she flew with it to a near tree and hid it in a fork of the branches, then went home, and, when her neighbor returned with his mate, was innocently employed about her own affairs. The proud male, finding his feather gone, came out of his box in a high state of excitement, and with wrath in his manner and accusation on his tongue, rushed into the cot of the female. Not finding his goods and chattels there as he had expected, he stormed around a while, abusing everybody in general and his neighbor in particular, and then went away as if to repair the loss. As soon as he was out of sight, the shrewd thief went and brought the feather home and lined her own domicile with it.

I was much amused one summer day in seeing a bluebird feeding her young one in the shaded street of a large town. She had captured a cicada or harvest-fly, and after bruising it a while on the ground flew with it to a tree and placed it in the beak of the young bird. It was a large morsel, and the mother seemed to have doubts of her chick's ability to dispose of it, for she stood near and watched its efforts with great solicitude. The young bird struggled valiantly with the cicada, but made no headway in swallowing it, when the mother took it from him and flew to the sidewalk, and proceeded to break and bruise it more thoroughly. Then she again placed it in his beak, and seemed to say, "There, try it now," and sympathized so thoroughly with his efforts that she repeated many of his motions and contortions. But the great fly was unyielding, and, indeed, seemed ridiculously disproportioned to the beak that held it. The young bird fluttered and fluttered, and screamed, "I'm stuck, I'm stuck," till the anxious parent again seized the morsel and carried it to an iron railing, where she came down upon it for the space of a minute with all the force and momentum her beak could command. Then she offered it to her young a third time, but with the same result as before, except that this time the bird dropped it; but she was to the ground as soon as the cicada was, and taking it in her beak flew some distance to a high board fence where she sat motionless for some moments. While pondering the problem how that fly should be broken, the male bluebird approached her, and said very plainly, and I thought rather curtly, "Give me that bug," but she quickly resented his interference and flew farther away, where she sat apparently quite discouraged when I last saw her.

The bluebird is a home bird, and I am never tired of recurring to him. His coming or reappearance in the spring marks a new chapter in the progress of the season; things are never quite the same after one has heard that note. The past spring the males came about a week in advance of the females. A fine male lingered about my grounds and orchard all that time, apparently waiting the arrival of his mate. He called and warbled every day, as if he felt sure she was within ear-shot, and could be hurried up. Now he warbled half-angrily or upbraidingly, then coaxingly, then cheerily and confidently, the next moment in a plaintive, far-away manner. He would half open his wings, and twinkle them caressingly, as if beckoning his mate to his heart. One morning she had come, but was shy and reserved. The fond male flew to a knot-hole in an old apple tree, and coaxed her to his side. I heard a fine confidential warble—the old, old story. But the female flew to a near tree, and uttered her plaintive, homesick note. The male went and got some dry grass or bark in his beak, and flew again to the hole in the old tree, and promised unremitting devotion, but the other said, "Nay," and flew away in the distance. When he saw her going, or rather heard her distant note, he dropped his stuff, and cried out in a tone that said plainly enough, "Wait a minute. One word, please," and flew swiftly in pursuit.

He won her before long, however, and early in April the pair were established in one of the four or five boxes I had put up for them, but not until they had changed their minds several times. As soon as the first brood had flown, and while they were yet under their parents' care, they began another nest in one of the other boxes, the female, as usual, doing all the work, and the male all the complimenting. A source of occasional great distress to the mother-bird was a white cat that sometimes followed me about. The cat had never been known to catch a bird, but she had a way of watching them that was very embarrassing to the bird. Whenever she appeared, the mother bluebird would set up that pitiful melodious plaint. One morning the cat was standing by me, when the bird came with her beak loaded with building material, and alighted above me to survey the place, before going into the box. When she saw the cat, she was greatly disturbed, and in her agitation could not keep her hold upon all her material. Straw after straw came eddying down, till not half her original burden remained. After the cat had gone away, the bird's alarm subsided, till, presently seeing the coast clear, she flew quickly to the box and pitched in the remaining straws with the greatest precipitation, and without going in to arrange them, as was her wont, flew away in evident relief.

In the cavity of an apple tree but a few yards off, and much nearer the house than they usually build, a pair of high-holes, or golden-shafted woodpeckers, took up their abode. A knot-hole which led to the decayed interior was enlarged, the live wood being cut away as clean as a squirrel would have done it. The inside preparations I could not witness, but day after day, as I passed near, I heard the bird hammering away, evidently beating down obstructions and shaping and enlarging the cavity. The chips were not brought out, but were used rather to floor the interior. The woodpeckers are not nest-builders, but rather nest-carvers. The time seemed very short before the voices of the young were heard in the heart of the old tree—at first feebly, but waxing stronger day by day until they could be heard many rods distant. When I put my hand upon the trunk of the tree, they would set up an eager, expectant chattering; but if I climbed up it toward the opening, they soon detected the unusual sound and would hush quickly, only now and then uttering a warning note. Long before they were fully fledged, they clambered up to the orifice to receive their food. As but one could stand in the opening at a time, there was a good deal of elbowing and struggling for this position. It was a very desirable one aside from the advantages it had when food was served; it looked out upon the great, shining world, into which the young birds seemed never tired of gazing. The fresh air must have been a consideration also, for the interior of a high-hole's dwelling is not sweet. When the parent birds came with food, the young one in the opening did not get it all, but after he had received a portion, either on his own motion or on a hint from the old one, he would give place to the one behind him. Still, one bird evidently outstripped his fellows, and in the race of life was two or three days in advance of them. His voice was loudest and his head oftenest at the window. But I noticed that when he had kept the position too long, the others evidently made it uncomfortable in his rear, and, after "fidgeting" about a while, he would be compelled to "back down." But

John Burroughs and children. Courtesy of the American Museum of Natural History.

retaliation was then easy, and I fear his mates spent few easy moments at that lookout. They would close their eyes and slide back into the cavity as if the world had suddenly lost all its charms for them.

This bird was, of course, the first to leave the nest. For two days before that event he kept his position in the opening most of the time and sent forth his strong voice incessantly. The old ones abstained from feeding him almost entirely, no doubt to encourage his exit. As I stood looking at him one afternoon and noting his progress, he suddenly reached a resolution — seconded, I have no doubt, from the rear — and launched forth upon his untried wings. They served him well and carried him about fifty yards up-hill the first heat. The second day after, the next in size and spirit left in the same manner; then another, till only one remained. The parent birds ceased their visits to him, and for one day he called and called till our ears were tired of the sound. His was the faintest heart of all. Then he had none to encourage him from behind. He left the nest and clung to the outer bole of the tree, and yelped and piped for an hour longer; then he committed himself to his wings and went his way like the rest.

A young farmer in the western part of New York, who has a sharp, discriminating eye, sends me some interesting notes about a tame high-hole he once had.

"Did you ever notice," says he,

that the high-hole never eats anything that he cannot pick up with his tongue? At least this was the case with a young one I took from the nest and tamed. He could thrust out his tongue two or three inches, and it was amusing to see his efforts to eat currants from the hand. He would run out his tongue and try to stick it to the currant; failing in that, he would bend his tongue around it like a hook and try to raise it by a sudden jerk. But he never succeeded, the round fruit would roll and slide away every time. He never seemed to think of taking it in his beak. His tongue was in constant use to find out the nature of everything he saw; a nail-hole in a board or any similar hole was carefully explored. If he was held near the face he would soon be attracted by the eye and thrust his tongue into it. In this way he gained the respect of a number of half-grown cats that were around the house. I wished to make them familiar to each other, so there would be less danger of their killing him. So I would take them both on my knee, when the bird would soon notice the kitten's eyes, and leveling his bill as carefully as a marksman levels his rifle, he would remain so a minute when he would dart his tongue into the cat's eye. This was held by the cats to be very mysterious; being struck in the eye by something invisible to them. They soon acquired such a terror of him that they would avoid him and run away whenever they saw his bill turned in their direction. He never would swallow a grasshopper even when it was placed in his throat; he would shake himself until he had thrown it out of his mouth. His 'best hold' was ants. He never was surprised at anything, and never was afraid of anything. He would drive the turkey gobbler and the rooster. He would advance upon them holding one wing up as high as possible, as if to strike with it, and shuffle along the ground toward them, scolding all the while in a harsh voice. I feared at first that they might kill him, but I soon found that he was able to take care of himself. I would turn over stones and dig into ant-hills for him, and he would lick up the ants so fast that a stream of them seemed going into his mouth unceasingly. I kept him till late in the fall, when he disappeared, probably going south, and I never saw him again.

My correspondent also sends me some interesting observations about the cuckoo. He says a large gooseberry-bush standing in the border of an old hedge-row, in the midst of open fields, and not far from his house, was occupied by a pair of cuckoos for two seasons in succession, and, after an interval of a year, for two seasons more. This gave him a good chance to observe them. He says the mother-bird lays a single egg, and sits upon it a number of days before laying the second, so that he has seen one young bird nearly grown, a second just hatched, and a whole egg all in the nest at once.

So far as I have seen this is the settled practice—the young leaving the nest one at a time to the number of six or eight. The young have quite the look of the young of the dove in many respects. When nearly grown they are covered with long blue pin-feathers as long as darning needles, without a bit of plumage on them. They part on the back and hang down on each side by their own weight. With its curious feathers and misshapen body the young bird is anything but handsome. They never open their mouths when approached, as many young birds do, but sit perfectly still, hardly moving when touched.

He also notes the unnatural indifference of the mother-bird when her nest and young are approached. She makes no sound, but sits quietly on a near branch in apparent perfect unconcern.

These observations, together with the fact that the egg of the cuckoo is occasionally found in the nests of other birds, raise the inquiry whether our bird is slowly relapsing into the habit of the European species, which always foists its egg upon other birds; or whether, on the other hand, it be not mending its manners in this respect. It has but little to unlearn or forget in the one case, but great progress to make in the other. How far is its rudimentary nest—a mere platform of coarse twigs and dry stalks of weeds—from the deep, compact, finely woven and finely modeled nest of the goldfinch or king-bird, and what a gulf between its indifference toward its young and their solicitude! Its irregular manner of laying also seems better suited to a parasite like our cow-bird, or the European cuckoo, than to a regular nest-builder.

This observer, like most sharp-eyed persons, sees plenty of interesting things as he goes about his work. He one day saw a white swallow, which is a rare occurrence. He saw a bird, a sparrow he thinks, fly against the side of a horse and fill his beak with hair from the loosened coat of the animal. He saw a shrike pursue a chickadee, when the latter escaped by taking refuge in a small hole in a tree. One day in early spring he saw two hen-hawks that were circling and screaming high in air approach each other, extend a claw and clasping them together, fall toward the earth flapping and struggling as if they were tied together; on nearing the ground they separated and soared aloft again. He supposed that it was not a passage of war but of love, and that the hawks were toying fondly with each other.

He further relates a curious circumstance of finding a humming-bird in the upper part of a barn with its bill stuck fast in a crack of one of the large timbers, dead, of course, with wings extended, and as dry as a chip. The bird seems to have died as it had lived, on the wing, and its last act was indeed a ghastly parody of its living career. Fancy this nimble, flashing sprite, whose life was passed probing the honeyed depths of flowers, at last thrusting its bill into a dry timber in a hay-loft, and, with spread wings, ending its existence!

When the air is damp and heavy, swallows frequently hawk for insects about cattle and moving herds in the field. My farmer describes how they attended him one foggy day, as he was mowing in the meadow with a mowing-machine. It had been foggy for two days, and the swallows were very hungry, and the insects stupid and inert. When the sound of his machine was heard, the swallows appeared and attended him like a brood of hungry chickens. He says there was a continued rush of purple wings over the "cut-bar," and just where it was causing the grass to tremble and fall. Without his assistance the swallows would doubtless have gone hungry yet another day. Of the hen-hawk, he has observed that both male and female take part in incubation. "I was rather surprised," he says, "on one occasion, to see how quickly they change places on the nest. The nest was in a tall beech, and the leaves were not yet fully out. I could see the head and neck of the hawk over the edge of the next, when I saw the other hawk coming down through the air at full speed. I expected he would alight near by, but instead of that he struck directly upon the nest, his mate getting out of the way barely in time to avoid being hit; it seemed almost as if he had knocked her off the nest. I hardly see how they can make such a rush on the nest without danger to the eggs."

The king-bird will worry the hawk as a whiffet dog will worry a bear. It is by his persistence and audacity, not by any injury he is capable of dealing his great antagonist. The king-bird seldom more than dogs the hawk, keeping above and between his wings, and making a great ado; but my correspondent says he once "saw a king-bird riding on a hawk's back. The hawk flew as fast as possible, and the king-bird sat upon his shoulders in triumph until they had passed out of sight," — tweaking his feathers, no doubt, and threatening to scalp him the next moment. That near relative of the king-bird, the great crested flycatcher, has one well-known peculiarity: he appears never to consider his nest finished until it contains a cast-off snake-skin. My alert correspondent one day saw him eagerly catch up an onion skin and make off with it, either deceived by it or else thinking it a good substitute for the coveted material.

One day in May, walking in the woods, I came upon the nest of a whip-poor-will, or rather its eggs, for it builds no nest — two elliptical whitish spotted eggs lying upon the dry leaves. My foot was within a yard of the mother-bird before she flew. I wondered what a sharp eye would detect curious or characteristic in the ways of the bird, so I came to the place many times and had a look. It was always a task to separate the bird from her surroundings, though I stood within a few feet of her, and knew exactly where to look. One had to bear on with his eye, as it were, and refuse to be baffled. The sticks and leaves and bits of black or dark-brown bark were all exactly copied in the bird's plumage. And then she did sit so close, and simulate so well a shapeless decaying piece of wood or bark! Twice I brought a companion, and guiding his eyes to the spot, noted how difficult it was for him to make out there, in full view upon the dry leaves, any semblance to a bird. When the bird returned after being disturbed, she would alight within a few inches of her eggs, and then, after a moment's pause, hobble awkwardly upon them.

After the young had appeared, all the wit of the bird came into play. I was on hand the next day, I think. The mother-bird sprang up when I was within a pace of her, and in doing so fanned the leaves with her wings till they sprang up too; as the leaves started, the young started, and, being of the same color, to tell which was the leaf and which the bird was a trying task to any eye. I came the next day, when the same tactics were repeated. Once a leaf fell upon one of the young birds and nearly hid it. The young are covered with a reddish down, like a young partridge, and soon follow their mother about. When disturbed, they gave but one leap, then settled down, perfectly motionless and stupid, with eyes closed. The parent bird, on these occasions, made frantic efforts to decoy me away from her young. She would fly a few paces and fall upon her breast, and a spasm, like that of death, would run through her tremulous outstretched wings and prostrate body. She kept a sharp eye out the meanwhile to see if the ruse took, and if it did not, she was quickly cured, and moving about to some other point, tried to draw my attention as before. When followed she always alighted upon the ground, dropping down in a sudden peculiar way. The second or third day both old and young had disappeared.

The whip-poor-will walks as awkwardly as a swallow, which is as awkward as a man in a bag, and yet she manages to lead her young about the woods. The latter, I think, move by leaps and sudden spurts, their protective coloring shielding them most effectively. Wilson once came upon the mother-bird and her brood in the woods, and, though they were at his very feet, was so baffled by the concealment of the young that he was about to give up the search, much disappointed, when he perceived something "like a slight moldiness among the withered leaves, and, on stooping down, discovered it to be a young whip-poor-will, seemingly asleep." Wilson's description of the young is very accurate, as its downy covering does look precisely like a "slight moldiness." Returning a few moments afterward to the spot to get a pencil he had forgotten, he could find neither old nor young.

It takes an eye to see a partridge in the woods, motionless upon the leaves; this sense needs to be as sharp as that of smell in hounds and pointers, and yet I know an unkempt youth that seldom fails to see the bird and shoot it before it takes wing. I think he sees it as soon as it sees him, and before its suspects itself seen. What a training to the eye is hunting! To pick out the game from its surroundings, the grouse from the leaves, the gray squirrel from the mossy oak limb it hugs so closely, the red fox from the ruddy or brown or gray field, the rabbit from the stubble, or the white hare from the snow, requires the best powers of this sense. A woodchuck motionless in the fields or upon a rock looks very much like a large stone or bowlder, yet a keen eye knows the difference at a glance, a quarter of a mile away.

A man has a sharper eye than a dog, or a fox, or than any of the wild creatures, but not so sharp an ear or nose. But in the bird he finds his match. How quickly the old turkey discovers the hawk, a mere speck against the sky, and how quickly the hawk discovers you if you happen to be secreted in the bushes, or behind the fence near which he alights. One advantage the bird surely has, and that is, owing to the form, structure, and position of the eye, it has a much larger field of vision—indeed, can probably see in nearly every direction at the same instant, behind as well as before. Man's field of vision embraces less than half a circle horizontally, and still less vertically; his brow and brain prevent him from seeing within many degrees of the zenith without a movement of the head; the bird, on the other hand, takes in nearly the whole sphere at a glance.

I find I see, almost without effort, nearly every bird within sight in the field or wood I pass through (a flit of the wing, a flirt of the tail are enough, though the flickering leaves do all conspire to hide them), and that with like ease the birds see me, though, unquestionably, the chances are immensely in their favor. The eye sees what it has the means of seeing, truly. You must have the bird in your heart before you can find it in the bush. The eye must have purpose and aim. No one ever yet found the walking fern who did not have the walking fern in his mind. A person whose eye is full of Indian relics picks them up in every field he walks through.

One season I was interested in the tree-frogs, especially the tiny pipers that one hears about the woods and brushy fields—the hyla of the swamps become a denizen of the trees; I had never seen him in this new role. But this season having them in mind, or rather being ripe for them, I several times came across them. One Sunday, walking amid some bushes, I captured two. They leaped before me as doubtless they had done many times before, but though not looking for or thinking of them, yet they were quickly recognized, because the eye had been commissioned to find them. On another occasion, not long afterward, I was hurriedly loading my gun in the October woods in hopes of overtaking a gray squirrel that was fast escaping through the tree tops, when one of those lilliput frogs, the color of the fast-yellowing leaves, leaped near me. I saw him only out of the corner of my eye and yet bagged him, because I had already made him my own.

Nevertheless, the habit of observation is the habit of clear and decisive gazing; not by a first casual glance, but by a steady deliberate aim of the eye are the rare and characteristic things discovered. You must look intently and hold your eye firmly to the spot, to see more than do the rank and file of mankind. The sharp-shooter picks out his man and knows him with fatal certainty from a stump, or a rock, or a cap on a pole. The phrenologists do well to locate not only form, color, weight, etc., in the region of the eye, but a faculty which they call individuality—that which separates, discriminates, and sees in every object its essential character. This is just as necessary to the naturalist as to the artist or the poet. The sharp eye notes specific points and differences—it seizes upon and preserves the individuality of the thing.

Persons frequently describe to me some bird they have seen or heard and ask me to name it, but in most cases the bird might be any one of a dozen, or else it is totally unlike any bird found on this continent. They have either seen falsely or else vaguely. Not so the farm youth who wrote me one winter day that he had seen a single pair of strange birds, which he describes as follows: "They were about the size of the 'chippie,' the tops of their heads were red, and the breast of the male was of the same color, while that of the female was much lighter; their rumps were also faintly tinged with red. If I have described them so that you would know them, please write me their names." There can be little doubt but the young observer had seen a pair of red-polls—a bird related to the goldfinch, and that occasionally comes down to us in the winter from the far north. Another time, the same youth wrote that he had seen a strange bird, the color of a sparrow, that alighted on fences and buildings as well as upon the ground and that walked. This last fact showed the youth's discriminating eye and settled the case. I knew it to be a species of lark, and from the size, color, season, etc., the tit-lark. But how many persons would have observed that the bird walked instead of hopped?

Some friends of mine who lived in the country tried to describe to me a bird that built a nest in a tree within a few feet of the house. As it was a brown bird, I should have taken it for a wood-thrush, had not the nest been described as so thin and loose that from beneath the eggs could be distinctly seen. The most pronounced feature in the description was the barred appearance of the underside of the bird's tail. I was quite at sea, until one day, when we were driving out, a cuckoo flew across the road in front of us, when my friends exclaimed, "There is our bird!" I had never known a cuckoo to build near a house, and I had never noted the appearance the tail presents when viewed from beneath; but if the bird had been described in its most obvious features, as slender, with a long tail, cinnamon brown above and white beneath, with a curved bill, anyone who knew the bird would have recognized the portrait.

We think we have looked at a thing sharply until we are asked for its specific features. I thought I knew exactly the form of the leaf of the tulip-tree, until one day a lady asked me to draw the outlines of one. A good observer is quick to take a hint and to follow it up. Most of the facts of nature, especially in the life of the birds and animals, are well screened. We do not see the play because we do not look intently enough. The other day I was sitting with a friend upon a high rock in the wood, near a small stream, when we saw a water-snake swimming across a pool toward the opposite bank. Any eye would have noted it, perhaps nothing more. A little close and sharper gaze revealed the fact that the snake bore something in its mouth, which, as we went down to investigate, proved to be a small catfish, three or four inches long. The snake had captured it in the pool, and, like any other fisherman, wanted to get its prey to dry land, although it itself lived mostly in the water. Here, we said, is being enacted a little tragedy that would have escaped any but sharp eyes. The snake, which was itself small, had the fish by the throat, the hold of vantage among all creatures, and clung to it with great tenacity. The snake knew that its best tactics was to get upon dry land as soon as possible. It could not swallow its victim alive, and it could not strangle it in the water. For a while it tried to kill its game by holding it up out of the water, but the fish grew heavy, and every few moments its struggles brought down the snake's head. This would not do. Compressing the fish's throat would not shut off its breath under such circumstances, so the wily serpent tried to get ashore with it, and after several attempts succeeded in effecting a landing on a flat rock. But the fish died hard. Catfish do not give up the ghost in a hurry. Its throat was becoming congested, but the snake's distended jaws must have ached. It was like a petrified gape. Then the spectators became very curious and close in their scrutiny, and the snake determined to withdraw from the public gaze and finish the business in hand to its own notions. But, when gently but firmly remonstrated with by my friend with his walking-stick, it dropped the fish and retreated in high dudgeon beneath a stone in the bed of the creek. The fish, with a swollen and angry throat, went its way also.

Birds, I say, have wonderfully keen eyes. Throw a fresh bone or a piece of meat upon the snow in winter, and see how soon the crows will discover it and be on hand. If it be near the house or barn, the crow that first discovers it will alight near it, to make sure he is not deceived; then he will go away, and soon return with a companion. The two alight a few yards from the bone, and after some delay, during which the vicinity is sharply scrutinized, one of the crows advances boldly to within a few feet of the coveted prize. Here he pauses, and if no trick is discovered, and the meat be indeed meat, he seizes it and makes off.

One midwinter, I cleared away the snow under an apple tree near the house and scattered some corn there. I had not seen a blue-jay for weeks, yet that very day they found my corn, and after that they came daily and partook of it, holding the kernels under their feet upon the limbs of the trees and pecking them vigorously.

Of course the woodpecker and his kind have sharp eyes; still I was surprised to see how quickly Downy found out some bones that were placed in a convenient place under the shed to be pounded up for the hens. In going out to the barn I often disturbed him making a meal off the bits of meat that still adhered to them.

"Look intently enough at anything," said a poet to me one day, "and you will see something that would otherwise escape you." I thought of the remark as I sat on a stump in an opening of the woods one spring day. I saw a small hawk approaching; he flew to a tall tulip-tree and alighted on a large limb near the top. He eyed me and I eyed him. Then the bird disclosed a trait that was new to me; he hopped along the limb to a small cavity near the trunk, when he thrust in his head and pulled out some small object and fell to eating it. After he had partaken of it for some minutes, he put the remainder back in his larder and flew away. I had seen something like feathers eddying slowly down as the hawk ate, and on approaching the spot found the feathers of a sparrow here and there clinging to the bushes beneath the tree. The hawk, then—commonly called the chicken hawk—is as provident as a mouse or squirrel, and lays by a store against a time of need, but I should not have discovered the fact had I not held my eye to him.

An observer of the birds is attracted by any unusual sound or commotion among them. In May or June, when other birds are most vocal, the jay is a silent bird; he goes sneaking about the orchards and the groves as silent as a pickpocket; he is robbing birds' nests, and he is very anxious that nothing should be said about it, but in the fall none so quick and loud to cry "Thief, thief" as he. One December morning a troop of them discovered a little screech-owl secreted in the hollow trunk of an old apple tree near my house. How they found the owl out is a mystery, since it never ventures forth in the light of day; but they did, and proclaimed the fact with great emphasis. I suspect the bluebirds first told them, for these birds are constantly peeping into holes and crannies, both spring and fall. Some unsuspecting bird probably entered the cavity prospecting for a place for next year's nest, or else looking out a likely place to pass a cold night, when it had rushed out with important news. A boy who should unwittingly venture into a bear's den when Bruin was at home could not be more astonished and alarmed than a bluebird would be on finding itself in the cavity of a decayed tree with an owl. At any rate the bluebirds joined the jays in calling the attention of all whom it might concern to the fact that a culprit of some sort was hiding from the light of day in the old apple tree. I heard the notes of warning and alarm and approached to within eye-shot. The bluebirds were cautious and hovered about uttering their peculiar twittering calls; but the jays were bolder and took turns looking in at the cavity, and deriding the poor, shrinking owl. A jay would alight in the entrance of the hole and flirt and peer and attitudinize, and then fly away crying "Thief, thief, thief," at the top of his voice.

I climbed up and peered into the opening, and could just descry the owl clinging to the inside of the tree. I reached in and took him out, giving little heed to the threatening snapping of his beak. He was as red as a fox and as yellow-eyed as a cat. He made no effort to escape, but planted his claws in my forefinger and clung there with a grip that soon grew uncomfortable. I placed him in the loft of an out-house in hopes of getting better acquainted with him. By day he was a very willing prisoner, scarcely moving at all, even when approached and touched with hand, but looking out upon the world with half-closed, sleepy eyes. But at night what a change; how alert, how wild, how active! He was like another bird; he darted about with wide, fearful eyes, and regarded me like a cornered cat. I opened the window, and swiftly, but as silent as a shadow, he glided out into the congenial darkness, and perhaps, ere this, has revenged himself upon the sleeping jay or bluebird that first betrayed his hiding-place.

Bird-Songs

I SUSPECT IT REQUIRES a special gift of grace to enable one to hear the bird-songs; some new power must be added to the ear, or some obstruction removed. There are not only scales upon our eyes so that we do not see; there are scales upon our ears so that we do not hear. A city woman who had spent much of her time in the country once asked a well-known ornithologist to take her where she could hear the bluebird. "What, never heard the bluebird!" said he. "I have not" said the woman. "Then you will never hear it," said the bird-lover; never hear it with that inward ear that gives beauty and meaning to the note. He could probably have taken her in a few minutes where she could have heard the call or warble of the bluebird; but it would have fallen upon unresponsive ears—upon ears that were not sensitized by love for the birds or associations with them. Bird-songs are not music, properly speaking, but only suggestions of music. A great many people whose attention would be quickly arrested by the same volume of sound made by a musical instrument or by artificial means never hear them at all. The sound of a boy's penny whistle there in the grove or the meadow would separate itself more from the background of nature, and be a greater challenge to the ear, than is the strain of the thrush or the song of the sparrow. There is something elusive, indefinite, neutral, about bird-songs that makes them strike obliquely, as it were, upon the ear; and we are very apt to miss them. They are a part of nature, the Nature that lies about us, entirely occupied with her own affairs, and quite regardless of our presence. Hence it is with bird-songs as it is with so many other things in nature—they are what we make them; the ear that hears them must be half-creative. I am always disturbed when persons not especially observant of birds ask me to take them where they can hear a particular bird, in whose song they have become interested through a description in some book. As I listen with them, I feel like apologizing for the bird: it has a bad cold, or has just heard some depressing news; it will not let itself out. The song seems so casual and

From *Ways of Nature*, 1905.

minor when you make a dead set at it. I have taken persons to hear the hermit thrush, and I have fancied that they were all the time saying to themselves, "Is that all?" But should one hear the bird in his walk, when the mind is attuned to simple things and is open and receptive, when expectation is not aroused and the song comes as a surprise out of the dusky silence of the woods, then one feels that it merits all the fine things that can be said of it.

One of our popular writers and lecturers upon birds told me this incident: He had engaged to take two city girls out for a walk in the country, to teach them the names of the birds they might see and hear. Before they started, he read to them Henry van Dyke's poem on the song sparrow—one of our best bird-poems—telling them that the song sparrow was one of the first birds they were likely to hear. As they proceeded with their walk, sure enough, there by the roadside was a sparrow in song. The bird man called the attention of his companions to it. It was some time before the unpracticed ears of the girls could make it out; then one of them said (the poem she had just heard, I suppose, still ringing in her ears), "What! that little squeaky thing?" The sparrow's song meant nothing to her at all, and how could she share the enthusiasm of the poet? Probably the warble of the robin or the call of the meadowlark or of the high-hole, if they chanced to hear them, meant no more to these girls. If we have no associations with these sounds, they will mean very little to us. Their merit as musical performances is very slight. It is as signs of joy and love in nature, as heralds of spring, and as the spirit of the woods and fields made audible, that they appeal to us. The drumming of the woodpeckers and of the ruffed grouse give great pleasure to a countryman, though these sounds have not the quality of real music. It is the same with the call of the migrating geese or the voice of any wild thing: our pleasure in them is entirely apart from any considerations of music. Why does the wild flower, as we chance upon it in the woods or bogs, give us more pleasure than the more elaborate flower of the garden or lawn? Because it comes as a surprise, offers a greater contrast with its surroundings, and suggests a spirit in wild nature that seems to take thought of itself and to aspire to beautiful forms.

The songs of caged birds are always disappointing, because such birds have nothing but their musical qualities to recommend them to us. We have separated them from that which gives quality and meaning to their songs. One recalls Emerson's lines:

> I thought the sparrow's note from heaven,
> Singing at dawn on the alder bough;
> I brought him home, in his nest, at even;

> He sings the song, but it cheers not now,
> For I did not bring home the river and sky;
> He sang to my ear—they sang to my eye.

I have never yet seen a caged bird that I wanted—at least, not on account of its song—nor a wild flower that I wished to transfer to my garden. A caged skylark will sing its song sitting on a bit of turf in the bottom of the cage; but you want to stop your ears, it is so harsh and sibilant and penetrating. But up there against the morning sky, and above the wide expanse of fields, what delight we have in it! It is not the concord of sweet sounds: it is the soaring spirit of gladness and ecstasy raining down upon us from "heaven's gate."

Then, if to the time and the place one could only add the association, or hear the bird through the vista of the years, the song touched with the magic of youthful memories! One season a friend in England sent me a score of skylarks in a cage. I gave them their liberty in a field near my place. They drifted away, and I never heard them or saw them again. But one Sunday a Scotchman from a neighboring city called upon me, and declared with visible excitement that on his way along the road he had heard a skylark. He was not dreaming; he knew it was a skylark—though he had not heard one since be had left the banks of the Doon, a quarter of a century or more before. What pleasure it gave him! How much more the song meant to him than it would have meant to me! For the moment he was on his native heath again. Then I told him about the larks I had liberated, and he seemed to enjoy it all over again with renewed appreciation.

Many years ago some skylarks were liberated on Long Island, and they became established there, and may now occasionally be heard in certain localities. One summer day a friend of mine was out there observing them; a lark was soaring and singing in the sky above him. An old Irishman came along, and suddenly stopped as if transfixed to the spot; a look of mingled delight and incredulity came into his face. Was he indeed hearing the bird of his youth? He took off his hat, turned his face skyward, and with moving lips and streaming eyes stood a long time regarding the bird. "Ah," my friend thought, "if I could only hear that song with his ears!" How it brought back his youth and all those long-gone days on his native hills!

The power of bird-songs over us is so much a matter of association that every traveler to other countries finds the feathered songsters of less merit than those he left behind. The stranger does not hear the birds in the same receptive, uncritical frame of mind as does the native; they are not in the same way the voices of the place and the season. What music can there be in that long, piercing, far-heard note of the first meadowlark in spring to any but a native, or in the *o-ka-lee* of the red-shouldered starling as he rests upon the willows in March? A stranger would probably recognize melody and a wild woodsy quality in the flutings of the veery thrush; but how much more they would mean to him after he had spent many successive Junes threading our northern trout-streams and encamping on their banks! The veery will come early in the morning, and again at sundown, and perch above your tent, and blow his soft, reverberant note for many minutes at a time. The strain repeats the echoes of the limpid stream in the halls and corridors of the leafy woods.

While in England in 1882, I rushed about two or three counties in late June and early July, bent on hearing the song of the nightingale, but missed it by a few days, and in some cases, as it seemed, only by a few hours. The nightingale seems to be wound up to go only so long, or till about the middle of June, and it is only by a rare chance that you hear one after that date. Then I came home to hear a nightingale in song one winter morning in a friend's house in the city. It was a curious let-down to my enthusiasm. A caged song in a city chamber in broad daylight, in lieu of the wild, free song in the gloaming of an English landscape! I closed my eyes, abstracted myself from my surroundings, and tried my best to fancy myself listening to the strain back there amid the scenes I had haunted about Hazlemere and Godalming, but with poor success, I suspect. The nightingale's song, like the lark's, needs vista, needs all the accessories of time and place. The song is not all in the singing, any more than the wit is all in the saying. It is in the occasion, the surroundings, the spirit of which it is the expression. My friend said that the bird did not fully let itself out. Its song was a brilliant medley of notes—no theme that I could detect—like the lark's song in this respect; all the notes of the field and forest appeared to be the gift of this bird, but what tone! what accent! like that of a great poet!

Nearly every May I am seized with an impulse to go back to the scenes of my youth, and hear the bobolinks in the home meadows once more. I am sure they sing there better than anywhere else. They probably drink nothing but dew, and the dew distilled in those high pastoral regions has surprising virtues. It gives a clear, full, vibrant quality to the birds' voices that I have never heard elsewhere. The night of my arrival, I leave my southern window open, so that the meadow chorus may come pouring in before I am up in the morning. How it does transport me athwart the years, and make me a boy again, sheltered by the paternal wing! On one occasion, the third morning after my arrival, a bobolink appeared with a new note in his song.

The note sounded like the word "baby" uttered with a peculiar, tender resonance: but it was clearly an interpolation; it did not belong there; it had no relation to the rest of the song. Yet the bird never failed to utter it with the same joy and confidence as the rest of his song. Maybe it was the beginning of a variation that will in time result in an entirely new bobolink song.

On my last spring visit to my native hills, my attention was attracted to another songster not seen or heard there in my youth, namely, the prairie horned lark. Flocks of these birds used to be seen in some of the northern States in the late fall during their southern migrations; but within the last twenty years they have become regular summer residents in the hilly parts of many sections of New York and New England. They are genuine skylarks, and lack only the powers of song to make them as attractive as their famous cousins of Europe.

The larks are ground-birds when they perch, and sky-birds when they sing; from the turf to the clouds—nothing between. Our horned lark mounts upward on quivering wing in the true lark fashion, and, spread out against the sky at an altitude of two or three hundred feet, hovers and sings. The watcher and listener below holds him in his eye, but the ear catches only a faint, broken, half-inarticulate note now and then—mere splinters, as it were, of the song of the skylark. The song of the latter is continuous, and is loud and humming; it is a fountain of jubilant song up there in the sky: but our lark sings in snatches; at each repetition of its notes it dips forward and downward a few feet, and then rises again. One day I kept my eye upon one until it had repeated its song one hundred and three times; then it closed its wings, and dropped toward the earth like a plummet, as does its European congener. While I was watching the bird, a bobolink flew over my head, between me and the lark, and poured out his voluble and copious strain. "What a contrast," I thought, "between the voice of the spluttering, tongue-tied lark, and the free, liquid, and varied song of the bobolink!"

I have heard of a curious fact in the life-histories of these larks in the West. A Michigan woman once wrote me that her brother, who was an engineer on an express train that made daily trips between two Western cities, reported that many birds were struck by the engine every day, and killed— often as many as thirty on a trip of sixty miles. Birds of many kinds were killed, but the most common was a bird that went in flocks, the description of which answered to the horned lark. Since then I have read in a Minnesota newspaper that many horned larks are killed by railroad locomotives in that State. It was thought that the birds sat behind the rails to get out of the wind, and on starting up in front of the advancing train, were struck down by the engine. The Michigan engineer referred to thought that the birds gathered upon the track to earth their wings, or else to pick up the grain that leaks out of the wheat-trains and sows the track from Dakota to the seaboard. Probably the wind which they might have to face in getting up was the prime cause of their being struck. One does not think of the lo-comotive as a bird-destroyer, though it is well known that many of the smaller mammals often fall beneath it.

A very interesting feature of our bird-songs is the wing-song, or song of ecstasy. It is not the gift of many of our birds. Indeed, less than a dozen species are known to me as ever singing on the wing. It seems to spring from more intense excitement and self-abandonment than the ordinary song delivered from the perch. When its joy reaches the point of rapture, the bird is literally carried off its feet, and up it goes into the air, pouring out its song as a rocket pours out its sparks. The skylark and the bobolink habitually do this, while a few others of our birds do it only on occasions. One summer, up in the Catskills, I added another name to my list of ec-static singers—that of the vesper sparrow. Several times I heard a new song in the air, and caught a glimpse of the bird as it dropped back to the earth. My attention would be attracted by a succession of hurried, chirping notes, followed by a brief burst of song, then by the vanishing form of the bird. One day I was lucky enough to see the bird as it was rising to its climax in the air, and to identify it as the vesper sparrow. The burst of song that crowned the upward flight of seventy-five or one hundred feet was brief; but it was brilliant and striking, and entirely unlike the leisurely chant of the bird while upon the ground. It suggested a lark, but was less buzzing or humming. The preliminary chirping notes, uttered faster and faster as the bird mounted in the air, were like the trail of sparks which a rocket emits before its grand burst of color at the top of its flight.

It is interesting to note that this bird is quite lark-like in its color and markings, having the two lateral white quills in the tail, and it has the habit of elevating the feathers on the top of the head so as to suggest a crest. The solitary skylark that I discovered several years ago in a field near me was seen on several occasions paying his addresses to one of these birds, but the vesper-bird was shy, and eluded all his advances.

Probably the perch-songster among our ordinary birds that is most regu-larly seized with the fit of ecstasy that results in this lyric burst in the air, as I described in my first book, *Wake-Robin,* over thirty years ago, is the oven-bird, or wood-accentor—the golden-crowned thrush of the old ornitholo-gists. Every loiterer about the woods knows this pretty, speckled-breasted, olive-backed little bird, which walks along over the dry leaves a few yards from him, moving its head as it walks, like a miniature domestic fowl. Most birds are very stiff-necked, like the robin, and as they run or hop upon the ground, carry the head as if it were riveted to the body. Not so the oven-bird, or the other birds that walk, as the cow-bunting, or the quail, or the crow. They move the head forward with the movement of the feet. The sharp, reiterated, almost screeching song of the oven-bird, as it perches on a limb a few feet from the ground, like the words, "preacher, preacher, preacher," or "teacher, teacher, teacher," uttered louder and louder, and re-peated six or seven times, is also familiar to most ears; but its wild, ringing, rapturous burst of song in the air high above the tree-tops is not so well known. From a very prosy, tiresome, unmelodious singer, it is suddenly transformed for a brief moment into a lyric poet of great power. It is a great surprise. The bird undergoes a complete transformation. Ordinarily it is a very quiet, demure sort of bird. It walks about over the leaves, moving its head like a little hen; then perches on a limb a few feet from the ground and sends forth its shrill, rather prosy, unmusical chant. Surely it is an ordinary, commonplace bird. But wait till the inspiration of its flight-song is upon it. What a change! Up it goes through the branches of the trees, leaping from limb to limb, faster and faster, till it shoots from the tree-tops fifty or more feet into the air above them, and bursts into an ecstasy of song, rapid, ring-ing, lyrical; no more like its habitual performance than a match is like a rocket; brief but thrilling; emphatic but musical. Having reached its climax of flight and song, the bird closes its wings and drops nearly perpendicularly downward like the skylark. If its song were more prolonged, it would rival the song of that famous bird. The bird does this many times a day during early June, but oftenest at twilight. The song in quality and general cast is like that of its congener, the water-accentor, which, however, I believe is never delivered on the wing. From its habit of singing at twilight, and from the swift, darting motions of the bird, I am inclined to think that in it we have solved the mystery of Thoreau's "night-warbler," that puzzled and eluded him for years. Emerson told him he must beware of finding and booking it, lest life should have nothing more to show him. The older or-nithologists must have heard this song many times, but they never seem to have suspected the identity of the singer.

Other birds that sing on the wing are the meadowlark, goldfinch, purple finch, indigo-bird, Maryland yellow-throat, and woodcock. The flight-song of the woodcock I have heard but twice in my life. The first time was in the evening twilight about the middle of April. The bird was calling in the dusk *yeap, yeap,* or *eap, seap,* from the ground—a peculiar, reedy call. Then, by and by, it started upward on an easy slant, that peculiar whistling of its wings alone heard; then, at an altitude of one hundred feet or more, it began to float about in wide circles and broke out in an ecstatic chipper, almost a warble at times, with a peculiar smacking musical quality; then, in a minute or so, it dropped back to the ground again, not straight down like the lark, but more spirally, and continued its call as before. In less than five minutes it was up again. The next time, a few years later, I heard the song in company with a friend, Dr. Clara Barrus. Let me give the woman's impression of the song as she afterward wrote it up for a popular journal.

> The sunset light was flooding all this May loveliness of field and farm and distant wood; song sparrows were blithely pouring out happiness by the throatful; peepers were piping and toads trilling, and we thought it no hardship to wait in such a place till the dusk should gather, and the wary woodcock announce his presence. But hark! while yet 'tis light, only a few rods distant, I hear that welcome 'seap . . . seap,'and lo! a chipper and a chirr, and past us he flies—a direct, slanting upward flight, somewhat labored—his bill showing long against the reddened sky. 'He has something in his mouth,' I start to say, when I bethink me what a long bill he has. Around, above us he flies in wide, ambitious circles, the while we are enveloped, as it were, in that hurried chippering sound—fine, elusive, now near, now distant. How rapid is the flight! Now it sounds faster and faster, 'like a whiplash flashed through the air,' said my friend; up, up he soars, till he becomes lost to sight at the instant that his song ends in that last mad ecstasy that just precedes his alighting.

The meadowlark sings in a level flight, half hovering in the air, giving voice to a rapid medley of lark-like notes. The goldfinch also sings in a level flight, beating the air slowly with its wings broadly open, and pouring out its jubilant, ecstatic strain. I think it indulges in this wing-song only in the early season. After the mother-bird has begun sitting, the male circles about within earshot of her, in that curious undulating flight, uttering his *per-chic-o-pee, per-chic-o-pee*, while the female calls back to him in the tenderest tones, "yes, lovie; I hear you." The indigo-bird and the purple finch, when their happiness becomes too full and buoyant for them longer to control it, launch into the air, and sing briefly, ecstatically, in a tremulous, hovering flight. The air-song of these birds does not differ essentially from the song delivered from the perch, except that it betrays more excitement, and hence is a more complete lyrical rapture.

The purple finch is our finest songster among the finches. Its strain is so soft and melodious, and touched with such a childlike gaiety and plaintiveness, that I think it might sound well even in a cage inside a room, if the bird would only sing with the same joyous abandonment, which, of course, it would not do.

It is not generally known that individual birds of the same species show different degrees of musical ability. This is often noticed in caged birds, among which the principle of variation seems more active; but an attentive observer notes the same fact in wild birds. Occasionally he hears one that in powers of song surpasses all its fellows. I have heard a sparrow, an oriole, and a wood thrush, each of which had a song of its own that far exceeded any other. I stood one day by a trout-stream, and suspended my fishing for several minutes to watch a song sparrow that was singing on a dry limb before me. He had five distinct songs, each as markedly different from the others as any human songs, which he repeated one after the other. He may have had a sixth or a seventh, but he bethought himself of some business in the next field, and flew away before he had exhausted his repertory. I once had a letter from Robert Louis Stevenson, who said he had read an account I had written of the song of the English blackbird. He said I might as well talk of the song of man; that every blackbird had its own song; and then he told me of a remarkable singer he used to hear somewhere amid the Scottish hills. But his singer was, of course, an exception; twenty-four blackbirds out of every twenty-five probably sing the same song, with no appreciable variations: but the twenty-fifth may show extraordinary powers. I told Stevenson that his famous singer had probably been to school to some nightingale on the Continent or in southern England. I might have told him of the robin I once heard here that sang with great spirit and accuracy the song of the brown thrasher, or of another that had the note of the whip-poor-will interpolated in the regular robin song, or of still another that had the call of the quail. In each case the bird had probably heard the song and learned it while very young. In the Trossachs, in Scotland, I followed a song thrush about for a long time, attracted by its peculiar song. It repeated over and over again three or four notes of a well-known air, which it might have caught from some shepherd boy whistling to his flock or to his cow.

The songless birds—why has Nature denied them this gift? But they nearly all have some musical call or impulse that serves them very well. The quail has his whistle, the woodpecker his drum, the pewee his plaintive cry, the chickadee his exquisitely sweet call, the high-hole his long, repeated *wick, wick, wick,* one of the most welcome sounds of spring, the jay his musical gurgle, the hawk his scream, the crow his sturdy caw. Only one of our pretty birds of the orchard is reduced to an all but inaudible note, and that is the cedar-bird.

The Exhilarations of the Road

Afoot and light-hearted I take to the open road.
— Walt Whitman

OCCASIONALLY ON THE SIDEWALK, amid the dapper, swiftly moving, high-heeled boots and gaiters, I catch a glimpse of the naked human foot. Nimbly it scuffs along, the toes spread, the sides flatten, the heel protrudes; it grasps the curbing, or bends to the form of the uneven surfaces — a thing sensuous and alive, that seems to take cognizance of whatever it touches or passes. How primitive and uncivil it looks in such company — a real barbarian in the parlor! We are so unused to the human anatomy, to simple, unadorned nature, that it looks a little repulsive; but it is beautiful for all that. Though it be a black foot and an unwashed foot, it shall be exalted. It is a thing of life amid leather, a free spirit amid cramped, a wild bird amid caged, an athlete amid consumptives. It is the symbol of my order, the Order of Walkers. That unhampered, vitally playing piece of anatomy is the type of the pedestrian, man returned to first principles, in direct contact and intercourse with the earth and the elements, his faculties unsheathed, his mind plastic, his body toughened, his heart light, his soul dilated; while those cramped and distorted members in the calf and kid are the unfortunate wretches doomed to carriages and cushions.

I am not going to advocate the disuse of boots and shoes, or the abandoning of the improved modes of travel; but I am going to brag as lustily as I can on behalf of the pedestrian, and show how all the shining angels second and accompany the man who goes afoot, while all the dark spirits are ever looking out for a chance to ride.

When I see the discomforts that able-bodied American men will put up with rather than go a mile or half a mile on foot, the abuses they will

From *Winter Sunshine,* 1875.

tolerate and encourage, crowding the street car on a little fall in the temperature or the appearance of an inch or two of snow, packing up to overflowing, dangling to the straps, treading on each other's toes, breathing each other's breaths, crushing the women and children, hanging by tooth and nail to a square inch of the platform, imperiling their limbs and killing the horses—I think the commonest tramp in the street has good reason to felicitate himself on his rare privilege of going afoot. Indeed, a race that neglects or despises this primitive gift, that fears the touch of the soil, that has no footpaths, no community of ownership in the land which they imply, that warns off the walker as a trespasser, that knows no way but the highway, the carriage-way, that forgets the stile, the foot-bridge, that even ignores the rights of the pedestrian in the public road, providing no escape for him but in the ditch or up the bank, is in a fair way to far more serious degeneracy.

Shakespeare makes the chief qualification of the walker a merry heart:

> Jog on, jog on, the footpath way,
> And merrily hent the stile-a;
> A merry heart goes all the day,
> Your sad tires in a mile-a.

The human body is a steed that goes freest and longest under a light rider, and the lightest of all riders is a cheerful heart. Your sad, or morose, or embittered, or preoccupied heart settles heavily into the saddle, and the poor beast, the body, breaks down the first mile. Indeed, the heaviest thing in the world is a heavy heart. Next to that, the most burdensome to the walker is a heart not in perfect sympathy and accord with the body—a reluctant or unwilling heart. The horse and rider must not only both be willing to go the same way, but the rider must lead the way and infuse his own lightness and eagerness into the steed.

Herein is no doubt our trouble, and one reason of the decay of the noble art in this country. We are unwilling walkers. We are not innocent and simple-hearted enough to enjoy a walk. We have fallen from that state of grace which capacity to enjoy a walk implies. It cannot be said that as a people we are so positively sad, or morose, or melancholic, as that we are vacant of that sportiveness and surplusage of animal spirits that characterized our ancestors, and that springs from full and harmonious life—a sound heart in accord with a sound body.

A man must invest himself near at hand and in common things, and be content with a steady and moderate return, if he would know the blessedness of a cheerful heart and the sweetness of a walk over the round earth. This is a lesson the American has yet to learn—capability of amusement on a low key. He expects rapid and extraordinary returns. He would make the very elemental laws pay usury. He has nothing to invest in a walk; it is too slow, too cheap. We crave the astonishing, the exciting, the far away, and do not know the highways of the gods when we see them—always a sign of the decay of the faith and simplicity of man.

If I say to my neighbor, "Come with me, I have great wonders to show you," he pricks up his ears and comes forthwith; but when I take him on the hills under the full blaze of the sun, or along the country road, our footsteps lighted by the moon and stars, and say to him, "Behold, these are the wonders, these are the circuits of the gods, this we now tread is a morning star," he feels defrauded, and as if I had played him a trick. And yet nothing less than dilatation and enthusiasm like this is the badge of the master walker.

If we are not sad, we are careworn, hurried, discontented, mortgaging the present for the promise of the future. If we take a walk, it is as we take a prescription, with about the same relish and with about the same purpose; and the more the fatigue, the greater our faith in the virtue of the medicine.

Of those gleesome saunters over the hills in spring, or those sallies of the body in winter, those excursions into space when the foot strikes fire at every step, when the air tastes like a new and finer mixture, when we accumulate force and gladness as we go along, when the sight of objects by the roadside and of the fields and woods pleases more than pictures or than all the art in the world—those ten- or twelve-mile dashes that are but the wit and effluence of the corporeal powers—of such diversion and open road entertainment, I say, most of us know very little.

I notice with astonishment that at our fashionable watering-places nobody walks; that, of all those vast crowds of health-seekers and lovers of country air, you can never catch one in the fields or woods, or guilty of trudging along the country road with dust on his shoes and sun-tan on his hands and face. The sole amusement seems to be to eat and dress and sit about the hotels and glare at each other. The men look bored, the women look tired, and all seem to sigh, "O Lord! what shall we do to be happy and not be vulgar?" Quite different from our British cousins across the water, who have plenty of amusement and hilarity, spending most of the time at their watering-places in the open air, strolling, picnicking, boating, climbing, briskly walking, apparently with little fear of sun-tan or of compromising their "gentility."

It is indeed astonishing with what ease and hilarity the English walk. To an American it seems a kind of infatuation. When Dickens was in this country, I imagine the aspirants to the honor of a walk with him were not numerous. In a pedestrian tour of England by an American, I read that, "after breakfast with the Independent minister, he walked with us for six miles out of town upon our road. Three little boys and girls, the youngest six years old, also accompanied us. They were romping and rambling about all the while, and their morning walk must have been as much as fifteen miles; but they thought nothing of it, and when we parted were apparently as fresh as when they started, and very loath to return."

I fear, also, the American is becoming disqualified for the manly art of walking by a falling off in the size of his foot. He cherishes and cultivates this part of his anatomy, and apparently thinks his taste and good breeding are to be inferred from its diminutive size. A small, trim foot, well booted or gaitered, is the national vanity. How we stare at the big feet of foreigners, and wonder what may be the price of leather in those countries, and where all the aristocratic blood is, that these plebeian extremities so predominate! If we were admitted to the confidences of the shoemaker to Her Majesty or to His Royal Highness, no doubt we should modify our views upon this latter point, for a truly large and royal nature is never stunted in the extremities; a little foot never yet supported a great character.

It is said that Englishmen, when they first come to this country, are for some time under the impression that American women all have deformed feet, they are so coy of them and so studiously careful to keep them hid. That there is an astonishing difference between the women of the two countries in this respect every traveler can testify; and that there is a difference equally astonishing between the pedestrian habits and capabilities of the rival sisters is also certain.

The English pedestrian, no doubt, has the advantage of us in the matter of climate; for, notwithstanding the traditional gloom and moroseness of English skies, they have in that country none of those relaxing, sinking, enervating days, of which we have so many here, and which seem especially trying to the female constitution—days which withdraw all support from the back and loins, and render walking of all things burdensome. Theirs is a climate of which it has been said that "it invites men abroad more days in the year and more hours in the day than that of any other country."

Then their land is threaded with paths which invite the walker, and which are scarcely less important than the highways. I heard of a surly nobleman near London who took it into his head to close a footpath that passed through his estate near his house, and open another a little farther off. The pedestrians objected; the matter got into the courts, and after protracted litigation the aristocrat was beaten. The path could not be closed or moved. The memory of man ran not to the time when there was not a footpath there, and every pedestrian should have the right of way there still.

I remember the pleasure I had in the path that connects Stratford-on-Avon with Shottery, Shakespeare's path when he went courting Anne Hathaway. By the king's highway the distance is some farther, so there is a well-worn path along the hedgerows and through the meadows and turnip patches. The traveler in it has the privilege of crossing the railroad track, an unusual privilege in England, and one denied to the lord in his carriage, who must either go over or under it. (It is a privilege, is it not, to be allowed the forbidden, even if it be the privilege of being run over by the engine?) In strolling over the South Downs, too, I was delighted to find that where the hill was steepest, some benefactor of the order of walkers had made notches in the sward, so that the foot could bite the better and firmer; the path became a kind of stairway, which I have no doubt the plowman respected.

When you see an English country church withdrawn, secluded, out of the reach of wheels, standing amid grassy graves and surrounded by noble trees, approached by paths and shaded lanes, you appreciate more than ever this beautiful habit of the people. Only a race that knows how to use its feet, and holds footpaths sacred, could put such a charm of privacy and humility into such a structure. I think I should be tempted to go to church myself if I saw all my neighbors starting off across the fields or along paths that led to such charmed spots, and were sure I should not be jostled or run over by the rival chariots of the worshipers at the temple doors. I think that is what ails our religion; humility and devoutness of heart leave one when he lays by his walking shoes and walking clothes, and sets out for church drawn by something.

Indeed, I think it would be tantamount to an astonishing revival of religion if the people would all walk to church on Sunday and walk home again. Think how the stones would preach to them by the wayside; how their benumbed minds would warm up beneath the friction of the gravel; how their vain and foolish thoughts, their desponding thoughts, their besetting demons of one kind and another, would drop behind them, unable to keep up or to endure the fresh air! They would walk away from their ennui, their worldly cares, their uncharitableness, their pride of dress; for these devils always want to ride, while the simple virtues are never so happy as when on foot. Let us walk by all means; but if we will ride, get an ass.

Then the English claim that they are a more hearty and robust people than we are. It is certain they are a plainer people, have plainer tastes, dress plainer, build plainer, speak plainer, keep closer to facts, wear broader shoes and coarser clothes, and place a lower estimate on themselves—all of which traits favor pedestrian habits. The English grandee is not confined to his carriage; but if the American aristocrat leaves his, he is ruined. Oh the weariness, the emptiness, the plotting, the seeking rest and finding none, that go by in the carriages! while your pedestrian is always cheerful, alert, re-freshed, with his heart in his hand and his hand free to all. He looks down upon nobody; he is on the common level. His pores are all open, his circu-lation is active, his digestion good. His heart is not cold, nor are his faculties asleep. He is the only real traveler; he alone tastes the "gay, fresh sentiment of the road." He is not isolated, but is at one with things, with the farms and the industries on either hand. The vital, universal currents play through him. He knows the ground is alive; he feels the pulses of the wind, and reads the mute language of things. His sympathies are all aroused; his senses are continually reporting messages to his mind. Wind, frost, rain, heat, cold are something to him. He is not merely a spectator of the panorama of na-ture, but a participator in it. He experiences the country he passes through —tastes it, feels it, absorbs it; the traveler in his fine carriage sees it merely. This gives the fresh charm to that class of books that may be called "Views Afoot," and to the narratives of hunters, naturalists, exploring parties, etc. The walker does not need a large territory. When you get into a railway car, you want a continent, the man in his carriage requires a township; but a walker like Thoreau finds as much and more along the shores of Walden Pond. The former, as it were, has merely time to glance at the headings of the chapters, while the latter need not miss a line, and Thoreau reads be-tween the lines. Then the walker has the privilege of the fields, the woods, the hills, the byways. The apples by the roadside are for him, and the berries, and the spring of water, and the friendly shelter; and if the weather is cold, he eats the frost grapes and the persimmons, or even the white-meated turnip, snatched from the field he passed through, with incredible relish.

Afoot and in the open road, one has a fair start in life at last. There is no hindrance now. Let him put his best foot forward. He is on the broadest human plane. This is on the level of all the great laws and heroic deeds. From this platform he is eligible to any good fortune. He was sighing for the golden age; let him walk to it. Every step brings him nearer. The youth of the world is but a few days' journey distant. Indeed, I know persons who think they have walked back to that fresh aforetime of a single bright Sun-day in autumn or early spring. Before noon they felt its airs upon their cheeks, and by nightfall, on the banks of some quiet stream, or along some path in the wood, or on some hilltop, aver they have heard the voices and felt the wonder and the mystery that so enchanted the early races of men.

I think if I could walk through a country, I should not only see many things and have adventures that I should otherwise miss, but that I should come into relations with that country at first hand, and with the men and women in it, in a way that would afford the deepest satisfaction. Hence I envy the good fortune of all walkers, and feel like joining myself to every tramp that comes along. I am jealous of the clergyman I read about the other day, who footed it from Edinburgh to London, as poor Effie Deans did, carrying her shoes in her hand most of the way, and over the ground that rugged Ben Jonson strode, larking it to Scotland, so long ago. I read with longing of the pedestrian feats of college youths, so gay and light-hearted, with their coarse shoes on their feet and their knapsacks on their backs. It would have been a good draught of the rugged cup to have walked with Wilson the ornithologist, deserted by his companions, from Niagara to Philadelphia through the snows of winter. I almost wish that I had been born to the career of a German mechanic, that I might have had that deli-cious adventurous year of wandering over my country before I settled down to work. I think how much richer and firmer-grained life would be to me if I could journey afoot through Florida and Texas, or follow the windings of the Platte or the Yellowstone, or stroll through Oregon, or browse for a sea-son about Canada. In the bright, inspiring days of autumn I only want the time and the companion to walk back to the natal spot, the family nest, across two States and into the mountains of a third. What adventures we would have by the way, what hard pulls, what prospects from hills, what spectacles we would behold of night and day, what passages with dogs, what glances, what peeps into windows, what characters we should fall in with, and how seasoned and hardy we should arrive at our destination!

For companion I should want a veteran of the war! Those marches put something into him I like. Even at this distance his mettle is but little soft-ened. As soon as he gets warmed up, it all comes back to him. He catches your step and away you go, a gay, adventurous, half-predatory couple. How quickly he falls into the old ways of jest and anecdote and song! You may have known him for years without having heard him hum an air, or more than casually revert to the subject of his experience during the war. You have even questioned and cross-questioned him without firing the train you wished. But get him out on a vacation tramp, and you can walk it all out of him. By the camp-fire at night, or swinging along the streams by day, song, anecdote, adventure, come to the surface, and you wonder how your companion has kept silent so long.

It is another proof of how walking brings out the true character of a man. The devil never yet asked his victims to take a walk with him. You will not be long in finding your companion out. All disguises will fall away from him. As his pores open, his character is laid bare. His deepest and most private self will come to the top. It matters little with whom you ride, so he be not a pickpocket; for both of you will, very likely, settle down closer and firmer in your reserve, shaken down like a measure of corn by the jolting as the journey proceeds. But walking is a more vital copartnership; the relation is a closer and more sympathetic one, and you do not feel like walking ten paces with a stranger without speaking to him.

Hence the fastidiousness of the professional walker in choosing or admitting a companion, and hence the truth of a remark of Emerson, that you will generally fare better to take your dog than to invite your neighbor. Your cur-dog is a true pedestrian, and your neighbor is very likely a small politician. The dog enters thoroughly into the spirit of the enterprise; he is not indifferent or preoccupied; he is constantly sniffing adventure, laps at every spring, looks upon every field and wood as a new world to be explored, is ever on some fresh trail, knows something important will happen a little farther on, gazes with the true wonder-seeing eyes, whatever the spot or whatever the road, finds it good to be there—in short, is just that happy, delicious, excursive vagabond that touches one at so many points, and whose human prototype in a companion robs miles and leagues of half their power to fatigue.

Persons who find themselves spent in a short walk to the market or the post-office, or to do a little shopping, wonder how it is that their pedestrian friends can compass so many weary miles and not fall down from sheer exhaustion; ignorant of the fact that the walker is a kind of projectile that drops far or near according to the expansive force of the motive that set it in motion, and that it is easy enough to regulate the charge according to the distance to be traversed. If I am loaded to carry only one mile and am compelled to walk three, I generally feel more fatigue than if I had walked six under the proper impetus of preadjusted resolution. In other words, the will or corporeal mainspring, whatever it be, is capable of being wound up to different degrees of tension, so that one may walk all day nearly as easy as half that time, if he is prepared beforehand. He knows his task, and he measures and distributes his powers accordingly. It is for this reason that an unknown road is always a long road. We cannot cast the mental eye along it and see the end from the beginning. We are fighting in the dark, and cannot take the measure of our foe. Every step must be preordained and provided for in the mind. Hence also the fact that to vanquish one mile in the woods seems equal to compassing three in the open country. The furlongs are ambushed, and we magnify them.

Then, again, how annoying to be told it is only five miles to the next place when it is really eight or ten! We fall short nearly half the distance, and are compelled to urge and roll the spent ball the rest of the way. In such a case walking degenerates from a fine art to a mechanic art; we walk merely; to get over the ground becomes the one serious and engrossing thought; whereas success in walking is not to let your right foot know what your left foot doeth. Your heart must furnish such music that in keeping time to it your feet will carry you around the globe without knowing it. The walker I would describe takes no note of distance, his walk is a sally, a *bon mot,* an unspoken *jeu d'esprit;* the ground is his butt, his provocation; it furnishes him the resistance his body craves; he rebounds upon it, he glances off and returns again, and uses it gayly as his tool.

I do not think I exaggerate the importance or the charms of pedestrianism, or our need as a people to cultivate the art. I think it would tend to soften the national manners, to teach us the meaning of leisure, to acquaint us with the charms of the open air, to strengthen and foster the tie between the race and the land. No one else looks out upon the world so kindly and charitably as the pedestrian; no one else gives and takes so much from the country he passes through. Next to the laborer in the fields, the walker holds the closest relation to the soil; and he holds a closer and more vital relation to nature because he is freer and his mind more at leisure.

Man takes root at his feet, and at best he is no more than a potted plant in his house or carriage till he has established communication with the soil by the loving and magnetic touch of his soles to it. Then the tie of association is born; then spring those invisible fibres and rootlets through which character comes to smack of the soil, and which make a man kindred to the spot of earth he inhabits.

The roads and paths you have walked along in summer and winter weather, the fields and hills which you have looked upon in lightness and gladness of heart, where fresh thoughts have come into your mind, or some noble prospect has opened before you, and especially the quiet ways where you have walked in sweet converse with your friend, pausing under the trees, drinking at the spring, henceforth they are not the same; a new charm is added; those thoughts spring there perennial, your friend walks there forever.

We have produced some good walkers and saunterers, and some noted climbers; but as a staple recreation, as a daily practice, the mass of the people dislike and despise walking. Thoreau said he was a good horse, but a poor roadster. I chant the virtues of the roadster as well. I sing of the sweetness of gravel, good sharp quartz-grit. It is the proper condiment for the sterner seasons, and many a human gizzard would be cured of half its ills by a suitable daily allowance of it. I think Thoreau himself would have profited immensely by it. His diet was too exclusively vegetable. A man cannot live on grass alone. If one has been a lotus-eater all summer, he must turn gravel-eater in the fall and winter. Those who have tried it know that gravel possesses an equal though an opposite charm. It spurs to action. The foot tastes it and henceforth rests not. The joy of moving and surmounting, of attrition and progression, the thirst for space, for miles and leagues of distance, for sights and prospects, to cross mountains and thread rivers, and defy frost, heat, snow, danger, difficulties, seizes it; and from that day forth its possessor is enrolled in the noble army of walkers.

The Bluebird

WHEN NATURE MADE THE BLUEBIRD she wished to propitiate both the sky and the earth, so she gave him the color of the one on his back and the hue of the other on his breast, and ordained that his appearance in spring should denote that the strife and war between these two elements was at an end. He is the peace-harbinger; in him the celestial and terrestrial strike hands and are fast friends. He means the furrow and he means the warmth; he means all the soft, wooing influences of the spring on the one hand, and the retreating footsteps of winter on the other.

It is sure to be a bright March morning when you first hear his note; and it is as if the milder influences up above had found a voice and let a word fall upon your ear, so tender is it and so prophetic, a hope tinged with a regret.

"Bermuda! Bermuda! Bermuda!" he seems to say, as if both invoking and lamenting, and, behold! Bermuda follows close, though the little pilgrim may be only repeating the tradition of his race, himself having come only from Florida, the Carolinas, or even from Virginia, where he has found his Bermuda on some broad sunny hillside thickly studded with cedars and persimmon-trees.

In New York and in New England the sap starts up in the sugar maple the very day the bluebird arrives, and sugar-making begins forthwith. The bird is generally a mere disembodied voice; a rumor in the air for two or three days before it takes visible shape before you. The males are the pioneers, and come several days in advance of the females. By the time both are here and the pairs have begun to prospect for a place to nest, sugar-making is over, the last vestige of snow has disappeared, and the plow is brightening its mould-board in the new furrow.

The bluebird enjoys the preeminence of being the first bit of color that cheers our northern landscape. The other birds that arrive about the same

From *Wake-Robin,* 1871.

time—the sparrow, the robin, the phoebe-bird—are clad in neutral tints, gray, brown, or russet; but the bluebird brings one of the primary hues and the divinest of them all.

This bird also has the distinction of answering very nearly to the robin redbreast of English memory, and was by the early settlers of New England christened the blue robin. It is a size or two larger, and the ruddy hue of its breast does not verge so nearly on an orange, but the manners and habits of the two birds are very much alike. Our bird has the softer voice, but the English redbreast is much the more skilled musician. He has indeed a fine, animated warble, heard nearly the year through about English gardens and along the old hedge-rows, that is quite beyond the compass of our bird's instrument. On the other hand, our bird is associated with the spring as the British species cannot be, being a winter resident also, while the brighter sun and sky of the New World have given him a coat that far surpasses that of his transatlantic cousin.

It is worthy of remark that among British birds there is no *blue* bird. The cerulean tint seems much rarer among the feathered tribes there than here. On this continent there are at least three species of the common bluebird, while in all our woods there is the blue jay and the indigo-bird, the latter so intensely blue as to fully justify its name. There is also the blue grosbeak, not much behind the indigo-bird in intensity of color; and among our warblers the blue tint is very common.

It is interesting to know that the bluebird is not confined to any one section of the country; and that when one goes west he will still have this favorite with him, though a little changed in voice and color, just enough to give variety without marring the identity.

The western bluebird is considered a distinct species, and is perhaps a little more brilliant and showy than its eastern brother; and Nuttall thinks its song is more varied, sweet, and tender. Its color approaches to ultramarine, while it has a sash of chestnut-red across its shoulders—all the effects, I suspect, of that wonderful air and sky of California, and of those great western plains; or, if one goes a little higher up into the mountainous regions of the West, he finds the Arctic bluebird, the ruddy brown on the breast changed to greenish blue, and the wings longer and more pointed; in other respects not differing much from our species.

The bluebird usually builds its nest in a hole in a stump or stub, or in an old cavity excavated by a woodpecker, when such can be had; but its first impulse seems to be to start in the world in much more style, and the happy pair make a great show of house-hunting about the farm buildings,

John Burroughs looking at birdhouse. Courtesy of the American Museum of Natural History.

now half persuaded to appropriate a dove-cote, then discussing in a lively manner a last year's swallow's nest, or proclaiming with much flourish and flutter that they have taken the wren's house, or the tenement of the purple martin; till finally nature becomes too urgent, when all this pretty make-believe ceases, and most of them settle back upon the old family stumps and knotholes in remote fields, and go to work in earnest.

In such situations the female is easily captured by approaching very stealthily and covering the entrance to the nest. The bird seldom makes any effort to escape, seeing how hopeless the case is, and keeps her place on the nest till she feels your hand closing around her. I have looked down into the cavity and seen the poor thing palpitating with fear and looking up with distended eyes, but never moving till I had withdrawn a few paces; then she rushes out with a cry that brings the male on the scene in a hurry. He warbles and lifts his wings beseechingly, but shows no anger or disposition to scold and complain like most birds. Indeed, this bird seems incapable of uttering a harsh note, or of doing a spiteful, ill-tempered thing.

The ground-builders all have some art or device to decoy one away from the nest, affecting lameness, a crippled wing, or a broken back, promising an easy capture if pursued. The tree-builders depend upon concealing the nest or placing it beyond reach. But the bluebird has no art either way, and its nest is easily found.

About the only enemies the sitting bird or the nest is in danger of are snakes and squirrels. I knew of a farm-boy who was in the habit of putting his hand down into a bluebird's nest and taking out the old bird whenever he came that way. One day he put his hand in, and, feeling something peculiar, withdrew it hastily, when it was instantly followed by the head and neck of an enormous black snake. The boy took to his heels and the snake gave chase, pressing him close till a plowman near by came to the rescue with his ox-whip.

There never was a happier or more devoted husband than the male bluebird is. But among nearly all our familiar birds the serious cares of life seem to devolve almost entirely upon the female. The male is hilarious and demonstrative, the female serious and anxious about her charge. The male is the attendant of the female, following her wherever she goes. He never leads, never directs, but only seconds and applauds. If his life is all poetry and romance, hers is all business and prose. She has no pleasure but her duty, and no duty but to look after her nest and brood. She shows no affection for the male, no pleasure in his society; she only tolerates him as a necessary evil, and, if he is killed, goes in quest of another in the most businesslike manner, as you would go for the plumber or the glazier. In most cases the male is the ornamental partner in the firm, and contributes little of the working capital. There seems to be more equality of the sexes among the woodpeckers, wrens, and swallows; while the contrast is greatest, perhaps, in the bobolink family, where the courting is done in the Arab fashion, the female fleeing with all her speed and the male pursuing with equal precipitation; and were it not for the broods of young birds that appear, it would be hard to believe that the intercourse ever ripened into anything more intimate.

With the bluebirds the male is useful as well as ornamental. He is the gay champion and escort of the female at all times, and while she is sitting, he feeds her regularly. It is very pretty to watch them building their nest. The male is very active in hunting out a place and exploring the boxes and cavities, but seems to have no choice in the matter and is anxious only to please and encourage his mate, who has the practical turn and knows what will do and what will not. After she has suited herself, he applauds her immensely, and away the two go in quest of material for the nest, the male acting as guard and flying above and in advance of the female. She brings all the material and does all the work of building, he looking on and encouraging her with gesture and song. He acts also as inspector of her work, but I fear is a very partial one. She enters the nest with her bit of dry grass or straw, and, having adjusted it to her notion, withdraws and waits near by while he goes in and looks it over. On coming out he exclaims very plainly, *Excellent! excellent!* and away the two go again for more material.

The bluebirds, when they build about the farm buildings, sometimes come in conflict with the swallows. The past season I knew a pair to take forcible possession of the domicile of a pair of the latter—the cliff species that now stick their nests under the eaves of the barn. The bluebirds had been broken up in a little bird-house near by, by the rats or perhaps a weasel, and being no doubt in a bad humor, and the season being well advanced, they made forcible entrance into the adobe tenement of their neighbors, and held possession of it for some days, but I believe finally withdrew, rather than live amid such a squeaky, noisy colony. I have heard that these swallows, when ejected from their homes in that way by the phoebe-bird, have been known to fall to and mason up the entrance to the nest while their enemy was inside, thus having a revenge as complete and cruel as anything in human annals.

The bluebirds and the house wrens more frequently come into collision. A few years ago I put up a little bird-house in the back end of my garden for the accommodation of the wrens, and every season a pair have taken up their abode there. One spring a pair of bluebirds looked into the tenement and lingered about several days, leading me to hope that they would conclude to occupy it. But they finally went away, and later in the season the wrens appeared, and, after a little coquetting, were regularly installed in their old quarters, and were as happy as only wrens can be.

One of our younger poets, Myron Benton, saw a little bird "Ruffled with whirlwind of his ecstasies," which must have been the wren, as I know of no other bird that so throbs and palpitates with music as this little vagabond. And the pair I speak of seemed exceptionally happy, and the male had a small tornado of song in his crop that kept him "ruffled" every moment in the day. But before their honeymoon was over, the bluebirds returned. I knew something was wrong before I was up in the morning. Instead of that voluble and gushing song outside the window, I heard the wrens scolding

and crying, at a fearful rate, and on going out saw the bluebirds in possession of the box. The poor wrens were in despair; they wrung their hands
and tore their hair, after the wren fashion, but chiefly did they rattle out
their disgust and wrath at the intruders. I have no doubt that, if it could
have been interpreted, it would have proven the rankest and most voluble
Billingsgate ever uttered. For the wren is saucy, and he has a tongue in his
head that can outwag any other tongue known to me.

The bluebirds said nothing, but the male kept an eye on Mr. Wren; and,
when he came too near, gave chase, driving him to cover under the fence, or
under a rubbish-heap or other object, where the wren would scold and rattle away—while his pursuer sat on the fence or the pea-brush waiting for
him to reappear.

Days passed, and the usurpers prospered and the outcasts were wretched;
but the latter lingered about, watching and abusing their enemies, and hoping, no doubt, that things would take a turn, as they presently did. The outraged wrens were fully avenged. The mother bluebird had laid her full
complement of eggs and was beginning to set, when one day, as her mate
was perched above her on the barn, along came a boy with one of those
wicked elastic slings and cut him down with a pebble. There he lay like a bit
of sky fallen upon the grass. The widowed bird seemed to understand what
had happened, and without much ado disappeared next day in quest of another mate. How she contrived to make her wants known, without trum-
peting them about, I am unable to say. But I presume the birds have a way
of advertising that answers the purpose well. Maybe she trusted to luck to
fall in with some stray bachelor or bereaved male who would undertake to
console a widow of one day's standing. I will say, in passing, that there are
no bachelors from choice among the birds; they are all rejected suitors,
while old maids are entirely unknown. There is a Jack to every Jill; and
some to boot.

The males, being more exposed by their song and plumage, and by being
the pioneers in migrating, seem to be slightly in excess lest the supply fall
short, and hence it sometimes happens that a few are bachelors perforce;
there are not females enough to go around, but before the season is over,
there are sure to be some vacancies in the marital ranks which they are
called on to fill.

In the meantime the wrens were beside themselves with delight; they
fairly screamed with joy. If the male was before "ruffled with whirlwind of
his ecstasies," he was now in danger of being rent asunder. He inflated his
throat and caroled as wren never caroled before. And the female, too, how

she cackled and darted about! How busy they both were! Rushing into the nest, they hustled those eggs out in less than a minute, wren time. They carried in new material, and by the third day were fairly installed again in their old quarters; but on the third day, so rapidly are these little dramas played, the female bluebird reappeared with another mate. Ah! how the wren stock went down then! What dismay and despair filled again those little breasts! It was pitiful. They did not scold as before, but after a day or two withdrew from the garden, dumb with grief, and gave up the struggle.

The bluebird, finding her eggs gone and her nest changed, seemed suddenly seized with alarm and shunned the box; or else, finding she had less need for another husband than she thought, repented her rashness and wanted to dissolve the compact. But the happy bridegroom would not take the hint, and exerted all his eloquence to comfort and reassure her. He was fresh and fond, and until this bereaved female found him, I am sure his suit had not prospered that season. He thought the box just the thing, and that there was no need of alarm, and spent days in trying to persuade the female back. Seeing he could not be a stepfather to a family, he was quite willing to assume a nearer relation. He hovered about the box, he went in and out, he called, he warbled, he entreated; the female would respond occasionally and come and alight near, and even peep into the nest, but would not enter it, and quickly flew away again. Her mate would reluctantly follow, but he was soon back, uttering the most confident and cheering calls. If she did not come he would perch above the nest and sound his loudest notes over and over again, looking in the direction of his mate and beckoning with every motion. But she responded less and less frequently. Some days I would see him only, but finally he gave it up; the pair disappeared, and the box remained deserted the rest of the summer.

Speckled Trout

THE LEGEND OF THE WARY TROUT, hinted at in the last sketch, is to be further illustrated in this and some following chapters. We shall get at more of the meaning of those dark water-lines, and I hope, also, not entirely miss the significance of the gold and silver spots and the glancing iridescent hues. The trout is dark and obscure above, but behind this foil there are wondrous tints that reward the believing eye. Those who seek him in his wild remote haunts are quite sure to get the full force of the sombre and uninviting aspects — the wet, the cold, the toil, the broken rest, and the huge, savage, uncompromising nature — but the true angler sees farther than these, and is never thwarted of his legitimate reward by them.

I have been a seeker of trout from my boyhood, and on all the expeditions in which this fish has been the ostensible purpose I have brought home more game than my creel showed. In fact, in my mature years I find I got more of nature into me, more of the woods, the wild, nearer to bird and beast, while threading my native streams for trout than in almost any other way. It furnished a good excuse to go forth; it pitched one in the right key; it sent one through the fat and marrowy places of field and wood. Then the fisherman has a harmless, preoccupied look; he is a kind of vagrant that nothing fears. He blends himself with the trees and the shadows. All his approaches are gentle and indirect. He times himself to the meandering, soliloquizing stream; its impulse bears him along. At the foot of the waterfall he sits sequestered and hidden in its volume of sound. The birds know he has no designs upon them, and the animals see that his mind is in the creek. His enthusiasm anneals him, and makes him pliable to the scenes and influences he moves among.

Then what acquaintance he makes with the stream! He addresses himself to it as a lover to his mistress; he woos it and stays with it till he knows its most hidden secrets. It runs through his thoughts not less than through its

From *Locusts and Wild Honey*, 1879.

banks there; he feels the fret and thrust of every bar and boulder. Where it deepens, his purpose deepens; where it is shallow, he is indifferent. He knows how to interpret its every glance and dimple; its beauty haunts him for days.

I am sure I run no risk of overpraising the charm and attractiveness of a well-fed trout stream, every drop of water in it as bright and pure as if the nymphs had brought it all the way from its source in crystal goblets, and as cool as if it had been hatched beneath a glacier. When the heated and soiled and jaded refugee from the city first sees one, he feels as if he would like to turn it into his bosom and let it flow through him a few hours, it suggests such healing freshness and newness. How his roily thoughts would run clear; how the sediment would go downstream! Could he ever have an impure or an unwholesome wish afterward? The next best thing he can do is to tramp along its banks and surrender himself to its influence. If he reads it intently enough, he will, in a measure, be taking it into his mind and heart, and experiencing its salutary ministrations.

Trout streams coursed through every valley my boyhood knew. I crossed them, and was often lured and detained by them, on my way to and from school. We bathed in them during the long summer noons, and felt for the trout under their banks. A holiday was a holiday indeed that brought permission to go fishing over on Rose's Brook, or up Hardscrabble, or in Meeker's Hollow; all-day trips, from morning till night, through meadows and pastures and beechen woods, wherever the shy, limpid stream led. What an appetite it developed! a hunger that was fierce and aboriginal, and that the wild strawberries we plucked as we crossed the hill teased rather than allayed. When but a few hours could be had, gained perhaps by doing some piece of work about the farm or garden in half the allotted time, the little creek that headed in the paternal domain was handy; when half a day was at one's disposal, there were the hemlocks, less than a mile distant, with their loitering, meditative, log-impeded stream and their dusky, fragrant depths. Alert and wide-eyed, one picked his way along, startled now and then by the sudden bursting-up of the partridge, or by the whistling wings of the "dropping snipe," pressing through the brush and the briers, or finding an easy passage over the trunk of a prostrate tree, carefully letting his hook down through some tangle into a still pool, or standing in some high, sombre avenue and watching his line float in and out amid the moss-covered boulders.

In my first essayings I used to go to the edge of these hemlocks, seldom dipping into them beyond the first pool where the stream swept under the roots of two large trees. From this point I could look back into the sunlit fields where the cattle were grazing; beyond, all was gloom and mystery; the trout were black, and to my young imagination the silence and the shadows were blacker. But gradually I yielded to the fascination and penetrated the woods farther and farther on each expedition, till the heart of the mystery was fairly plucked out. During the second or third year of my piscatorial experience I went through them, and through the pasture and meadow beyond, and through another strip of hemlocks, to where the little stream joined the main creek of the valley.

In June, when my trout fever ran pretty high, and an auspicious day arrived, I would make a trip to a stream a couple of miles distant, that came down out of a comparatively new settlement. It was a rapid mountain brook presenting many difficult problems to the young angler, but a very enticing stream for all that, with its two saw-mill dams, its pretty cascades, its high, shelving rocks sheltering the mossy nests of the phoebe-bird—and its general wild and forbidding aspects.

But a meadow brook was always a favorite. The trout like meadows; doubtless their food is more abundant there, and, usually, the good hiding-places are more numerous. As soon as you strike a meadow, the character of the creek changes: it goes slower and lies deeper; it tarries to enjoy the high, cool banks and to half hide beneath them; it loves the willows, or rather the willows love it and shelter it from the sun; its spring runs are kept cool by the overhanging grass, and the heavy turf that faces its open banks is not cut away by the sharp hoofs of the grazing cattle. Then there are the bobolinks and the starlings and the meadowlarks, always interested spectators of the angler; there are also the marsh marigolds, the buttercups, or the spotted lilies, and the good angler is always an interested spectator of them. In fact, the patches of meadow land that lie in the angler's course are like the happy experiences in his own life, or like the fine passages in the poem he is reading; the pasture oftener contains the shallow and monotonous places. In the small streams the cattle scare the fish, and soil their element and break down their retreats under the banks. Woodland alternates the best with meadow: the creek loves to burrow under the roots of a great tree, to scoop out a pool after leaping over the prostrate trunk of one, and to pause at the foot of a ledge of moss-covered rocks, with ice-cold water dripping down. How straight the current goes for the rock! Note its corrugated, muscular appearance; it strikes and glances off, but accumulates, deepens with well-defined eddies above and to one side; on the edge of these the trout lurk and spring upon their prey.

The angler learns that it is generally some obstacle or hindrance that makes a deep place in the creek, as in a brave life; and his ideal brook is one that lies in deep, well-defined banks, yet makes many a shift from right to left, meets with many rebuffs and adventures, hurled back upon itself by rocks, waylaid by snags and trees, tripped up by precipices, but sooner or later reposing under meadow banks, deepening and eddying beneath bridges, or prosperous and strong in some level stretch of cultivated land with great elms shading it here and there.

But I early learned that from almost any stream in a trout country the true angler could take trout, and that the great secret was this, that, whatever bait you used, worm, grasshopper, grub, or fly, there was one thing you must always put upon your hook, namely, your heart: when you bait your hook with your heart, the fish always bite; they will jump clear from the water after it; they will dispute with each other over it; it is a morsel they love above everything else. With such bait I have seen the born angler (my grandfather was one) take a noble string of trout from the most unpromising waters, and on the most unpromising day. He used his hook so coyly and tenderly, he approached the fish with such address and insinuation, he divined the exact spot where they lay: if they were not eager, he humored them and seemed to steal by them; if they were playful and coquettish, he would suit his mood to theirs; if they were frank and sincere, he met them halfway; he was so patient and considerate, so entirely devoted to pleasing the critical trout, and so successful in his efforts—surely his heart was upon his hook—and it was a tender, unctuous heart, too, as that of every angler is. How nicely he would measure the distance! how dexterously he would avoid an overhanging limb or bush and drop the line exactly in the right spot! Of course there was a pulse of feeling and sympathy to the extremity of that line. If your heart is a stone, however, or an empty husk, there is no use to put it upon your hook; it will not tempt the fish; the bait must be quick and fresh. Indeed, a certain quality of youth is indispensable to the successful angler, a certain unworldliness and readiness to invest yourself in an enterprise that doesn't pay in the current coin. Not only is the angler, like the poet, born and not made, as Walton says, but there is a deal of the poet in him, and he is to be judged no more harshly; he is the victim of his genius: those wild streams, how they haunt him! he will play truant to dull care, and flee to them; their waters impart somewhat of their own perpetual youth to him. My grandfather when he was eighty years old would take down his pole as eagerly as any boy, and step off with wonderful elasticity toward the beloved streams; it used to try my young legs a good deal to

follow him, specially on the return trip. And no poet was ever more innocent of worldly success or ambition. For, to paraphrase Tennyson,

> Lusty trout to him were scrip and share,
> And babbling waters more than cent for cent.

He laid up treasures, but they were not in this world. In fact, though the
kindest of husbands, I fear he was not what the country people call a "good
provider," except in providing trout in their season, though it is doubtful if
there was always fat in the house to fry them in. But he could tell you they
were worse off than that at Valley Forge, and that trout, or any other fish,
were good roasted in the ashes under the coals. He had the Walton requisite
of loving quietness and contemplation, and was devout withal. Indeed, in
many ways he was akin to those Galilee fishermen who were called to be
fishers of men. How he read the Book and pored over it, even at times, I
suspect, nodding over it, and laying it down only to take up his rod, over
which, unless the trout were very dilatory and the journey very fatiguing, he
never nodded!

II

The Delaware is one of our minor rivers, but it is a stream beloved of the
trout. Nearly all its remote branches head in mountain springs, and its collected waters, even when warmed by the summer sun, are as sweet and
wholesome as dew swept from the grass. The Hudson wins from it two
streams that are fathered by the mountains from whose loins most of its beginnings issue, namely, the Rondout and the Esopus. These swell a more illustrious current than the Delaware, but the Rondout, one of the finest
trout streams in the world, makes an uncanny alliance before it reaches its
destination, namely, with the malarious Wallkill.

In the same nest of mountains from which they start are born the Neversink and the Beaverkill, streams of wondrous beauty that flow south and
west into the Delaware. From my native hills I could catch glimpses of the
mountains in whose laps these creeks were cradled, but it was not till after
many years, and after dwelling in a country where trout are not found, that
I returned to pay my respects to them as an angler.

My first acquaintance with the Neversink was made in company with
some friends in 1869. We passed up the valley of the Big Ingin, marveling
at its copious ice-cold springs, and its immense sweep of heavy-timbered
mountain-sides. Crossing the range at its head, we struck the Neversink

quite unexpectedly about the middle of the afternoon, at a point where it was a good-sized trout stream. It proved to be one of those black mountain brooks born of innumerable ice-cold springs, nourished in the shade, and shod, as it were, with thick-matted moss, that every camper-out remembers. The fish are as black as the stream and very wild. They dart from beneath the fringed rocks, or dive with the hook into the dusky depths—an integral part of the silence and the shadows. The spell of the moss is over all. The fisherman's tread is noiseless, as he leaps from stone to stone and from ledge to ledge along the bed of the stream. How cool it is! He looks up the dark, silent defile, hears the solitary voice of the water, sees the decayed trunks of fallen trees bridging the stream, and all he has dreamed, when a boy, of the haunts of beasts of prey—the crouching feline tribes, especially if it be near nightfall and the gloom already deepening in the woods— comes freshly to mind, and he presses on, wary and alert, and speaking to his companions in low tones.

After an hour or so the trout became less abundant, and with nearly a hundred of the black sprites in our baskets we turned back. Here and there I saw the abandoned nests of the pigeons, sometimes half a dozen in one tree. In a yellow birch which the floods had uprooted, a number of nests were still in place, little shelves or platforms of twigs loosely arranged, and affording little or no protection to the eggs or the young birds against inclement weather.

Before we had reached our companions the rain set in again and forced us to take shelter under a balsam. When it slackened, we moved on and soon came up with Aaron, who had caught his first trout, and, considerably drenched, was making his way toward camp, which one of the party had gone forward to build. After traveling less than a mile, we saw a smoke struggling up through the dripping trees, and in a few moments were all standing round a blazing fire. But the rain now commenced again, and fairly poured down through the trees, rendering the prospect of cooking and eating our supper there in the woods, and of passing the night on the ground without tent or cover of any kind, rather disheartening. We had been told of a bark shanty a couple of miles farther down the creek, and thitherward we speedily took up our line of march. When we were on the point of discontinuing the search, thinking we had been misinformed or had passed it by, we came in sight of a bark-peeling, in the midst of which a small log house lifted its naked rafters toward the now breaking sky. It had neither floor nor roof, and was less inviting on first sight than the open woods. But a board partition was still standing, out of which we built a rude porch on the east side of the house, large enough for us all to sleep under if well packed, and eat under if we stood up. There was plenty of well-seasoned timber lying about, and a fire was soon burning in front of our quarters that made the scene social and picturesque, especially when the frying-pans were brought into requisition, and the coffee, in charge of Aaron, who was an artist in this line, mingled its aroma with the wild-wood air. At dusk a balsam was felled, and the tips of the branches used to make a bed, which was more fragrant than soft; hemlock is better, because its needles are finer and its branches more elastic.

There was a spirt or two of rain during the night, but not enough to find out the leaks in our roof. It took the shower or series of showers of the next day to do that. They commenced about two o'clock in the afternoon. The forenoon had been fine, and we had brought into camp nearly three hundred trout; but before they were half dressed, or the panfuls fried, the rain set in. First came short dashes, then a gleam of treacherous sunshine followed by more and heavier dashes. The wind was in the southwest, and to rain seemed the easiest thing in the world. From fitful dashes to a pour the transition was natural. We stood huddled together, stark and grim, under our cover, like hens under a cart. The fire fought bravely for a time, and retaliated with sparks and spiteful tongues of flame; but gradually its spirit was broken, only a heavy body of coal and half-consumed logs in the centre holding out against all odds. The simmering fish were soon floating about in a yellow liquid that did not look in the least appetizing. Point after point gave way in our cover, till standing between the drops was no longer possible. The water coursed down the underside of the boards, and dripped in our necks and formed puddles on our hat-brims. We shifted our guns and traps and viands, till there was no longer any choice of position, when the loaves and the fishes, the salt and the sugar, the pork and the butter, shared the same watery fate. The fire was gasping its last. Little rivulets coursed about it, and bore away the quenched but steaming coals on their bosoms. The spring run in the rear of our camp swelled so rapidly that part of the trout that had been hastily left lying on its banks again found themselves quite at home. For over two hours the floods came down. About four o'clock, Orville, who had not yet come from the day's sport, appeared. To say Orville was wet is not much; he was better than that—he had been washed and rinsed in at least half a dozen waters, and the trout that he bore dangling at the end of a string hardly knew that they had been out of their proper element.

But he brought welcome news. He had been two or three miles down the creek, and had seen a log building—whether house or stable he did not

know, but it had the appearance of having a good roof, which was induce-
ment enough for us instantly to leave our present quarters. Our course lay
along an old wood-road, and much of the time we were to our knees in
water. The woods were literally flooded everywhere. Every little rill and
springlet ran like a mill-tail, while the main stream rushed and roared,
foaming, leaping, lashing, its volume increased fifty-fold. The water was not
roily, but of a rich coffee-color, from the leachings of the woods. No more
trout for the next three days! we thought, as we looked upon the rampant
stream.

After we had labored and floundered along for about an hour, the road
turned to the left, and in a little stumpy clearing near the creek a gable up-
rose on our view. It did not prove to be just such a place as poets love to
contemplate. It required a greater effort of the imagination than any of us
were then capable of to believe it had ever been a favorite resort of wood-
nymphs or sylvan deities. It savored rather of the equine and the bovine.
The bark-men had kept their teams there, horses on the one side and oxen
on the other, and no Hercules had ever done duty in cleansing the stables.

But there was a dry loft overhead with some straw, where we might get
some sleep, in spite of the rain and the midges; a double layer of boards,
standing at a very acute angle, would keep off the former, while the mingled
refuse hay and muck beneath would nurse a smoke that would prove a
thorough protection against the latter. And then, when Jim, the two-
handed, mounting the trunk of a prostrate maple near by, had severed it
thrice with easy and familiar stroke, and, rolling the logs in front of the
shanty, had kindled a fire which, getting the better of the dampness, soon
cast a bright glow over all, shedding warmth and light even into the dingy
stable, I consented to unsling my knapsack and accept the situation. The
rain had ceased, and the sun shone out behind the woods. We had trout
sufficient for present needs; and after my first meal in an ox-stall, I strolled
out on the rude log bridge to watch the angry Neversink rush by. Its waters
fell quite as rapidly as they rose, and before sundown it looked as if we
might have fishing again on the morrow.

We had better sleep that night than either night before, though there
were two disturbing causes—the smoke in the early part of it, and the cold
in the latter. The "no-see-ems" left in disgust; and, though disgusted myself,
I swallowed the smoke as best I could, and hugged my pallet of straw the
closer. But the day dawned bright, and a plunge in the Neversink set me all
right again. The creek, to our surprise and gratification, was only a little
higher than before the rain, and some of the finest trout we had yet seen we
caught that morning near camp.

We tarried yet another day and night at the old stable, but taking our meals outside squatted on the ground, which had now become quite dry. Part of the day I spent strolling about the woods, looking up old acquaintances among the birds, and, as always, half expectant of making some new ones. Curiously enough, the most abundant species were among those I had found rare in most other localities, namely, the small water-wagtail, the mourning ground warbler, and the yellow-bellied woodpecker. The latter seems to be the prevailing woodpecker through the woods of this region.

That night the midges, those motes that sting, held high carnival. We learned afterward, in the settlement below and from the bark-peelers, that it was the worst night ever experienced in that valley. We had done no fishing during the day, but had anticipated some fine sport about sundown. Accordingly Aaron and I started off between six and seven o'clock, one going upstream and the other down. The scene was charming. The sun shot up great spokes of light from behind the woods, and beauty, like a presence, pervaded the atmosphere. But torment, multiplied as the sands of the seashore, lurked in every tangle and thicket. In a thoughtless moment I removed my shoes and socks, and waded in the water to secure a fine trout that had accidentally slipped from my string and was helplessly floating with the current. This caused some delay and gave the gnats time to accumulate. Before I had got one foot half dressed I was enveloped in a black mist that settled upon my hands and neck and face, filling my ears with infinitesimal pipings and covering my flesh with infinitesimal bitings. I thought I should have to flee to the friendly fumes of the old stable, with "one stocking off and one stocking on"; but I got my shoe on at last, though not without many amusing interruptions and digressions.

In a few moments after this adventure I was in rapid retreat toward camp. Just as I reached the path leading from the shanty to the creek, my companion in the same ignoble flight reached it also, his hat broken and rumpled, and his sanguine countenance looking more sanguinary than I had ever before seen it, and his speech, also, in the highest degree inflammatory. His face and forehead were as blotched and swollen as if he had just run his head into a hornets' nest, and his manner as precipitate as if the whole swarm was still at his back.

No smoke or smudge which we ourselves could endure was sufficient in the earlier part of that evening to prevent serious annoyance from the same cause; but later a respite was granted us. About ten o'clock, as we stood round our campfire, we were startled by a brief but striking display of the aurora borealis. My imagination had already been excited by talk of legends and of weird shapes and appearances, and when, on looking up toward the sky, I saw those pale, phantasmal waves of magnetic light chasing each other across the little opening above our heads, and at first sight seeming barely to clear the treetops, I was as vividly impressed as if I had caught a glimpse of a veritable spectre of the Neversink. The sky shook and trembled like a great white curtain.

After we had climbed to our loft and had lain down to sleep, another adventure befell us. This time a new and uninviting customer appeared upon the scene, the *genius loci* of the old stable, namely, the "fretful porcupine." We had seen the marks and work of these animals about the shanty, and had been careful each night to hang our traps, guns, etc., beyond their reach, but of the prickly night-walker himself we feared we should not get a view.

We had lain down some half hour, and I was just on the threshold of sleep, ready, as it were, to pass through the open door into the land of dreams, when I heard outside somewhere that curious sound—a sound which I had heard every night I spent in these woods, not only on this but on former expeditions, and which I had settled in my mind as proceeding from the porcupine, since I knew the sounds our other common animals were likely to make—a sound that might be either a gnawing on some hard, dry substance, or a grating of teeth, or a shrill grunting.

Orville heard it also, and, raising up on his elbow, asked, "What is that?"

"What the hunters call a 'porcupig,'" said I.

"Sure?"

"Entirely so."

"Why does he make that noise?"

"It is a way he has of cursing our fire," I replied. "I heard him last night also."

"Where do you suppose he is?" inquired my companion, showing a disposition to look him up.

"Not far off, perhaps fifteen or twenty yards from our fire, where the shadows begin to deepen."

Orville slipped into his trousers, felt for my gun, and in a moment had disappeared down through the scuttle hole. I had no disposition to follow him, but was rather annoyed than otherwise at the disturbance. Getting the direction of the sound, he went picking his way over the rough, uneven ground, and, when he got where the light failed him, poking every doubtful object with the end of his gun. Presently he poked a light grayish object, like a large round stone, which surprised him by moving off. On this hint he fired, making an incurable wound in the "porcupig," which, nevertheless, tried harder than ever to escape. I lay listening, when, close on the heels of the report of the gun, came excited shouts for a revolver. Snatching up my Smith and Wesson, I hastened, shoeless and hatless, to the scene of action, wondering what was up. I found my companion struggling to detain, with the end of the gun, an uncertain object that was trying to crawl off into the darkness. "Look out!" said Orville, as he saw my bare feet, "the quills are lying thick around here."

And so they were; he had blown or beaten them nearly all off the poor creature's back, and was in a fair way completely to disable my gun, the ramrod of which was already broken and splintered clubbing his victim. But a couple of shots from the revolver, sighted by a lighted match, at the head of the animal, quickly settled him.

He proved to be an unusually large Canada porcupine—an old patriarch, gray and venerable, with spines three inches long, and weighing, I should say, twenty pounds. The build of this animal is much like that of the woodchuck, that is, heavy and pouchy. The nose is blunter than that of the woodchuck, the limbs stronger, and the tail broader and heavier. Indeed, the latter appendage is quite clublike, and the animal can, no doubt, deal a smart blow with it. An old hunter with whom I talked thought it aided them in climbing. They are inveterate gnawers, and spend much of their time in trees gnawing the bark. In winter one will take up its abode in a hemlock, and continue there till the tree is quite denuded. The carcass emitted a peculiar, offensive odor, and, though very fat, was not in the least inviting as game. If it is part of the economy of nature for one animal to prey upon some other beneath it, then the poor devil has indeed a mouthful that makes a meal off the porcupine. Panthers and lynxes have essayed it, but have invariably left off at the first course, and have afterwards been found dead, or nearly so, with their heads puffed up like a pincushion, and the quills protruding on all sides. A dog that understands the business will manoeuvre round the porcupine till he gets an opportunity to throw it over on its back, when he fastens on its quill-less underbody. Aaron was puzzled to know how long-parted friends could embrace, when it was suggested that the quills could be depressed or elevated at pleasure.

The next morning boded rain; but we had become thoroughly sated with the delights of our present quarters, outside and in, and packed up our traps to leave. Before we had reached the clearing, three miles below, the rain set in, keeping up a lazy monotonous drizzle till the afternoon.

The clearing was quite a recent one, made mostly by barkpeelers, who followed their calling in the mountains round about in summer, and worked in their shops making shingle in winter. The Biscuit Brook came in here from the west—a fine, rapid trout stream six or eight miles in length, with plenty of deer in the mountains about its head. On its banks we found the house of an old woodman, to whom we had been directed for information about the section we proposed to traverse.

"Is the way very difficult," we inquired, "across from the Neversink into the head of the Beaverkill?"

"Not to me; I could go it the darkest night ever was. And I can direct you so you can find the way without any trouble. You go down the Neversink about a mile, when you come to Highfall Brook, the first stream that comes down on the right. Follow up it to Jim Reed's shanty, about three miles. Then cross the stream, and on the left bank, pretty well up on the side of the mountain, you will find a wood-road, which was made by a fellow below here who stole some ash logs off the top of the ridge last winter and drew them out on the snow. When the road first begins to tilt over the mountain, strike down to your left, and you can reach the Beaverkill before sundown."

As it was then after two o'clock, and as the distance was six or eight of these terrible hunters' miles, we concluded to take a whole day to it, and wait till next morning. The Beaverkill flowed west, the Neversink south, and I had a mortal dread of getting entangled amid the mountains and valleys that lie in either angle.

Besides, I was glad of another and final opportunity to pay my respects to the finny tribes of the Neversink. At this point it was one of the finest trout streams I had ever beheld. It was so sparkling, its bed so free from sediment or impurities of any kind, that it had a new look, as if it had just come from the hand of its Creator. I tramped along its margin upward of a mile that afternoon, part of the time wading to my knees, and casting my hook, baited only with a trout's fin, to the opposite bank. Trout are real cannibals, and make no bones, and break none either, in lunching on each other. A friend of mine had several in his spring, when one day a large female trout gulped down one of her male friends, nearly one third her own size, and went around for two days with the tail of her liege lord protruding from her mouth! A fish's eye will do for bait, though the anal fin is better. One of the natives here told me that when he wished to catch large trout (and I judged he never fished for any other—I never do), he used for bait the bullhead, or dart, a little fish an inch and a half or two inches long, that rests on the pebbles near shore and darts quickly, when disturbed, from point to point. "Put that on your hook," said he, "and if there is a big fish in the creek, he is bound to have it." But the darts were not easily found; the big fish, I concluded, had cleaned them all out; and, then, it was easy enough to supply our wants with a fin.

Declining the hospitable offers of the settlers, we spread our blankets that night in a dilapidated shingle-shop on the banks of the Biscuit Brook, first flooring the damp ground with the new shingle that lay piled in one corner. The place had a great-throated chimney with a tremendous expanse of fire-place within, that cried "More!" at every morsel of wood we gave it.

But I must hasten over this part of the ground, nor let the delicious flavor of the milk we had that morning for breakfast, and that was so delectable after four days of fish, linger on my tongue; nor yet tarry to set down the talk of that honest, weather-worn passer-by who paused before our door, and every moment on the point of resuming his way, yet stood for an hour and recited his adventures hunting deer and bears on these mountains. Having replenished our stock of bread and salt pork at the house of one of the settlers, midday found us at Reed's shanty—one of those temporary structures erected by the bark jobber to lodge and board his "hands" near their work. Jim not being at home, we could gain no information from the "women folks" about the way, nor from the men who had just come in to dinner; so we pushed on, as near as we could, according to the instructions we had previously received. Crossing the creek, we forced way up the side of the mountain, through a perfect *cheval-de-frise* of fallen and peeled hem-locks, and, entering the dense woods above, began to look anxiously about for the wood-road. My companions at first could see no trace of it; but knowing that a casual wood-road cut in winter, when there was likely to be two or three feet of snow on the ground, would present only the slightest indications to the eye in summer, I looked a little closer, and could make out a mark or two here and there. The larger trees had been avoided, and the axe used only on the small saplings and underbrush, which had been lopped a couple of feet from the ground. By being constantly on the alert, we followed it till near the top of the mountain; but, when looking to see it "tilt" over the other side, it disappeared altogether. Some stumps of the black cherry were found, and a solid pair of snow-shoes was hanging high and dry on a branch, but no further trace of human hands could we see. While we were resting here, a couple of hermit thrushes, one of them with some sad defect in his vocal powers which barred him from uttering more than a few notes of his song, gave voice to solitude of the place. This was the second instance in which I have observed a song-bird with apparently some organic defect in its instrument. The other case was that of a bobolink, which, hover in mid-air and inflate its throat as it might, could only force out a few incoherent notes. But the bird in each case presented this striking contrast to human examples of the kind, that it was apparently just as proud of itself, and just as well satisfied with its performance, as were its more successful rivals.

After deliberating some time over a pocket compass which I carried, we decided upon our course, and held on to the west. The descent was very gradual. Traces of bear and deer were noted at different points, but not a live animal was seen.

About four o'clock we reached the bank of a stream flowing west. Hail to the Beaverkill! and we pushed on along its banks. The trout were plenty, and rose quickly to the hook; but we held on our way, designing to go into camp about six o'clock. Many inviting places, first on one bank, then on the other, made us linger, till finally we reached a smooth, dry place over-shadowed by balsam and hemlock, where the creek bent around a little flat, which was so entirely to our fancy that we unslung our knapsacks at once. While my companions were cutting wood and making other preparations for the night, it fell to my lot, as the most successful angler, to provide the trout for supper and breakfast. How shall I describe that wild, beautiful stream, with features so like those of all other mountain streams? And yet, as I saw it in the deep twilight of those woods on that June afternoon, with its steady, even flow, and its tranquil, many-voiced murmur, it made an impression upon my mind distinct and peculiar, fraught in an eminent degree with the charm of seclusion and remoteness. The solitude was perfect, and I felt that strangeness and insignificance which the civilized man must always feel when opposing himself to such a vast scene of silence and wildness. The trout were quite black, like all wood trout, and took the bait eagerly. I followed the stream till the deepening shadows warned me to turn back. As I neared camp, the fire shone far through the trees, dispelling the gathering gloom, but blinding my eyes to all obstacles at my feet.

I was seriously disturbed on arriving to find that one of my companions had cut an ugly gash in his shin with the axe while felling a tree. As we did not carry a fifth wheel, it was not just the time or place to have any of our members crippled, and I had bodings of evil. But, thanks to the healing virtues of the balsam which must have adhered to the blade of the axe, and double thanks to the court-plaster with which Orville had supplied himself before leaving home, the wounded leg, by being favored that night and the next day, gave us little trouble.

That night we had our first fair-and-square camping out—that is, sleeping on the ground with no shelter over us but the trees—and it was in many respects the pleasantest night we spent in the woods. The weather was perfect and the place was perfect, and for the first time we were exempt from the midges and smoke; and then we appreciated the clean new page we had to work on. Nothing is so acceptable to the camper-out as a pure article in the way of woods and waters. Any admixture of human relics mars the spirit of the scene. Yet I am willing to confess that, before we were through those woods, the marks of an axe in a tree were a welcome sight. On resuming our march next day we followed the right bank of the Beaverkill, in order to strike a stream which flowed in from the north, and which was the outlet of Balsam Lake, the objective point of that day's march. The distance to the lake from our camp could not have been over six or seven miles; yet, traveling as we did, without path or guide, climbing up banks, plunging into ravines, making detours around swampy places, and forcing our way through woods choked up with much fallen and decayed timber, it seemed at least twice that distance, and the mid-afternoon sun was shining when we emerged into what is called the "Quaker Clearing," ground that I had been over nine years before, and that lies about two miles south of the lake. From this point we had a well-worn path that led us up a sharp rise of ground, then through level woods till we saw the bright gleam of the water through the trees.

I am always struck, on approaching these little mountain lakes, with the extensive preparation that is made for them in the conformation of the ground. I am thinking of a depression, or natural basin, in the side of the mountain or on its top, the brink of which I shall reach after a little steep climbing; but instead of that, after I have accomplished the ascent, I find a broad sweep of level or gently undulating woodland that brings me after a half hour or so to the lake, which lies in this vast lap like a drop of water in the palm of a man's hand.

Balsam Lake was oval-shaped, scarcely more than half a mile long and a quarter of a mile wide, but presented a charming picture, with a group of dark gray hemlocks filling the valley about its head, and the mountains rising above and beyond. We found a bough house in good repair, also a dug-out and paddle and several floats of logs. In the dug-out I was soon creeping along the shady side of the lake, where the trout were incessantly jumping for a species of black fly, that, sheltered from the slight breeze, were dancing in swarms just above the surface of the water. The gnats were there in swarms also, and did their best toward balancing the accounts by preying upon me while I preyed upon the trout which preyed upon the flies. But by dint of keeping my hands, face, and neck constantly wet, I am convinced that the balance of blood was on my side. The trout jumped most within a foot or two of shore, where the water was only a few inches deep. The shallowness of the water, perhaps, accounted for the inability of the fish to do more than lift their heads above the surface. They came up mouths wide open, and dropped back again in the most impotent manner. Where there is any depth of water, a trout will jump several feet into the air; and where there is a solid, unbroken sheet or column, they will scale falls and dams fifteen feet high.

We had the very cream and flower of our trout-fishing at this lake. For the first time we could use the fly to advantage; and then the contrast between laborious tramping along shore, on the one hand, and sitting in one end of a dug-out and casting your line right and left with no fear of entanglement in brush or branch, while you were gently propelled along, on the other, was of the most pleasing character.

There were two varieties of trout in the lake, what it seems proper to call silver trout and golden trout; the former were the slimmer, and seemed to keep apart from the latter. Starting from the outlet and working round on the eastern side toward the head, we invariably caught these first. They glanced in the sun like bars of silver. Their sides and bellies were indeed as white as new silver. As we neared the head, and especially as we came near a space occupied by some kind of water-grass that grew in the deeper part of the lake, the other variety would begin to take the hook, their bellies a bright gold color, which became a deep orange on their fins; and as we returned to the place of departure with the bottom of the boat strewn with these bright forms intermingled, it was a sight not soon to be forgotten. It pleased my eye so that I would fain linger over them, arranging them in rows and studying the various hues and tints. They were of nearly a uniform size, rarely one over ten or under eight inches in length, and it seemed as if the hues of all the precious metals and stones were reflected from their sides. The flesh was deep salmon-color; that of brook trout is generally much lighter. Some hunters and fishers from the valley of the Mill Brook, whom we met here, told us the trout were much larger in the lake, though far less numerous than they used to be. Brook trout do not grow large till they become scarce. It is only in streams that have been long and much fished that I have caught them as much as sixteen inches in length.

The "porcupigs" were numerous about the lake, and not at all shy. One night the heat became so intolerable in our oven-shaped bough house that

I was obliged to withdraw from under its cover and lie down a little to one side. Just at daybreak, as I lay rolled in my blanket, something awoke me. Lifting up my head, there was a porcupine with his forepaws on my hips. He was apparently as much surprised as I was; and to my inquiry as to what he at that moment might be looking for, he did not pause to reply, but hitting me a slap with his tail which left three or four quills in my blanket, he scampered off down the hill into the brush.

Being an observer of the birds, of course every curious incident connected with them fell under my notice. Hence, as we stood about our camp-fire one afternoon looking out over the lake, I was the only one to see a little commotion in the water, half hidden by the near branches, as of some tiny swimmer struggling to reach the shore. Rushing to its rescue in the canoe, I found a yellow-rumped warbler, quite exhausted, clinging to a twig that hung down into the water. I brought the drenched and helpless thing to camp, and, putting it into a basket, hung it up to dry.

An hour or two afterward I heard it fluttering in its prison, and cautiously lifted the lid to get a better glimpse of the lucky captive, when it darted out and was gone in a twinkling. How came it in the water? That was my wonder, and I can only guess that it was a young bird that had never before flown over a pond of water, and, seeing the clouds and blue sky so perfect down there, thought it was a vast opening or gateway into another summer land, perhaps a short cut to the tropics, and so got itself into trouble. How my eye was delighted also with the redbird that alighted for a moment on a dry branch above the lake, just where a ray of light from the setting sun fell full upon it! A mere crimson point, and yet how it offset that dark, sombre background!

I have thus run over some of the features of an ordinary trouting excursion to the woods. People inexperienced in such matters, sitting in their rooms and thinking of these things, of all the poets have sung and romancers written, are apt to get sadly taken in when they attempt to realize their dreams. They expect to enter a sylvan paradise of trout, cool retreats, laughing brooks, picturesque views, and balsamic couches, instead of which they find hunger, rain, smoke, toil, gnats, mosquitoes, dirt, broken rest, vulgar guides, and salt pork; and they are very apt not to see where the fun comes in. But he who goes in a right spirit will not be disappointed, and will find the taste of this kind of life better, though bitterer, than the writers have described.

The Crow

ONE VERY COLD WINTER'S MORNING, after a fall of nearly two feet of snow, as I came out of my door, three crows were perched in an apple tree but a few rods away. One of them uttered a peculiar caw as they saw me, but they did not fly away. It was not the usual high-keyed note of alarm. It may have meant "Look out!" yet it seemed to me like the asking of alms: "Here we are, three hungry neighbors of yours; give us food." So I brought out the entrails and legs of a chicken, and placed them upon the snow. The crows very soon discovered what I had done, and with the usual suspicious movement of the closed wings which has the effect of emphasizing the birds' alertness, approached and devoured the food or carried it away.

But there was not the least strife or dispute among them over the food. Indeed, each seemed ready to give precedence to the others. In fact, the crow is a courtly, fine-mannered bird. Birds of prey will rend one another over their food; even buzzards will make some show of mauling one another with their wings; but I have yet to see anything of the kind with that gentle freebooter, the crow. Yet suspicion is his dominant trait. Anything that looks like design puts him on his guard. The simplest device in a cornfield usually suffices to keep him away. He suspects a trap. His wit is not deep, but it is quick, and ever on the alert.

One of our natural-history romancers makes the crows flock in June. But the truth is, they do not flock till September. Through the summer the different families keep pretty well together. You may see the old ones with their young foraging about the fields, the young often being fed by their parents.

From my boyhood I have seen the yearly meeting of the crows in September or October, on a high grassy hill or a wooded ridge. Apparently, all the crows from a large area assemble at these times; you may see them

From *Ways of Nature,* 1905.

coming, singly or in loose bands, from all directions to the rendezvous, till there are hundreds of them together. They make black an acre or two of ground. At intervals they all rise in the air, and wheel about, all cawing at once. Then to the ground again, or to the tree-tops, as the case may be; then, rising again, they send forth the voice of the multitude. What does it all mean? I notice that this rally is always preliminary to their going into winter quarters. It would be interesting to know just the nature of the communication that takes place between them. Not long afterwards, or early in October, they may be seen morning and evening going to and from their rookeries. The matter seems to be settled in these September gatherings of the clan. Was the spot agreed upon beforehand and notice served upon all the members of the tribe? Our "school-of-the-woods" professors would probably infer something of the kind. I suspect it is all brought about as naturally as any other aggregation of animals. A few crows meet on the hill; they attract others and still others. The rising of a body of them in the air, the circling and cawing, may be an instinctive act to advertise the meeting to all the crows within sight or hearing. At any rate, it has this effect, and they come hurrying from all points.

What their various calls mean, who shall tell? That lusty *caw-aw, caw-aw* that one hears in spring and summer, like the voice of authority or command, what does it mean? I never could find out. It is doubtless from the male. A crow will utter it while sitting alone on the fence in the pasture, as well as when flying through the air. The crow's cry of alarm is easily distinguished; all the other birds and wild creatures know it, and the hunter who is stalking his game is apt to swear when he hears it. I have heard two crows in the spring, seated on a limb close together, give utterance to many curious, guttural, gurgling, ventriloquial sounds. What were they saying? It was probably some form of the language of love.

I venture to say that no one has ever yet heard the crow utter a complaining or a disconsolate note. He is always cheery, he is always self-possessed, he is a great success. Nothing in Bermuda made me feel so much at home as a flock of half a dozen of our crows which I saw and heard there. At one time they were very numerous on the island, but they have been persecuted till only a remnant of the tribe remains.

I

My friend and neighbor through the year,
Self-appointed overseer

Of my crops of fruit and grain,
Of my woods and furrowed plain,

Claim thy tithings right and left,
I shall never call it theft.

Nature wisely made the law,
And I fail to find a flaw

In thy title to the earth,
And all it holds of any worth.

I like thy self-complacent air,
I like thy ways so free from care,

Thy landlord stroll about my fields,
Quickly noting what each yields;

Thy courtly mien and bearing bold,
As if thy claim were bought with gold;

Thy floating shape against the sky,
When days are calm and clouds sail high—

Thy thrifty flight ere rise of sun,
Thy homing clans when day is done.

Hues protective are not thine,
So sleek thy coat each quill doth shine.

Diamond black to end of toe,
Thy counter-point the crystal snow.

II

Never plaintive nor appealing,
Quite at home when thou art stealing,

Always groomed to tip of feather,
Calm and trim in every weather,

Morn till night my woods policing,
Every sound thy watch increasing.

Hawk and owl in tree-top hiding
Feel the shame of thy deriding.

Naught escapes thy observation,
None but dread thy accusation.

Hunters, prowlers, woodland lovers
Vainly seek the leafy covers.

III

Noisy, scheming, and predacious,
With demeanor almost gracious,

Dowered with leisure, void of hurry,
Void of fuss and void of worry,

Friendly bandit, Robin Hood,
Judge and jury of the wood,

Or Captain Kidd of sable quill,
Hiding treasures in the hill,

Nature made thee for each season,
Gave thee wit for ample reason

Good crow wit that's always burnished
Like the coat her care has furnished.

May thy numbers ne'er diminish,
I'll befriend thee till life's finish.

May I never cease to meet thee,
May I never have to eat thee.

And mayest thou never have to fare so
That thou playest the part of scarecrow.

Part Two

Farming and Rural Life

Phases of Farm Life

I HAVE THOUGHT THAT a good test of civilization, perhaps one of the best, is country life. Where country life is safe and enjoyable, where many of the conveniences and appliances of the town are joined to the large freedom and large benefits of the country, a high state of civilization prevails. Is there any proper country life in Spain, in Mexico, in the South American States? Man has always dwelt in cities, but he has not always in the same sense been a dweller in the country. Rude and barbarous people build cities. Hence, paradoxical as it may seem, the city is older than the country. Truly, man made the city, and after he became sufficiently civilized, not afraid of solitude, and knew on what terms to live with nature, God promoted him to life in the country. The necessities of defense, the fear of enemies, built the first city, built Athens, Rome, Carthage, Paris. The weaker the law, the stronger the city. After Cain slew Abel, he went out and built a city, and murder or the fear of murder, robbery or the fear of robbery have built most of the cities since. Penetrate into the heart of Africa, and you will find the people, or tribes, all living in villages or little cities. You step from the jungle or the forest into the town; there is no country. The best and most hopeful feature in any people is undoubtedly the instinct that leads them to the country and to take root there, and not that which sends them flocking to the town and its distractions.

The lighter the snow, the more it drifts; and the more frivolous the people, the more they are blown by one wind or another into towns and cities. The only notable exception I recall to city life preceding country life is furnished by the ancient Germans, of whom Tacitus says that they had no cities or contiguous settlements. "They dwell scattered and separate, as a spring, a meadow, or a grove may chance to invite them. Their villages are laid out, not like ours [the Romans] in rows of adjoining buildings, but every one surrounds his house with a vacant space, either by way of security, or against fire, or through ignorance of the art of building."

From *Signs and Seasons,* 1886.

These ancient Germans were indeed true countrymen. Little wonder that they overran the empire of the city-loving Romans, and finally sacked Rome itself. How hairy and hardy and virile they were! In the same way is the more fresh and vigorous blood of the country always making eruptions into the city. The Goths and Vandals from the woods and the farms—what would Rome do without them, after all? The city rapidly uses men up; families run out, man becomes sophisticated and feeble. A fresh stream of humanity is always setting from the country into the city; a stream not so fresh flows back again into the country, a stream for the most part of jaded and pale humanity. It is arterial blood when it flows in, and venous blood when it comes back.

A nation always begins to rot first in its great cities, is indeed perhaps always rotting there, and is saved only by the antiseptic virtues of fresh supplies of country blood.

But it is not of country life in general that I am to speak, but of some phases of farm life, and of farm life in my native State. Many of the early settlers of New York were from New England, Connecticut perhaps sending out the most. My own ancestors were from the latter State. The Connecticut emigrant usually made his first stop in our river counties, Putnam, Dutchess, or Columbia. If he failed to find his place there, he made another flight to Orange, to Delaware, or to Schoharie County, where he generally stuck. But the State early had one element introduced into its rural and farm life not found farther east, namely, the Holland Dutch. These gave features more or less picturesque to the country that are not observable in New England. The Dutch took root at various points along the Hudson, and about Albany and in the Mohawk valley, and remnants of their rural and domestic architecture may still be seen in these sections of the State. A Dutch barn became proverbial. "As broad as a Dutch barn" was a phrase that, when applied to the person of a man or woman, left room for little more to be said. The main feature of these barns was their enormous expansion of roof. It was a comfort to look at them, they suggested such shelter and protection. The eaves were very low and the ridge-pole very high. Long rafters and short posts gave them a quaint, short-waisted, grandmotherly look. They were nearly square, and stood very broad upon the ground. Their form was doubtless suggested by the damper climate of the Old World, where the grain and hay, instead of being packed in deep solid mows, used to be spread upon poles and exposed to the currents of air under the roof. Surface and not cubic capacity is more important in these matters in Holland than in this country. Our farmers have found that, in a climate where there is so much weather as with us, the less roof you have the better. Roofs will leak, and cured hay will keep sweet in a mow of any depth and size in our dry atmosphere.

The Dutch barn was the most picturesque barn that has been built, especially when thatched with straw, as they nearly all were, and forming one side of an inclosure of lower roofs or sheds also covered with straw, beneath which the cattle took refuge from the winter storms. Its immense, unpainted gable, cut with holes for the swallows, was like a section of a respectable-sized hill, and its roof like its slope. Its great doors always had a hood projecting over them, and the doors themselves were divided horizontally into upper and lower halves; the upper halves very frequently being left open, through which you caught a glimpse of the mows of hay, or the twinkle of flails when the grain was being threshed.

The old Dutch farmhouses, too, were always pleasing to look upon. They were low, often made of stone, with deep window-jambs and great family fireplaces. The outside door, like that of the barn, was always divided into upper and lower halves. When the weather permitted, the upper half could stand open, giving light and air without the cold draught over the floor where the children were playing that our wide-swung doors admit. This feature of the Dutch house and barn certainly merits preservation in our modern buildings.

The large, unpainted timber barns that succeeded the first Yankee settlers' log stables were also picturesque, especially when a lean-to for the cowstable was added, and the roof carried down with a long sweep over it; or when the barn was flanked by an open shed with a hayloft above it, where the hens cackled and hid their nests, and from the open window of which the hay was always hanging.

Then the great timbers of these barns and the Dutch barn, hewn from maple or birch or oak trees from the primitive woods, and put in place by the combined strength of all the brawny arms in the neighborhood when the barn was raised—timbers strong enough and heavy enough for docks and quays, and that have absorbed the odors of the hay and grain until they look ripe and mellow and full of the pleasing sentiment of the great, sturdy, bountiful interior! The "big beam" has become smooth and polished from the hay that has been pitched over it, and the sweaty, sturdy forms that have crossed it. One feels that he would like a piece of furniture—a chair, or a table, or a writing-desk, a bedstead, or a wainscoting—made from these long-seasoned, long-tried, richly toned timbers of the old barn. But the smart-painted, natty barn that follows the humbler structure, with its glazed windows, its ornamented ventilator and gilded weather vane—who cares to contemplate it? The wise human eye loves modesty and humility;

loves plain, simple structures; loves the unpainted barn that took no thought of itself, or the dwelling that looks inward and not outward; is offended when the farm-buildings get above their business and aspire to be something on their own account, suggesting, not cattle and crops and plain living, but the vanities of the town and the pride of dress and equipage.

Indeed, the picturesque in human affairs and occupations is always born of love and humility, as it is in art or literature; and it quickly takes to itself

John Burroughs with hoe. Courtesy of the American Museum of Natural History.

wings and flies away at the advent of pride, or any selfish or unworthy motive. The more directly the farm savors of the farmer, the more the fields and buildings are redolent of human care and toil, without any thought of the passer-by, the more we delight in the contemplation of it.

It is unquestionably true that farm life and farm scenes in this country are less picturesque than they were fifty or one hundred years ago. This is owing partly to the advent of machinery, which enables the farmer to do so much of his work by proxy, and hence removes him farther from the soil, and partly to the growing distaste for the occupation among our people. The old settlers—our fathers and grandfathers—loved the farm, and had no thoughts above it; but the later generations are looking to the town and its fashions, and only waiting for a chance to flee thither. Then pioneer life is always more or less picturesque; there is no room for vain and foolish thoughts; it is a hard battle, and the people have no time to think about appearances. When my grandfather and grandmother came into the country where they reared their family and passed their days, they cut a road through the woods and brought all their worldly gear on a sled drawn by a yoke of oxen. Their neighbors helped them build a house of logs, with a roof of black-ash bark and a floor of hewn white-ash plank. A great stone chimney and fireplace—the mortar of red clay—gave light and warmth, and cooked the meat and baked the bread, when there was any to cook or to bake. Here they lived and reared their family, and found life sweet. Their unworthy descendant, yielding to the inherited love of the soil, flees the city and its artificial ways, and gets a few acres in the country, where he proposes to engage in the pursuit supposed to be free to every American citizen—the pursuit of happiness. The humble old farmhouse is discarded, and a smart, modern country-house put up. Walks and roads are made and graveled; trees and hedges are planted; the rustic old barn is rehabilitated; and, after it is all fixed, the uneasy proprietor stands off and looks, and calculates by how much he has missed the picturesque, at which he aimed. Our new houses undoubtedly have greater comforts and conveniences than the old; and, if we could keep our pride and vanity in abeyance and forget that all the world is looking on, they might have beauty also.

The man that forgets himself, he is the man we like; and the dwelling that forgets itself, in its purpose to shelter and protect its inmates and make them feel at home in it, is the dwelling that fills the eye. When you see one of the great cathedrals, you know that it was not pride that animated these builders, but fear and worship; but when you see the house of the rich farmer, or of the millionaire from the city, you see the pride of money and the insolence of social power.

Machinery, I say, has taken away some of the picturesque features of farm life. How much soever we may admire machinery and the faculty of mechanical invention, there is no machine like a man; and the work done directly by his hands, the things made or fashioned by them, have a virtue and a quality that cannot be imparted by machinery. The line of mowers in the meadows, with the straight swaths behind them, is more picturesque than the "Clipper" or "Buckeye" mower, with its team and driver. So are the flails of the threshers, chasing each other through the air, more pleasing to the eye and the ear than the machine, with its uproar, its choking clouds of dust, and its general hurly-burly.

Sometimes the threshing was done in the open air, upon a broad rock, or a smooth, dry plat of greensward; and it is occasionally done there yet, especially the threshing of the buckwheat crop, by a farmer who has not a good barn floor, or who cannot afford to hire the machine. The flail makes a louder *thud* in the fields than you would imagine; and in the splendid October weather it is a pleasing spectacle to behold the gathering of the ruddy crop, and three or four lithe figures beating out the grain with their flails in some sheltered nook, or some grassy lane lined with cedars. When there are three flails beating together, it makes lively music; and when there are four, they follow each other so fast that it is a continuous roll of sound, and it requires a very steady stroke not to hit or get hit by the others. There is just room and time to get your blow in, and that is all. When one flail is upon the straw, another has just left it, another is halfway down, and the fourth is high and straight in the air. It is like a swiftly revolving wheel that delivers four blows at each revolution. Threshing, like mowing, goes much easier in company than when alone; yet many a farmer or laborer spends nearly all the late fall and winter days shut in the barn, pounding doggedly upon the endless sheaves of oats and rye.

When the farmers made "bees," as they did a generation or two ago much more than they do now, a picturesque element was added. There was the stone bee, the husking bee, the "raising," the "moving," etc. When the carpenters had got the timbers of the house or the barn ready, and the foundation was prepared, then the neighbors for miles about were invited to come to the "raisin'." The afternoon was the time chosen. The forenoon was occupied by the carpenter and the farm hands in putting the sills and "sleepers" in place ("sleepers," what a good name for those rude hewn timbers that lie under the floor in the darkness and silence!). When the hands arrived, the great beams and posts and joists and braces were carried to their place on the platform, and the first "bent," as it was called, was put together and pinned by oak pins that the boys brought. Then pike poles were distributed, the men, fifteen or twenty of them, arranged in a line abreast of the bent; the boss carpenter steadied and guided the corner post and gave the word of command—"Take holt, boys!" "Now, set her up!" "Up with her!" "Up she goes!"

When it gets shoulder high, it becomes heavy, and there is a pause. The pikes are brought into requisition; every man gets a good hold and braces himself, and waits for the words. "All together now!" shouts the captain; "Heave her up!" "He-o-he!" (heave all, heave), "hie-o-he," at the top of his voice, every man doing his best. Slowly the great timbers go up; louder grows the word of command, till the bent is up. Then it is plumbed and stay-lathed, and another is put together and raised in the same way, till they are all up. Then comes the putting on the great plates—timbers that run lengthwise of the building and match the sills below. Then, if there is time, the putting up of the rafters. In every neighborhood there was always some man who was especially useful at "raisin's." He was bold and strong and quick. He helped guide and superintend the work. He was the first one up on the bent, catching a pin or a brace and putting it in place. He walked the lofty and perilous plate with the great beetle in hand, put the pins in the holes, and, swinging the heavy instrument through the air, drove the pins home. He was as much at home up there as a squirrel.

Now that balloon frames are mainly used for houses, and lighter sawed timbers for barns, the old-fashioned raising is rarely witnessed.

Then the moving was an event, too. A farmer had a barn to move, or wanted to build a new house on the site of the old one, and the latter must be drawn to one side. Now this work is done with pulleys and rollers by a few men and a horse; then the building was drawn by sheer bovine strength. Every man that had a yoke of cattle in the country round about was invited to assist. The barn or house was pried up and great runners, cut in the woods, placed under it, and under the runners were placed skids. To these runners it was securely chained and pinned; then the cattle—stags, steers, and oxen, in two long lines, one at each runner—were hitched fast, and, while men and boys aided with great levers, the word to go was given. Slowly the two lines of bulky cattle straightened and settled into their bows; the big chains that wrapped the runners tightened, a dozen or more "gads" were flourished, a dozen or more lusty throats urged their teams at the top of their voices, when there was a creak or a groan as the building stirred. Then the drivers redoubled their efforts; there was a perfect Babel of discordant sounds; the oxen bent to the work, their eyes bulged, their nostrils distended; the lookers-on cheered, and away went the old house or barn as nimbly as a boy on a handsled. Not always, however; sometimes the chains would break, or one runner strike a rock, or bury itself in the earth. There were generally enough mishaps or delays to make it interesting.

In the section of the State of which I write, flax used to be grown, and cloth for shirts and trousers, and towels and sheets, woven from it. It was no laughing matter for the farm-boy to break in his shirt or trousers, those days. The hair shirts in which the old monks used to mortify the flesh could not have been much before them in this mortifying particular. But after the bits of shives and sticks were subdued, and the knots humbled by use and the washboard, they were good garments. If you lost your hold in a tree and your shirt caught on a knot or limb, it would save you.

But when has any one seen a crackle, or a swingling-knife, or a hetchel, or a distaff, and where can one get some tow for strings or for gun-wadding, or some swingling-tow for a bonfire? The quill-wheel, and the spinning-wheel, and the loom are heard no more among us. The last I knew of a certain hetchel, it was nailed up behind the old sheep that did the churning; and when he was disposed to shirk or hang back and stop the machine, it was always ready to spur him up in no uncertain manner. The old loom became a hen-roost in an outbuilding; and the crackle upon which the flax was broken—where, oh, where is it?

When the produce of the farm was taken a long distance to market—that was an event, too; the carrying away of the butter in the fall, for instance, to the river, a journey that occupied both ways four days. Then the family marketing was done in a few groceries. Some cloth, new caps and boots for the boys, and a dress, or a shawl, or a cloak for the girls were brought back, besides news and adventure, and strange tidings of the distant world. The farmer was days in getting ready to start; food was prepared and put in a box to stand him on the journey, so as to lessen the hotel expenses, and oats were put up for the horses. The butter was loaded up overnight, and in the cold November morning, long before it was light, he was up and off. I seem to hear the wagon yet, its slow rattle over the frozen ground diminishing in the distance. On the fourth day toward night all grew expectant of his return, but it was usually dark before his wagon was heard coming down the hill, or his voice from before the door summoning a light. When the boys got big enough, one after the other accompanied him each year, until all had made the famous journey and seen the great river and the steamboats, and the thousand and one marvels of the far-away town. When it came my turn to go, I was in a great state of excitement for a week beforehand, for fear my clothes would not be ready, or else that it would be too cold, or else that the world would come to an end before the time fixed for starting. The day previous I roamed the woods in quest of game to supply my bill of fare on the way, and was lucky enough to shoot a partridge and an owl, though the latter I did not take. Perched high on a "springboard" I made the journey, and saw more sights and wonders than I have ever seen on a journey since, or ever expect to again.

But now all this is changed. The railroad has found its way through or near every settlement, and marvels and wonders are cheap. Still, the essential charm of the farm remains and always will remain: the care of crops, and of cattle, and of orchards, bees, and fowls; the clearing and improving of the ground; the building of barns and houses; the direct contact with the soil and with the elements; the watching of the clouds and of the weather; the privacies with nature, with bird, beast, and plant; and the close acquaintance with the heart and virtue of the world. The farmer should be the true naturalist; the book in which it is all written is open before him night and day, and how sweet and wholesome all his knowledge is!

The predominant feature of farm life in New York, as in other States, is always given by some local industry of one kind or another. In many of the high, cold counties in the eastern centre of the State, this ruling industry is hop growing; in the western, it is grain and fruit growing; in sections along the Hudson, it is small-fruit growing, as berries, currants, grapes; in other counties, it is milk and butter; in others, quarrying flagging-stone. I recently visited a section of Ulster County, where everybody seemed getting out hoop-poles and making hoops. The only talk was of hoops, hoops! Every team that went by had a load or was going for a load of hoops. The principal fuel was hoop-shavings or discarded hoop-poles. No man had any money until he sold his hoops. When a farmer went to town to get some grain, or a pair of boots, or a dress for his wife, he took a load of hoops. People stole hoops and poached for hoops, and bought, and sold, and speculated in hoops. If there was a corner, it was in hoops; big hoops, little hoops, hoops for kegs, and firkins, and barrels, and hogsheads, and pipes; hickory hoops, birch hoops, ash hoops, chestnut hoops, hoops enough to go around the world. Another place it was shingle, shingle; everybody was shaving hemlock shingle.

In most of the eastern counties of the State, the interest and profit of the farm revolve about the cow. The dairy is the one great matter—for milk, when milk can be shipped to the New York market, and for butter when it cannot. Great barns and stables and milking-sheds, and immense meadows and cattle on a thousand hills, are the prominent agricultural features of these sections of the country. Good grass and good water are the two indispensables to successful dairying. And the two generally go together. Where there are plenty of copious cold springs, there is no dearth of grass. When the cattle are compelled to browse upon weeds and various wild growths, the milk and butter will betray it in the flavor. Tender, juicy grass, the ruddy blossoming clover, or the fragrant, well-cured hay, make the delicious milk and the sweet butter. Then there is a charm about a natural pastoral country that belongs to no other. Go through Orange County in May and see the vivid emerald of the smooth fields and hills. It is a new experience of the beauty and effectiveness of simple grass. And this grass has rare virtues, too, and imparts a flavor to the milk and butter that has made them famous.

Along all the sources of the Delaware the land flows with milk, if not with honey. The grass is excellent, except in times of protracted drought, and then the browsings in the beech and birch woods are a good substitute. Butter is the staple product. Every housewife is or wants to be a famous butter-maker, and Delaware County butter rivals that of Orange in market. Delaware is a high, cool grazing country. The farms lie tilted up against the sides of the mountain or lapping over the hills, striped or checked with stone walls, and presenting to the eye long stretches of pasture and meadow land, alternating with plowed fields and patches of waving grain. Few of their features are picturesque; they are bare, broad, and simple. The farmhouse gets itself a coat of white paint, and green blinds to the windows, and the barn and wagon-house a coat of red paint with white trimmings, as soon as possible. A penstock flows by the doorway, rows of tin pans sun themselves in the yard, and the great wheel of the churning machine flanks the milk-house, or rattles behind it. The winters are severe, the snow deep. The principal fuel is still wood—beech, birch, and maple. It is hauled off the mountain in great logs when the first November or December snows come, and cut up and piled in the wood-houses and under a shed. Here the axe still rules the winter, and it may be heard all day and every day upon the woodpile, or echoing through the frost-bound wood, the coat of the chopper hanging to a limb, and his white chips strewing the snow.

Many cattle need much hay; hence in dairy sections haying is the period of "storm and stress" in the farmer's year. To get the hay in, in good condition, and before the grass gets too ripe, is a great matter. All the energies and resources of the farm are bent to this purpose. It is a thirty or forty days' war, in which the farmer and his "hands" are pitted against the heat and the rain and the legions of timothy and clover. Everything about it has the urge, the hurry, the excitement of a battle. Outside help is procured; men flock in from adjoining counties, where the ruling industry is something else and is less imperative; coopers, blacksmiths, and laborers of various kinds drop their tools, and take down their scythes and go in quest of a job in haying. Every man is expected to pitch his endeavors in a little higher key than at any other kind of work. The wages are extra, and the work must correspond. The men are in the meadow by half-past four or five in the morning, and mow an hour or two before breakfast. A good mower is proud of his skill. He does not "lop in," and his "pointing out" is perfect, and you can hardly see the ribs of his swath. He stands up to his grass and strikes level and sure. He will turn a double down through the stoutest grass, and when the hay is raked away, you will not find a spear left standing. The Americans are — or were — the best mowers. A foreigner could never quite give the masterly touch.

The hayfield has its code. One man must not take another's swath unless he expects to be crowded. Each expects to take his turn leading the band. The scythe may be so whetted as to ring out a saucy challenge to the rest. It is not good manners to mow up too close to your neighbor, unless you are trying to keep out of the way of the man behind you. Many a race has been brought on by some one being a little indiscreet in this respect. Two men may mow all day together under the impression that each is trying to put the other through. The one that leads strikes out briskly, and the other, not to be outdone, follows close. Thus the blood of each is soon up; a little heat begets more heat, and it is fairly a race before long. It is a great ignominy to be mowed out of your swath.

Hay-gathering is clean, manly work all through. Young fellows work in haying who do not do another stroke on the farm, the whole year. It is a gymnasium in the meadows and under the summer sky. How full of pictures, too! — the smooth slopes dotted with cocks with lengthening shadows; the great, broad-backed, soft-cheeked loads, moving along the lanes and brushing under the trees; the unfinished stacks with forkfuls of hay being handed up its sides to the builder, and when finished the shape of a great pear, with a pole in the top for the stem. Maybe in the fall and winter the calves and yearlings will hover around it and gnaw its base until it overhangs them and shelters them from the storm. Or the farmer will "fodder" his cows there — one of the most picturesque scenes to be witnessed on the farm — twenty or thirty or forty milchers filing along toward the stack in the field, or clustered about it, waiting the promised bite. In great, green flakes the hay is rolled off, and distributed about in small heaps upon the unspotted snow. After the cattle have eaten, the birds—snow buntings and red-polls—come and pick up the crumbs, the seeds of the grasses and weeds. At night the fox and the owl come for mice.

What a beautiful path the cows make through the snow to the stack or to the spring under the hill!—always more or less wayward, but broad and firm, and carved and indented by a multitude of rounded hoofs. In fact, the cow is the true pathfinder and pathmaker. She has the leisurely, deliberate movement that insures an easy and a safe way. Follow her trail through the woods, and you have the best, if not the shortest, course. How she beats down the brush and briers and wears away even the roots of the trees! A herd of cows left to themselves fall naturally into single file, and a hundred or more hoofs are not long in smoothing and compacting almost any surface.

Indeed, all the ways and doings of cattle are pleasant to look upon, whether grazing in the pasture, or browsing in the woods, or ruminating under the trees, or feeding in the stall, or reposing upon the knolls. There is virtue in the cow; she is full of goodness; a wholesome odor exhales from her; the whole landscape looks out of her soft eyes; the quality and the aroma of miles of meadow and pasture lands are in her presence and products. I had rather have the care of cattle than be the keeper of the great seal of the nation. Where the cow is, there is Arcadia; so far as her influence prevails, there is contentment, humility, and sweet, homely life.

Blessed is he whose youth was passed upon the farm, and if it was a dairy farm, his memories will be all the more fragrant. The driving of the cows to and from the pasture, every day and every season for years—how much of summer and of nature he got into him on these journeys! What rambles and excursions did this errand furnish the excuse for! The birds and birds' nests, the berries, the squirrels, the woodchucks, the beech woods with their treasures into which the cows loved so to wander and to browse, the fragrant wintergreens and a hundred nameless adventures, all strung upon that brief journey of half a mile to and from the remote pastures. Sometimes a cow or two will be missing when the herd is brought home at night; then to hunt them up is another adventure. My grandfather went out one night to look up an absentee from the yard, when he heard something in the brush, and out stepped a bear into the path before him.

Every Sunday morning the cows were salted. The farm-boy would take a pail with three or four quarts of coarse salt, and, followed by the eager herd, go to the field and deposit the salt in handfuls upon smooth stones and rocks and upon clean places on the turf. If you want to know how good salt is, see a cow eat it. She gives the true saline smack. How she dwells upon it, and gnaws the sward and licks the stones where it has been deposited! The cow is the most delightful feeder among animals. It makes one's mouth water to see her eat pumpkins, and to see her at a pile of apples is distracting. How she sweeps off the delectable grass! The sound of her grazing is appetizing; the grass betrays all its sweetness and succulency in parting under her sickle.

The region of which I write abounds in sheep also. Sheep love high, cool, breezy lands. Their range is generally much above that of cattle. Their sharp noses will find picking where a cow would fare poorly indeed. Hence most farmers utilize their high, wild, and mountain lands by keeping a small flock of sheep. But they are the outlaws of the farm and are seldom within bounds. They make many lively expeditions for the farm-boy, driving them out of mischief, hunting them up in the mountains, or salting them on the breezy hills. Then there is the annual sheep-washing, when on a warm day in May or early June the whole herd is driven a mile or more to a suitable pool in the creek, and one by one doused and washed and rinsed in the water. We used to wash below an old gristmill, and it was a pleasing spectacle — the mill, the dam, the overhanging rocks and trees, the round, deep pool, and the huddled and frightened sheep.

One of the features of farm life peculiar to this country, and one of the most picturesque of them all, is sugar-making in the maple woods in spring. This is the first work of the season, and to the boys is more play than work. In the Old World, and in more simple and imaginative times, how such an occupation as this would have got into literature, and how many legends and associations would have clustered around it! It is woodsy, and savors of the trees; it is an encampment among the maples. Before the bud swells, before the grass springs, before the plow is started, comes the sugar harvest. It is the sequel of the bitter frost; a sap run is the sweet goodbye of winter. It denotes a certain equipoise of the season; the heat of the day fully balances the frost of the night. In New York and New England, the time of the sap hovers about the vernal equinox, beginning a week or ten days before, and continuing a week or ten days after. As the days and nights get equal, the heat and cold get equal, and the sap mounts. A day that brings the bees out of the hive will bring the sap out of the maple-tree. It is the fruit of the equal marriage of the sun and the frost. When the frost is all out of the ground, and all the snow gone from its surface, the flow stops. The thermometer must not rise above 38° or 40° by day, or sink below 24° or 25° at night, with wind in the northwest; a relaxing south wind, and the run is over for the present. Sugar weather is crisp weather. How the tin buckets glisten in the gray woods; how the robins laugh; how the nuthatches call; how lightly the thin blue smoke rises among the trees! The squirrels are out of their dens; the migrating water-fowls are streaming northward; the sheep and cattle look wistfully toward the bare fields; the tide of the season, in fact, is just beginning to rise.

Sap-letting does not seem to be an exhaustive process to the trees, as the trees of a sugar-bush appear to be as thrifty and as long-lived as other trees. They come to have a maternal, large-waisted look, from the wounds of the axe or the auger, and that is about all.

In my sugar-making days, the sap was carried to the boiling-place in pails by the aid of a neck-yoke and stored in hogsheads, and boiled or evaporated in immense kettles or caldrons set in huge stone arches; now, the hogshead goes to the trees hauled upon a sled by a team, and the sap is evaporated in broad, shallow, sheet-iron pans—a great saving of fuel and of labor.

Many a farmer sits up all night boiling his sap, when the run has been an extra good one, and a lonely vigil he has of it amid the silent trees and beside his wild hearth. If he has a sap-house, as is now so common, he may make himself fairly comfortable; and if a companion, he may have a good time or a glorious wake.

Maple sugar in its perfection is rarely seen, perhaps never seen, in the market. When made in large quantities and indifferently, it is dark and coarse; but when made in small quantities—that is, quickly from the first run of sap and properly treated—it has a wild delicacy of flavor that no other sweet can match. What you smell in freshly cut maple-wood, or taste in the blossom of the tree, is in it. It is then, indeed, the distilled essence of the tree. Made into syrup, it is white and clear as clover-honey; and crystallized into sugar, it is as pure as the wax. The way to attain this result is to evaporate the sap under cover in an enameled kettle; when reduced about twelve times, allow it to settle half a day or more; then clarify with milk or the white of an egg. The product is virgin syrup or sugar worthy the table of the gods.

Perhaps the most heavy and laborious work of the farm in the section of the State of which I write is fence-building. But it is not unproductive labor as in the South or West, for the fence is of stone, and the capacity of the soil for grass or grain is of course increased by its construction. It is killing two birds with one stone: a fence is had, the best in the world, while the available area of the field is enlarged. In fact, if there are ever sermons in stones, it is when they are built into a stone wall—turning your hindrances into helps, shielding your crops behind the obstacles to your husbandry, making the enemies of the plow stand guard over its products. This is the kind of farming worth imitating. A stone wall with a good rock bottom will stand as long as a man lasts. Its only enemy is the frost, and it works so gently that it is not till after many years that its effect is perceptible. An old farmer will walk with you through his fields and say, "This wall I built at such and such a time, or the first year I came on the farm, or when I owned such and such a span of horses," indicating a period thirty, forty, or fifty years back. "This other, we built the summer so and so worked for me," and he relates some incident, or mishap, or comical adventures that the memory calls up. Every line of fence has a history; the mark of his plow or his crowbar is upon the stones; the sweat of his early manhood put them in place; in fact, the long black line covered with lichens and in places tottering to the fall revives long-gone scenes and events in the life of the farm.

The time for fence-building is usually between seed-time and harvest, May and June; or in the fall after the crops are gathered. The work has its picturesque features — the prying of rocks; supple forms climbing or swinging from the end of the great levers; or the blasting of the rocks with powder, the hauling of them into position with oxen or horses, or with both; the picking of the stone from the greensward; the bending, athletic forms of the wall-layers; the snug new fence creeping slowly up the hill or across the field, absorbing the windrow of loose stones; and, when the work is done, much ground reclaimed to the plow and the grass, and a strong barrier erected.

It is a common complaint that the farm and farm life are not appreciated by our people. We long for the more elegant pursuits, or the ways and fashions of the town. But the farmer has the most sane and natural occupation, and ought to find life sweeter, if less highly seasoned, than any other. He alone, strictly speaking, has a home. How can a man take root and thrive without land? He writes his history upon his field. How many ties, how many resources, he has — his friendships with his cattle, his team, his dog, his trees, the satisfaction in his growing crops, in his improved fields; his intimacy with nature, with bird and beast, and with the quickening elemental forces; his cooperations with the clouds, the sun, the seasons, heat, wind, rain, frost! Nothing will take the various social distempers which the city and artificial life breed out of a man like farming, like direct and loving contact with the soil. It draws out the poison. It humbles him, teaches him patience and reverence, and restores the proper tone to his system.

Cling to the farm, make much of it, put yourself into it, bestow your heart and your brain upon it, so that it shall savor of you and radiate your virtue after your day's work is done!

Be thou diligent to know the state of thy flocks, and look well to thy herds.

For riches are not forever; and doth the crown endure to every generation?

The hay appeareth, and the tender grass showeth itself, and herbs of the mountains are gathered.

The lambs are for thy clothing, and the goats are the price of the field.

And thou shalt have goat's milk enough for thy food, for the food of thy household, and for the maintenance for thy maidens.

A Walk in the Fields

L ET US GO AND WALK IN THE FIELDS. It is the middle of a very early March—a March that has in some way cut out April and got into its place.

I knew an Irish laborer, who during his last illness thought, when spring came, if he could walk in the fields, he would get well. I have observed that farmers, when harassed by trouble, or weighed down by grief, are often wont to go and walk alone in the fields. They find dumb sympathy and companionship there. I knew a farmer who, after the death of his only son, would frequently get up in the middle of the night and go and walk in his fields. It was said that he had been harsh and unjust to his son, and, during the last day the latter had worked and when the fatal illness was coming upon him, the father had severely upbraided him because he left his task and sat for a while under the fence. One can fancy him going to this very spot in his midnight wanderings, and standing in mute agony where the cruel words had been spoken, or throwing himself upon the ground, pleading in vain at the door of the irrevocable past. That door never opens again, plead you there till your heart breaks.

A farmer's fields become in time almost a part of himself: his life history is written all over them; virtue has gone out of himself into them; he has fertilized them with the sweat of his brow; he knows the look and the quality of each one. This one he reclaimed from the wilderness when he came on the farm as a young man; he sowed rye among the stumps and scratched it in with a thorn brush; as the years went by he saw the stumps slowly decay; he would send his boys to set fire to them in the dry spring weather. I was one of those boys, and it seems as if I could smell the pungent odor of those burning stumps at this moment: now this field is one of his smoothest, finest meadows. This one was once a rough pasture; he pried up

From *Leaf and Tendril,* 1908.

or blasted out the rocks, and with his oxen drew them into a line along the border of the woods, and with stone picked or dug from the surface built upon them a solid four-foot wall; now the mowing-machine runs evenly where once the cattle grazed with difficulty.

I was a boy when that field was cleaned up. I took a hand—a boy's hand—in the work. I helped pick up the loose stone, which we drew upon a stone-boat shod with green poles. It was back-aching work, and it soon wore the skin thin on the ends of the fingers. How the crickets and ants and beetles would rush about when we uncovered them! They no doubt looked upon the stone that sheltered them as an old institution that we had no right to remove. No right, my little folk, only the might of the stronger. Sometimes a flat stone would prove the roof of a mouse-nest—a blinking, bead-eyed, meadow-mouse. What consternation would seize him, too, as he would rush off along the little round beaten ways under the dry grass and weeds! Many of the large bowlders were deeply imbedded in the soil, and only stuck their noses or heads, so to speak, up through the turf. These we would first tackle with the big lever, a long, dry, ironwood pole, as heavy as one could handle, shod with a horseshoe. With the end of this thrust under the end or edge of a bowlder, and resting upon a stone for a fulcrum, we would begin the assault. Inch by inch the turf-bound rock would yield. Sometimes the lever would slip its hold, and come down upon our heads if we were not watchful. As the rock yielded, the lever required more bait, as the farmer calls it—an addition to the fulcrum.

After the rock was raised sufficiently, we would prop it up with stones, arrange a skid or skids under it—green beech poles cut in the woods—wrap a chain around it, and hitch the oxen to it, directing them to the right or left to turn the bowlder out of its bed and place it on the surface of the ground. When this was accomplished, then came the dead straight pull to the line of the fence. An old, experienced ox-team know what is before them, or rather behind them; they have felt the bowlder and sized it up. At the word and the crack of the whip they bend their heads and throw their weight upon the yoke. Now the hickory bows settle into their shoulders, they kink their tails and hump their backs, their sharp hoofs cut the turf, and the great inert mass moves. Tearing up the sod, grinding over stones, the shouts of the excited driver urging them on, away they go toward the line. The peculiar and agreeable odor of burnt and ground stone arises from the rear. Only a few yards at a time; how the oxen puff as they halt to take breath and lap their tongues out over their moist muzzles! Then they bend to the work again, the muscular effort reaching their very tails. Thus the work goes on for several days or a week, till the row of bottom rocks is complete. If there are others remaining in the field, then the row is doubled up till the land is cleaned.

What a torn and wounded appearance that section of ground presents, its surface everywhere marked with red stripes or bands, each ending in or starting from a large and deep red cavity in the sward! But soon the plow will come, equalizing and obliterating and writing another history upon the page.

There is something to me peculiarly interesting in stone walls—a kind of rude human expression to them, suggesting the face of the old farmer himself. How they climb the hills and sweep through the valleys. They decay not, yet they grow old and decrepit; little by little they lose their precision and firmness, they stagger, then fall. In a still, early spring morning or April twilight one often hears a rattle of stones in a distant field; some bit of old wall is falling. The lifetime of the best of them is rarely threescore and ten. The other day, along the highway, I saw an old man re-laying a dilapidated stone wall. "Fifty-three years ago," he said, "I laid this wall. When it is laid again, I shan't have the job." It is rarely now that one sees a new wall going up. The fences have all been built, and the farmer has only to keep them in repair.

When you build a field or a highway wall, do not make the top of it level across the little hollows; let it bend to the uneven surface, let it look flexible and alive. A foundation wall, with its horizontal lines, looks stiff and formal, but a wall that undulates along like a live thing pleases the eye.

When I was a boy upon the old farm, my father always "laid out" to build forty or fifty rods of new wall, or rebuild as many rods of old wall, each spring. It is true husbandry to fence your field with the stones that incumber it, to utilize obstacles. The walls upon the old farm of which I am thinking have each a history. This one, along the lower side of the road, was built in '46. I remember the man who laid it. I even remember something of the complexion of the May days when the work was going on. It was built from a still older wall, and new material added. It leans and staggers in places now like an old man, but it is still a substantial fence. This one upon the upper side of the road, my father told me he built the year he came upon the farm, which was in '28. He paid twenty cents a rod for having it laid to a man whose grandchildren are now gray-haired men. The wall has a rock foundation, and it still holds its course without much wavering.

The more padding there is in a stone wall, the less enduring it is. Let your stone reach clean through. A smooth face will not save it; a loose and cobbly interior will be its ruin. Let there be a broad foundation, let the parts be well bound together, let the joints be carefully broken, and, above all, let its height not be too great for its width. If it is too high, it will topple over; if its interior is defective, it will spread and collapse. Time searches out its every weakness, and respects only good material and good workmanship.

A Cow in the Capital

I HAVE OWNED BUT THREE COWS and loved but one. That was the first one, Chloe, a bright red, curlypated, golden-skinned Devonshire cow, that an ocean steamer landed for me upon the banks of the Potomac one bright May Day many clover summers ago. She came from the north, from the pastoral regions of the Catskills, to graze upon the broad commons of the national capital. I was then the fortunate and happy lessee of an old place with an acre of ground attached, almost within the shadow of the dome of the Capitol. Behind a high but aged and decrepit board fence I indulged my rural and unclerical tastes. I could look up from my homely tasks and cast a potato almost in the midst of that cataract of marble steps that flows out of the north wing of the patriotic pile. Ah! when that creaking and sagging back gate closed behind me in the evening, I was happy; and when it opened for my egress thence in the morning, I was not happy. Inside that gate was a miniature farm, redolent of homely, primitive life, a tumble-down house and stables and implements of agriculture and horticulture, broods of chickens, and growing pumpkins, and a thousand antidotes to the weariness of an artificial life. Outside of it were the marble-and-iron palaces, the paved and blistering streets, and the high, vacant mahogany desk of a government clerk. In that ancient inclosure I took an earth bath twice a day. I planted myself as deep in the soil as I could, to restore the normal tone and freshness of my system, impaired by the above-mentioned government mahogany. I have found there is nothing like the earth to draw the various social distempers out of one. The blue devils take flight at once if they see you mean to bury them and make compost of them. Emerson intimates that the scholar had better not try to have two gardens; but I could never spend an hour hoeing up dock and red-root and twitch-grass without in some way getting rid of many weeds and fungi—

From "Our Rural Divinity," in *Birds and Poets,* 1877.

unwholesome growths that a petty indoor life is forever fostering in my moral and intellectual nature.

But the finishing touch was not given till Chloe came. She was the jewel for which this homely setting waited. My agriculture had some object then. The old gate never opened with such alacrity as when she paused before it. How we waited for her coming! Should I send Drewer, the colored patriarch, for her? No; the master of the house himself should receive Juno at the capital.

"One cask for you," said the clerk, referring to the steamerbill of lading.

"Then I hope it's a cask of milk," I said. " I expected a cow."

"One cask, it says here."

"Well, let's see it; I'll warrant it has horns and is tied by a rope"; which proved to be the case, for there stood the only object that bore my name, chewing its cud, on the forward deck. How she liked the voyage I could not find out; but she seemed to relish so much the feeling of solid ground beneath her feet once more, that she led me a lively step all the way home. She cut capers in front of the White House, and tried twice to wind me up in the rope as we passed the Treasury. She kicked up her heels on the broad avenue, and became very coltish as she came under the walls of the Capitol. But that night the long-vacant stall in the old stable was filled, and the next morning the coffee had met with a change of heart. I had to go out twice with the lantern and survey my treasure before I went to bed. Did she not come from the delectable mountains, and did I not have a sort of filial regard for her as toward my foster-mother?

This was during the Arcadian age at the capital, before the easy-going Southern ways had gone out and the prim new Northern ways had come in, and when the domestic animals were treated with distinguished consideration and granted the freedom of the city. There was a charm of cattle in the street and upon the commons: goats cropped your rose bushes through the pickets, and nooned upon your front porch; and pigs dreamed Arcadian dreams under your garden fence, or languidly frescoed it with pigments from the nearest pool. It was a time of peace; it was the poor man's golden age. Your cow, your goat, your pig led vagrant, wandering lives, and picked up a subsistence wherever they could, like the bees, which was almost everywhere. Your cow went forth in the morning and came home fraught with milk at night, and you never troubled yourself where she went or how far she roamed.

Chloe took very naturally to this kind of life. At first I had to go with her a few times and pilot her to the nearest commons, and then I left her to her own wit, which never failed her. What adventures she had, what acquaintances she made, how far she wandered, I never knew. I never came across her in my walks or rambles. Indeed, on several occasions I thought I would look her up and see her feeding in national pastures, but I never could find her. There were plenty of cows, but they were all strangers. But punctually, between four and five o'clock in the afternoon, her white horns would be seen tossing above the gate and her impatient low be heard. Sometimes, when I turned her forth in the morning, she would pause and apparently consider which way she would go. Should she go toward Kendall Green today, or follow the Tiber, or over by the Big Spring, or out around Lincoln Hospital? She seldom reached a conclusion till she had stretched forth her neck and blown a blast on her trumpet that awoke the echoes in the very lantern on the dome of the Capitol. Then, after one or two licks, she would

John Burroughs weeding. Courtesy of the Jones Library, Amherst, Massachusetts. Photograph by Clifton Johnson.

disappear around the corner. Later in the season, when the grass was parched or poor on the commons, and the corn and cabbage tempting in the garden, Chloe was loath to depart in the morning, and her deliberations were longer than ever, and very often I had to aid her in coming to a decision.

For two summers she was a wellspring of pleasure and profit in my farm of one acre, when, in an evil moment, I resolved to part with her and try another. In an evil moment, I say, for from that time my luck in cattle left me. The goddess never forgave me the execution of that rash and cruel resolve.

The day is indelibly stamped on my memory when I exposed my Chloe for sale in the public market-place. It was in November, a bright, dreamy, Indian summer day. A sadness oppressed me, not unmixed with guilt and remorse. An old Irish woman came to the market also with her pets to sell, a sow and five pigs, and took up a position next me. We condoled with each other; we bewailed the fate of our darlings together; we berated in chorus the white-aproned but blood-stained fraternity who prowled about us. When she went away for a moment, I minded the pigs, and when I strolled about, she minded my cow.

How shy the innocent beast was of those carnal marketmen! How she would shrink away from them! When they put out a hand to feel her condition, she would "scrooch" down her back, or bend this way or that, as if the hand were a branding iron. So long as I stood by her head she felt safe—deluded creature!—and chewed the cud of sweet content; but the moment I left her side she seemed filled with apprehension, and followed me with her eyes, lowing softly and entreatingly till I returned.

At last the money was counted out for her, and her rope surrendered to the hand of another. How that last look of alarm and incredulity, which I caught as I turned for a parting glance, went to my heart!

Part Three

Far from Home

꙰

From "In Green Alaska"

O N JUNE 1st, after touching at Victoria, we were fairly launched upon
our voyage. Before us was a cruise of several thousand miles, one
thousand of which was through probably the finest scenery of the kind in
the world that can be viewed from the deck of a ship—the scenery of fiords
and mountain-locked bays and arms of the sea. Day after day a panorama
unrolls before us with features that might have been gathered from the
Highlands of the Hudson, from Lake George, from the Thousand Islands,
the Saguenay, and the Rangeley Lakes in Maine, with the addition of towering snowcapped peaks thrown in for a background. The edge of this part
of the continent for a thousand miles has been broken into fragments, small
and great, as by the stroke of some earth-cracking hammer, and into the
openings and channels thus formed the sea flows freely, often at a depth of
from one to two thousand feet. It is along these inland ocean highways,
through tortuous narrows, up smooth, placid inlets, across broad island-
studded gulfs and bays, with now and then the mighty throb of the Pacific
felt for an hour or two through some open door in the wall of islands, that
our course lay.

꙰   ꙰   ꙰

The next day found us in Glacier Bay on our way to the Muir Glacier. Our
course was up an arm of the sea, dotted with masses of floating ice, till in
the distance we saw the great glacier itself. Its front looked gray and dim
there twenty miles away, but in the background the mountains that feed it
lifted up vast masses of snow in the afternoon sun. At five o'clock we
dropped anchor about two miles from its front, in eighty fathoms of water,
abreast of the little cabin on the east shore built by John Muir some years
ago. Not till after repeated soundings did we find bottom within reach of

From *Far and Near* (1904); first appeared in *Harriman Alaska Expedition*, I (1901), ed.
C. Wright Merriam. These are representative selections from a narrative of more than one
hundred pages.

our anchor cables. Could the inlet have been emptied of its water for a moment, we should have seen before us a palisade of ice nearly one thousand feet higher and over two miles long, with a turbid river, possibly half a mile wide, boiling up from beneath it. Could we have been here many centuries ago, we should have seen, much farther down the valley, a palisade of ice two or three thousand feet high. Many of these Alaskan glaciers are rapidly melting and are now but the fragments of their former selves. From observations made here twenty years ago by John Muir, it is known that the position of the front of the Muir Glacier at that time was about two miles below its present position, which would indicate a rate of recession of about one mile in ten years.

What we saw on that June afternoon was a broken and crumbling wall of ice two hundred and fifty feet high in our front, stretching across the inlet and running down to a low, dirty, crumbling line where it ended on the shore on our left, and where it disappeared behind high gray gravelly banks on our right. The inlet near the glacier was choked with icebergs.

What is that roar or explosion that salutes our ears before our anchor has found bottom? It is the downpour of an enormous mass of ice from the glacier's front, making it for the moment as active as Niagara. Other and still other downpours follow at intervals of a few minutes, with deep explosive sounds and the rising up of great clouds of spray, and we quickly realize that here is indeed a new kind of Niagara, a cataract the like of which we have not before seen, a mighty congealed river that discharges into the bay intermittently in ice avalanches that shoot down its own precipitous front. The mass of ice below the water line is vastly greater than that above, and when the upper portions fall away, enormous bergs are liberated and rise up from the bottom. They rise slowly and majestically, like huge monsters of the deep, lifting themselves up to a height of fifty or a hundred feet, the water pouring off them in white sheets. Then they subside again and float away with a huge wave in front. Nothing we had read or heard had prepared us for the color of the ice, especially of the newly exposed parts and of the bergs that rose from beneath the water — its deep, almost indigo blue. Huge bergs were floating about that suggested masses of blue vitriol.

As soon as practicable, many of us went ashore in the naphtha launches, and were soon hurrying over the great plateau of sand, gravel, and boulders which the retreating glacier had left, and which forms its vast terminal moraine.

Many of the rocks and stones on the surface were sharp and angular, others were smooth and rounded. These latter had evidently passed, as it were,

John Burroughs and John Muir at Muir Glacier. Courtesy of the American Museum of Natural History.

through the gizzard of the huge monster, while the others had been carried on its back. A walk of a mile or more brought us much nearer the glacier's front, and standing high on the bank of the moraine we could observe it at our leisure. The roar that followed the discharge of ice from its front constantly suggested the blasting in mines or in railroad cuts. The spray often rose nearly to the top of the glacier. Night and day, summer and winter, this intermittent and explosive discharge of the ice into the inlet goes on and has gone on for centuries. When we awoke in the night, we heard its muffled thunder, sometimes so loud as to jar the windows in our staterooms, while the swells caused by the falling and rising masses rocked the ship. Probably few more strange and impressive spectacles than this glacier affords can be found on the continent. It has a curious fascination. Impending cataclysms are in its look. In a moment or two one knows some part of it will topple or slide into the sea.

ᴣ^{*}   ᴣ^{*}   ᴣ^{*}

We saw the world-shaping forces at work; we scrambled over plains they had built but yesterday. We saw them transport enormous rocks and tons on tons of soil and debris from the distant mountains; we saw the remains of extensive forests they had engulfed probably within the century, and were now uncovering again; we saw their turbid rushing streams loaded with newly ground rocks and soil-making material; we saw the beginnings of vegetation in the tracks of the retreating glacier; our dredgers brought up the first forms of sea life along the shore; we witnessed the formation of the low mounds and ridges and bowl-shaped depressions that so often diversify our landscapes—all the while with the muffled thunder of the falling bergs in our ears.

We were really in one of the workshops and laboratories of the elder gods, but only in the glacier's front was there present evidence that they were still at work. I wanted to see them opening crevasses in the ice, dropping the soil and rocks they had transported, polishing the mountains, or blocking the streams, but I could not. They seemed to knock off work when we were watching them. One day I climbed up to the shoulder of a huge granite ridge on the west, against which the glacier pressed and over which it broke. Huge masses of ice had recently toppled over, a great fragment of rock hung on the very edge, ready to be deposited upon the ridge, windrows of soil and gravel and boulders were clinging to the margin of the ice, but while I stayed, not a pebble moved, all was silence and inertia. And I could look down between the glacier and the polished mountain-side; they were not in contact; the hand of the sculptor was raised, as it were, but he did not strike while I was around. In front of me upon the glacier for many miles was a perfect wilderness of crevasses, the ice was ridged and contorted like an angry sea, but not a sound, not a movement anywhere.

In Yakutat Bay

In the afternoon we moved to the vicinity of the Hubbard Glacier, where the ship took a fresh supply of water from a mountain torrent, while the glacier hunters viewed the Nunatak Glacier, and the mineralogists with their hammers prowled upon the shore. My own diversion that afternoon was to climb one of the near mountains to an altitude of about twenty-five hundred feet, where I looked down at a fearful angle into the sea, and where I found my first titlark's nest. The bird with her shining eyes looked out upon me, and upon the sublime scene, from a little cavity in a mossy bank near the snow-line. Her nest held six dark-brown eggs. Some pussy willows near by were just starting. I thought to reach the peak of the mountain up a broad and very steep band of snow, but I looked back once too often. The descent to the sea was too easy and too fearful for my imagination, so I cautiously turned back. In a large patch of alders at the foot of the mountain four or five species of birds were nesting and in song. The most welcome sight to me was a solitary barn swallow skimming along as one might have seen it at home—no barns within hundreds of miles, yet the little swallow seemed quite at her ease.

$*$ $*$ $*$

The next day, which was thick and rainy, we picked up our party at Virgin Bay, and steamed back to Orca to mend our broken propeller. I wondered how it could be done, as there is no dry dock there, but the problem proved an easy one. The tide is so great in these waters that every shelving beach becomes a dry dock at low tide. In the morning our steamer lay in shallow water on the beach at Orca. A low scaffolding was built around her propeller, and very soon the broken blade was replaced by a new one.

While this was being done, many of us viewed the process of salmon canning. Some of the fish lay piled up on the dock, and were being loaded into wheelbarrows with a one-tined pitchfork, and wheeled in to the cleaners. Most of the work was done by Chinamen from San Francisco. It was positively fascinating to see the skill and swiftness with which some of these men worked; only two used knives—long, thin blades, which they kept very sharp. They cut off the fins, severed the head and tail, and did the disemboweling with lightninglike rapidity. It was like the tricks of jugglers. There was a gleam of steel about the fish half a moment, and the work was done. One had to be very intent to follow the movements. The fish were then washed and scraped and passed on to workmen inside, where they were cut and packed by machinery. Every second all day long a pound can, snugly packed, drops from the ingenious mechanism.

For some reason the looker-on soon loses his taste for salmon, there is such a world of it. It is as common as chips; it is kicked about under foot; it lies in great sweltering heaps; many of the fish, while lying upon the beach before they are brought in, are pecked and bruised by gulls and ravens; the air is redolent of an odor far different from that of roses or new-mown hay, and very shortly one turns away to the woods or to the unpolluted beach.

✳ ✳ ✳

On the morning of the 8th we were tied up at the pier in Dutch Harbor, Unalaska, amid a world of green hills and meadows like those at Kadiak. It was warm and cloudy, with light rain. We tarried here half a day, taking in coal and water, visiting the old Russian town of Iliuliuk a couple of miles away at the head of another indentation in the harbor, strolling through the wild meadows, or climbing the emerald heights.

One new bird, the Lapland longspur, which in color, flight, and song suggested our bobolink, attracted our attention here. As we came "cross lots" over the flower-besprinkled, undulating plain from the old town to the new, this bird was in song all about us, hovering in the air, pouring out its liquid, bubbling song, and dropping down in the grass again in a way very suggestive of the home bird, so much so that it may be fitly called the northland bobolink.

To the Lapland Longspur

Oh! thou northland bobolink,
 Looking over summer's brink,
Up to winter, worn and dim,
 Peering down from mountain rim,
Peering out on Bering Sea,
 To higher lands where he may flee—
Something takes me in thy note,
 Quivering wing and bubbling throat,
Something moves me in thy ways,
 Bird, rejoicing in thy days,
In thy upward hovering flight,
 In thy suit of black and white,
Chestnut cape and circled crown,
 In thy mate of speckled brown;
Surely I may pause and think
 Of my boyhood's bobolink.

Soaring over meadows wild,
 (Greener pastures never smiled)
Raining music from above—
 Full of rapture, full of love;
Frolic, gay, and debonair,
 Yet not all exempt from care,

For thy nest is in the grass,
    And thou worriest as I pass
But no hand nor foot of mine
    Shall do harm to thee or thine
I, musing, only pause to think
    Of my boyhood's bobolink.

But no bobolink of mine
    Ever sang o'er mead so fine,
Starred with flowers of every hue,
    Gold and purple, white and blue.
Painted cup, anemone,
    Jacob's ladder, fleur-de-lis,
Orchid, harebell, shooting-star,
    Crane's bill, lupine, seen afar,
Primrose, rubus, saxifrage,
    Pictured type on Nature's page,
These and others, here unnamed,
    In northland gardens, yet untamed,
Deck the fields where thou dost sing,
    Mounting up on trembling wing
Yet in wistful mood I think
    Of my boyhood's bobolink.

On Unalaska's emerald lea,
    On lonely isles in Bering Sea,
On far Siberia's barren shore,
    On north Alaska's tundra floor;
At morn, at noon, in pallid night,
    We heard thy song and saw thy flight,
While I, sighing, could but think
    Of my boyhood's bobolink.

On the higher peaks, amid lingering snow-banks, Mr. Ridgway found the snow bunting and the titlark nesting. Unalaska looked quite as interesting as Kadiak, and I longed to spend some days there in the privacy of its green solitudes, following its limpid trout streams, climbing its lofty peaks, and listening to the music of the longspur. I had seen much, but had been intimate with little; now if I could only have a few days of that kind of intimacy with this new nature which the saunterer, the camper-out, the stroller through fields in the summer twilight has, I should be more content; but in the afternoon the ship was off into Bering Sea, headed for the Seal Islands, and I was aboard her, but with wistful and reverted eyes.

∗ ∗ ∗

In the afternoon we anchored off a deserted Indian village north of Cape Fox. There was a row of a dozen houses on the beach of a little bay, with nineteen totem poles standing along their fronts. These totem poles were the attraction. There was a rumor that the Indians had nearly all died of smallpox a few years before, and that the few survivors had left under a superstitious fear, never to return. It was evident that the village had not been occupied for seven or eight years. Why not, therefore, secure some of these totem poles for the museums of the various colleges represented by members of the expedition? This was finally agreed upon, and all hands, including the ship's crew, fell to digging up and floating to the ship five or six of the more striking poles. This occupied us till the night of the 27th.

Under this date I find this entry in my note-book: "All day on shore by the deserted Indian village. Clear and hot. I sit in the shade of the spruces amid huge logs of driftwood on the upper edge of the beach, with several Indian graves at my back, under the trees, and write up my notes—the ship at anchor out in the bay a mile away. Aided by the sailors, the men are taking down totem poles and towing them to the ship with the naphtha launches. As I write, there are many birds in the trees and bushes near me— the rufous hummer, the rufous-backed chickadee, the golden-crowned kinglet, the pine siskin. Back in the woods I hear the russet-backed thrush and Steller's jay. With my lunch I have some salmon-berries gathered near by.

July 28. Woke up this morning hearing the birds sing through my open window. I looked out into the dusky wooded side of a mountain nearly within a stone's throw. We were in Grenville Channel, the skies clear, the sun shining full upon the opposite shore. Presently we were passing one of those bewitching alcoves or recesses in the shore where the mountains form a loop miles deep around an inlet of blue sea, with snow-crowned peaks above great curves of naked rock at the head of it. Then we cut one of those curious tide-lines, where two currents of water of different colors meet. The dividing line is sharp and clear for a long distance.

The next day, which was still bright and warm, there was a film of smoke in the air in the morning, which increased as we went south. We were nearing the region of forest fires. When we reached Seattle on July 30, this smoke had so increased that all the great mountains were hidden by it as effectually as they had been by the clouds when we entered upon the voyage.

We had three tons of coal left in our bunkers, but of our little stock farm down below only the milch cow remained. She had been to Siberia and back, and had given milk all the way.

No voyagers were ever more fortunate than we. No storms, no winds, no delays nor accidents to speak of, no illness. We had gone far and fared well.

A Hunt for the Nightingale

WHILE I LINGERED AWAY the latter half of May in Scotland, and the first half of June in northern England and finally in London, intent on seeing the land leisurely and as the mood suited, the thought never occurred to me that I was in danger of missing one of the chief pleasures I had promised myself in crossing the Atlantic, namely, the hearing of the song of the nightingale. Hence, when on the 17th of June I found myself down among the copses near Hazlemere, on the borders of Surrey and Sussex, and was told by the old farmer, to whose house I had been recommended by friends in London, that I was too late, that the season of the nightingale was over, I was a good deal disturbed.

"I think she be done singing now, Sir; I ain't heered her in some time, Sir," said my farmer, as we sat down to get acquainted over a mug of the hardest cider I ever attempted to drink.

"Too late!" I said in deep chagrin, "and I might have been here weeks ago."

"Yeas, Sir, she be done now; May is the time to hear her. The cuckoo is done too, sir; and you don't hear the nightingale after the cuckoo is gone, sir."

(The country people in this part of England sir one at the end of every sentence, and talk with an indescribable drawl.)

But I had heard a cuckoo that very afternoon, and I took heart from the fact. I afterward learned that the country people everywhere associate these two birds in this way; you will not hear the one after the other has ceased. But I heard the cuckoo almost daily till the middle of July. Matthew Arnold reflects the popular opinion when in one of his poems ("Thyrsis") he makes the cuckoo say in early June, "The bloom is gone, and with the bloom go I!"

From *Fresh Fields*, 1884.

The explanation is to be found in Shakespeare, who says,

> The cuckoo is in June
> Heard, not regarded,

as the bird really does not go till August. I got out my Gilbert White, as I should have done at an earlier day, and was still more disturbed to find that he limited the singing of the nightingale to June 15. But seasons differ, I thought, and it can't be possible that any class of feathered songsters all stop on a given day. There is a tradition that when George I died the nightingales all ceased singing for the year out of grief at the sad event; but his majesty did not die till June 21. This would give me a margin of several days. Then, when I looked further in White, and found that he says the chaffinch ceases to sing the beginning of June, I took more courage, for I had that day heard the chaffinch also. But it was evident I had no time to lose; I was just on the dividing line, and any day might witness the cessation of the last songster.

For it seems that the nightingale ceases singing the moment her brood is hatched. After that event, you hear only a harsh chiding or anxious note. Hence the poets, who attribute her melancholy strains to sorrow for the loss of her young, are entirely at fault.

As it was mid-afternoon, I could only compose myself till nightfall. I accompanied the farmer to the hayfield and saw the working of his mowing machine, a rare implement in England, as most of the grass is still cut by hand, and raked by hand also. The disturbed skylarks were hovering above the falling grass, full of anxiety for their nests, as one may note the bobolinks on like occasions at home. The weather is so uncertain in England, and it is so impossible to predict its complexion, not only from day to day but from hour to hour, that the farmers appear to consider it a suitable time to cut grass when it is not actually raining. They slash away without reference to the aspects of the sky, and when the field is down trust to luck to be able to cure the hay, or get it ready to "carry" between the showers. The clouds were lowering and the air was damp now, and it was Saturday afternoon; but the farmer said they would never get their hay if they minded such things. The farm had seen better days; so had the farmer; both were slightly down at the heel. Too high rent and too much hard cider were working their effects upon both. The farm had been in the family many generations, but it was now about to be sold and to pass into other hands, and my host said he was glad of it. There was no money in farming any more; no money in anything. I asked him what were the main sources of profit on such a farm.

"Well," he said, "sometimes the wheat pops up, and the barley drops in, and the pigs come on, and we picks up a little money, sir, but not much, sir. Pigs is doing well naow. But they brings so much wheat from Ameriky, and our weather is so bad that we can't get a good sample, sir, one year in three, that there is no money made in growing wheat, sir." And the "wuts" (oats) were not much better. "Theys as would buy hain't got no money, sir." "Up to the top of the nip," for top of the hill, was one of his expressions. Tennyson had a summer residence at Blackdown, not far off. "One of the Queen's poets, I believe, sir." "Yes, I often see him riding about, sir."

After an hour or two with the farmer, I walked out to take a survey of the surrounding country. It was quite wild and irregular, full of bushy fields and overgrown hedge-rows, and looked to me very nightingaly. I followed for a mile or two a road that led by tangled groves and woods and copses, with a still meadow trout stream in the gentle valley below. I inquired for nightingales of every boy and laboring-man I met or saw. I got but little encouragement; it was too late.

"She be about done singing now, sir." A boy whom I met in a footpath that ran through a pasture beside a copse said, after reflecting a moment, that he had heard one in that very copse two mornings before—"About seven o'clock, sir, while I was on my way to my work, sir." Then I would try my luck in said copse and in the adjoining thickets that night and the next morning. The railway ran near, but perhaps that might serve to keep the birds awake.

These copses in this part of England look strange enough to American eyes. What thriftless farming! the first thought is; behold the fields grown up to bushes, as if the land had relapsed to a state of nature again. Adjoining meadows and grain-fields, one may see an enclosure of many acres covered with a thick growth of oak and chestnut sprouts, six or eight or twelve feet high. These are the copses one has so often heard about, and they are a valuable and productive part of the farm.

They are planted and preserved as carefully as we plant an orchard or a vineyard. Once in so many years, perhaps five or six, the copse is cut and every twig is saved; it is a woodland harvest that in our own country is gathered in the forest itself. The larger poles are tied up in bundles and sold for hoop-poles; the fine branches and shoots are made into brooms in the neighboring cottages and hamlets, or used as material for thatching. The refuse is used as wood.

About eight o'clock in the evening I sallied forth, taking my way over the ground I had explored a few hours before. The gloaming, which at this season lasts till after ten o'clock, dragged its slow length along. Nine o'clock came, and, though my ear was attuned, the songster was tardy. I hovered about the copses and hedge-rows like one meditating some dark deed; I lingered in a grove and about an overgrown garden and a neglected orchard; I sat on stiles and leaned on wickets, mentally speeding the darkness that should bring my singer out. The weather was damp and chilly, and the tryst grew tiresome. I had brought a rubber water-proof, but not an overcoat. Lining the back of the rubber with a newspaper, I wrapped it about me and sat down, determined to lay siege to my bird. A footpath that ran along the fields and bushes on the other side of the little valley showed every few minutes a woman or girl, or boy or laborer, passing along it. A path near me also had its frequent figures moving along in the dusk. In this country people travel in footpaths as much as in highways. The paths give a private, human touch to the landscape that the roads do not. They are sacred to the human foot. They have the sentiment of domesticity, and suggest the way to cottage doors and to simple, primitive times.

Presently a man with a fishing-rod, and capped, coated, and booted for the work, came through the meadow and began casting for trout in the stream below me. How he gave himself to the work! how oblivious he was of everything but the one matter in hand! I doubt if he was conscious of the train that passed within a few rods of him. Your born angler is like a hound that scents no game but that which he is in pursuit of. Every sense and faculty were concentrated upon that hovering fly. This man wooed the stream, quivering with pleasure and expectation. Every foot of it he tickled with his decoy. His close was evidently a short one, and he made the most of it. He lingered over every cast, and repeated it again and again. An American angler would have been out of sight downstream long ago. But this fisherman was not going to bolt his preserve; his line should taste every drop of it. His eager, stealthy movements denoted his enjoyment and his absorption. When a trout was caught, it was quickly rapped on the head and slipped into his basket, as if in punishment for its tardiness in jumping. "Be quicker next time, will you?" (British trout, by the way, are not so beautiful as our own. They have more of a domesticated look. They are less brilliantly marked, and have much coarser scales. There is no gold or vermilion in their coloring.)

Presently there arose from a bushy corner of a near field a low, peculiar purring or humming sound, that sent a thrill through me; of course, I thought my bird was inflating her throat. Then the sound increased, and was answered or repeated in various other directions. It had a curious ventriloquial effect. I presently knew it to be the nightjar or goatsucker, a bird that answers to our whip-poor-will. Very soon the sound seemed to be floating all about me—*Jr-r-r-r-r* or *Chr-r-r-r-r,* slightly suggesting the call of our toads, but more vague as to direction.

Then as it grew darker, the birds ceased; the fisherman reeled up and left. No sound was now heard—not even the voice of a solitary frog anywhere. I never heard a frog in England. About eleven o'clock I moved down by a wood, and stood for an hour on a bridge over the railroad. No voice of bird greeted me till the sedge-warbler struck up her curious nocturne in a hedge near by. It was a singular medley of notes, hurried chirps, trills, calls, warbles, snatched from the songs of other birds, with a half-chiding, remonstrating tone or air running through it all. As there was no other sound to be heard, and as the darkness was complete, it had the effect of a very private and whimsical performance—as if the little bird had secluded herself there, and was giving vent to her emotions in the most copious and vehement manner. I listened till after midnight, and till the rain began to fall, and the vivacious warbler never ceased for a moment. White says that if it stops, a stone tossed into the bush near it will set it going again. Its voice is not musical; the quality of it is like that of the loquacious English house sparrows; but its song or medley is so persistently animated, and in such contrast to the gloom and the darkness, that the effect is decidedly pleasing.

This and the nightjar were the only nightingales I heard that night. I returned home, a good deal disappointed, but slept upon my arms, as it were, and was out upon the chase again at four o'clock in the morning. This time I passed down a lane by the neglected garden and orchard, where I was told the birds had sung for weeks past; then under the railroad by a cluster of laborers' cottages, and along a road with many copses and bushy fence corners on either hand, for two miles, but I heard no nightingales. A boy of whom I inquired seemed half frightened, and went into the house without answering.

After a late breakfast I sallied out again, going farther in the same direction, and was overtaken by several showers. I heard many and frequent birdsong—the lark, the wren, the thrush, the black-bird, the whitethroat, the greenfinch, and the hoarse, guttural cooing of the wood-pigeons—but not the note I was in quest of. I passed up a road that was a deep trench in the side of a hill overgrown with low beeches. The roots of the trees formed a network on the side of the bank, as their branches did above. In a framework of roots, within reach of my hand, I spied a wren's nest, a round hole leading to the interior of a large mass of soft green moss, a structure displaying the taste and neatness of the daintiest of bird architects, and the depth and warmth and snugness of the most ingenious mouse habitation. While lingering here, a young countryman came along whom I engaged in conversation. No, he had not heard the nightingale for a few days; but the previous week he had been in camp with the militia near Guildford, and while on picket duty had heard her nearly all night. "'Don't she sing splendid to-night?' the boys would say." This was tantalizing; Guildford was within easy reach; but the previous week, that could not be reached. However, he encouraged me by saying he did not think they were done singing yet, as he had often heard them during haying-time. I inquired for the blackcap, but saw he did not know this bird, and thought I referred to a species of tomtit, which also has a black cap. The woodlark I was also on the lookout for, but he did not know this bird either, and during my various rambles in England I found but one person who did. In Scotland it was confounded with the titlark or pipit.

I next met a man and boy, a villager with a stove-pipe hat on—and, as it turned out, a man of many trades, tailor, barber, painter, etc.—from Hazlemere. The absorbing inquiry was put to him also. No, not that day, but a few mornings before he had. But—he could easily call one out, if there were any about, as he could imitate them. Plucking a spear of grass, he adjusted it behind his teeth and startled me with the shrill, rapid notes he poured forth. I at once recognized its resemblance to the descriptions I had read of the opening part of the nightingale song, what is called "the challenge." The boy said, and he himself averred, that it was an exact imitation. The *chew, chew, chew,* and some other parts, were very birdlike, and I had no doubt were correct. I was astonished at the strong, piercing quality of the strain. It echoed in the woods and copses about, but, though oft repeated, brought forth no response. With this man I made an engagement to take a walk that evening at eight o'clock along a certain route where he had heard plenty of nightingales but a few days before. He was confident he could call them out; so was I.

In the afternoon, which had gleams of warm sunshine, I made another excursion, less in hopes of hearing my bird than of finding someone who could direct me to the right spot. Once I thought the game was very near. I met a boy who told me he had heard a nightingale only fifteen minutes before, "on Polecat Hill, sir, just this side the Devil's Punch-bowl, sir!" I had heard of his majesty's punch-bowl before, and of the gibbets near it where three murderers were executed nearly a hundred years ago, but Polecat Hill was a new name to me. The combination did not seem a likely place for nightingales, but I walked rapidly thitherward. I heard several warblers, but not Philomel, and was forced to conclude that probably I had crossed the sea to miss my bird by just fifteen minutes. I met many other boys (is there any country where boys do not prowl about in small bands of a Sunday?) and advertised the object of my search freely among them, offering a reward that made their eyes glisten for the bird in song; but nothing ever came of it. In my desperation, I even presented a letter I had brought to the village squire, just as, in company with his wife, he was about to leave his door for church. He turned back, and, hearing my quest, volunteered to take me on a long walk through the wet grass and bushes of his fields and copses, where he knew the birds were wont to sing.

"Too late," he said, and so it did appear. He showed me a fine old edition of White's "Selborne," with notes by some editor whose name I have forgotten. This editor had extended White's date of June 15 to July 1, as the time to which the nightingale continues in song, and I felt like thanking him for it, as it gave me renewed hope. The squire thought there was a chance yet; and in case my man with the spear of grass behind his teeth failed me, he gave me a card to an old naturalist and taxidermist at Godalming, a town nine miles above, who, he felt sure, could put me on the right track if anybody could.

At eight o'clock, the sun yet some distance above the horizon, I was at the door of the barber in Hazlemere. He led the way along one of those delightful footpaths with which this country is threaded, extending to a neighboring village several miles distant. It left the street at Hazlemere, cutting through the houses diagonally, as if the brick walls had made way for it, passed between gardens, through wickets, over stiles, across the highway and railroad, through cultivated fields and a gentleman's park, and on toward its destination—a broad, well-kept path, that seemed to have the same inevitable right of way as a brook. I was told that it was repaired and looked after the same as the highway. Indeed, it was a public way, public to pedestrians only, and no man could stop or turn it aside.

We followed it along the side of a steep hill, with copses and groves sweeping down into the valley below us. It was as wild and picturesque a spot as I had seen in England. The foxglove pierced the lower foliage and wild growths everywhere with its tall spires of purple flowers; the wild honeysuckle, with a ranker and coarser fragrance than our cultivated species, was just opening along the hedges. We paused here, and my guide blew his shrill call; he blew it again and again. How it awoke the echoes, and how it awoke all the other songsters! The valley below us and the slope beyond, which before were silent, were soon musical. The chaffinch, the robin, the blackbird, the thrush — the last, the loudest and most copious — seemed to vie with each other and with the loud whistler above them. But we listened in vain for the nightingale's note. Twice my guide struck an attitude and said, impressively, "There! I believe I 'erd 'er." But we were obliged to give it up. A shower came on, and after it had passed we moved to another part of the landscape and repeated our call, but got no response, and as darkness set in we returned to the village.

The situation began to look serious. I knew there was a nightingale somewhere whose brood had been delayed from some cause or other, and who was therefore still in song, but I could not get a clew to the spot. I renewed the search late that night, and again the next morning; I inquired of every man and boy I saw.

I soon learned to distrust young fellows and their girls who had heard nightingales in the gloaming. I knew one's ears could not always be depended upon on such occasions, nor his eyes either. Larks are seen in buntings, and a wren's song entrances like Philomel's. A young couple of whom I inquired in the train, on my way to Godalming, said Yes, they had heard nightingales just a few moments before on their way to the station, and described the spot, so I could find it if I returned that way. They left the train at the same point I did, and walked up the street in advance of me. I had lost sight of them till they beckoned to me from the corner of the street, near the church, where the prospect opens with a view of a near meadow and a stream shaded by pollard willows. "We heard one now, just there," they said, as I came up. They passed on, and I bent my ear eagerly in the direction. Then I walked farther on, following one of those inevitable footpaths to where it cuts diagonally through the cemetery behind the old church, but I heard nothing save a few notes of the thrush. My ear was too critical and exacting.

Then I sought out the old naturalist and taxidermist to whom I had a card from the squire. He was a short, stout man, racy both in look and speech, and kindly. He had a fine collection of birds and animals, in which he took great pride. He pointed out the woodlark and the blackcap to me, and told me where he had seen and heard them. He said I was too late for the nightingale, though I might possibly find one yet in song. But he said she grew hoarse late in the season, and did not sing as a few weeks earlier.

He thought our cardinal grosbeak—which he called the Virginia nightingale—as fine a whistler as the nightingale herself. He could not go with me that day, but he would send his boy. Summoning the lad, he gave him minute directions where to take me—over by Easing, around by Shackerford church, etc., a circuit of four or five miles.

Leaving the picturesque old town, we took a road over a broad, gentle hill, lined with great trees—beeches, elms, oaks—with rich, cultivated fields beyond. The air of peaceful and prosperous human occupancy which everywhere pervades this land seemed especially pronounced through all this section. The sentiment of parks and lawns, easy, large, basking, indifferent of admiration, self-sufficing, and full, everywhere prevailed. The road was like the most perfect private carriage-way. Homeliness, in its true sense, is a word that applies to nearly all English country scenes; homelike, redolent of affectionate care and toil, saturated with rural and domestic contentment; beauty without pride, order without stiffness, age without decay. This people love the country, because it would seem as if the country must first have loved them. In a field I saw for the first time a new species of clover, much grown in parts of England as green fodder for horses. The farmers call it trifolium, probably *Trifolium incarnatum.* The head is two or three inches long, and as red as blood. A field of it under the sunlight presents a most brilliant appearance. As we walked along, I got also my first view of the British blue jay—a slightly larger bird than ours, with a hoarser voice and much duller plumage. Blue, the tint of the sky, is not so common, and is not found in any such perfection among the British birds as among the American.

My boy companion was worthy of observation also. He was a curious specimen, ready and officious, but, as one soon found out, full of duplicity. I questioned him about himself. "I helps he, sir; sometimes I shows people about, and sometimes I does errands. I gets three a week, sir, and lunch and tea. I lives with my grandmother, but I calls her mother, sir. The master and the rector they gives me a character, says I am a good, honest boy, and that it is well I went to school in my youth. I am ten, sir. Last year I had the measles, sir, and I thought I should die; but I got hold of a bottle of medicine, and it tasted like honey, and I takes the whole of it, and it made me well, sir. I never lies, Sir. It is good to tell the truth."

And yet he would slide off into a lie as if the track in that direction was always greased. Indeed, there was a kind of fluent, unctuous, obsequious effrontery in all he said and did. As the day was warm for that climate, he soon grew tired of the chase. At one point we skirted the grounds of a large house, as thickly planted with trees and shrubs as a forest; many birds were singing there, and for a moment my guide made me believe that among them he recognized the notes of the nightingale. Failing in this, he coolly assured me that the swallow that skimmed along the road in front of us was the nightingale!

We presently left the highway and took a footpath. It led along the margin of a large plowed field, shut in by rows of noble trees, the soil of which looked as if it might have been a garden of untold generations. Then the path led through a wicket, and down the side of a wooded hill to a large stream and to the hamlet of Easing. A boy fishing said indifferently that he had heard nightingales there that morning. He had caught a little fish which he said was a gudgeon. "Yes," said my companion in response to a remark of mine, "they is little; but you can eat they if they *is* little." Then we went toward Shackerford church. The road, like most roads in the south of England, was a deep trench. The banks on either side rose fifteen feet, covered with ivy, moss, wild flowers, and the roots of trees. England's best defense against an invading foe is her sunken roads. Whole armies might be ambushed in these trenches, while an enemy moving across the open plain would very often find himself plunging headlong into these hidden pitfalls. Indeed, between the subterranean character of the roads in some places and the high-walled or high-hedged character of it in others, the pedestrian about England is shut out from much he would like to see. I used to envy the bicyclists, perched high upon their rolling stilts. But the footpaths escape the barriers, and one need walk nowhere else if he choose.

Around Shackerford church are copses, and large pine and fir woods. The place was full of birds. My guide threw a stone at a small bird which he declared was a nightingale; and though the missile did not come within three yards of it, yet he said he had hit it, and pretended to search for it on the ground. He must needs invent an opportunity for lying. I told him here I had no further use for him, and he turned cheerfully back, with my shilling in his pocket. I spent the afternoon about the woods and copses near Shackerford. The day was bright and the air balmy. I heard the cuckoo call and the chaffinch sing, both of which I considered good omens. The little chiffchaff was chiffchaffing in the pine woods. The whitethroat, with his quick, emphatic *Chew-che-rick* or *Che-rick-a-rew,* flitted and ducked and hid among the low bushes by the roadside. A girl told me she had heard the nightingale yesterday on her way to Sunday-school, and pointed out the spot. It was in some bushes near a house. I hovered about this place till I was afraid the woman, who saw me from the window, would think I had some designs upon her premises. But I managed to look very indifferent or abstracted when I passed. I am quite sure I heard the chiding, guttural note of the bird I was after. Doubtless her brood had come out that very day. Another girl had heard a nightingale on her way to school that morning, and directed me to the road; still another pointed out to me the whitethroat and said that was my bird. This last was a rude shock to my faith in the ornithology of schoolgirls.

Finally, I found a laborer breaking stone by the roadside—a serious, honest-faced man, who said he had heard my bird that morning on his way to work; he heard her every morning, and nearly every night, too. He heard her last night after the shower (just at the hour when my barber and I were trying to awaken her near Hazlemere), and she sang as finely as ever she did. This was a great lift. I felt that I could trust this man. He said that after his day's work was done, that is, at five o'clock, if I chose to accompany him on his way home, he would show me where he had heard the bird. This I gladly agreed to, and, remembering that I had had no dinner, I sought out the inn in the village and asked for something to eat. The unwonted request so startled the landlord that he came out from behind his inclosed bar and confronted me with good-humored curiosity. These back-country English inns, as I several times found to my discomfiture, are only drinking-places for the accommodation of local customers, mainly of the laboring class. Instead of standing conspicuously on some street corner, as with us, they usually stand on some byway, or some little paved court away from the main thoroughfare. I could have plenty of beer, said the landlord, but he had not a mouthful of meat in the house. I urged my needs, and finally got some rye-bread and cheese. With this and a glass of home-brewed beer I was fairly well fortified. At the appointed time I met the cottager and went with him on his way home. We walked two miles or more along a charming road, full of wooded nooks and arborlike vistas. Why do English trees always look so sturdy, and exhibit such massive repose, so unlike, in this latter respect, to the nervous and agitated expression of most of our own foliage? Probably because they have been a long time out of the woods, and have had plenty of room in which to develop individual traits and peculiarities; then, in a deep fertile soil, and a climate that does not hurry or overtax, they grow slow and last long, and come to have the picturesqueness of age without its infirmities. The oak, the elm, the beech, all have more striking profiles than in our country.

Presently my companion pointed out to me a small wood below the road that had a wide fringe of bushes and saplings connecting it with a meadow, amid which stood the tree-embowered house of a city man, where he had heard the nightingale in the morning; and then, farther along, showed me, near his own cottage, where he had heard one the evening before. It was now only six o'clock, and I had two or three hours to wait before I could reasonably expect to hear her. "It gets to be into the hevening," said my new friend, "when she sings the most, you know." I whiled away the time as best I could. If I had been an artist, I should have brought away a sketch of a picturesque old cottage near by, that bore the date of 1688 on its wall. I was obliged to keep moving most of the time to keep warm. Yet the "no-see-'ems," or midges, annoyed me, in a temperature which at home would have chilled them buzzless and biteless.

Finally, I leaped the smooth masonry of the stone wall and ambushed myself amid the tall ferns under a pine-tree, where the nightingale had been heard in the morning. If the keeper had seen me, he would probably have taken me for a poacher. I sat shivering there till nine o'clock, listening to the cooing of the wood-pigeons, watching the motions of a jay that, I suspect, had a nest near by, and taking note of various other birds. The song-thrush and the robins soon made such a musical uproar along the borders of a grove, across an adjoining field, as quite put me out. It might veil and obscure the one voice I wanted to hear. The robin continued to sing quite into the darkness. This bird is related to the nightingale, and looks and acts like it at a little distance; and some of its notes are remarkably piercing and musical.

When my patience was about exhausted, I was startled by a quick, brilliant call or whistle, a few rods from me, that at once recalled my barber with his blade of grass, and I knew my long-sought bird was inflating her throat. How it woke me up! It had the quality that startles; it pierced the gathering gloom like a rocket. Then it ceased. Suspecting I was too near the singer, I moved away cautiously, and stood in a lane beside the wood, where a loping hare regarded me a few paces away. Then my singer struck up again, but I could see did not let herself out; just tuning her instrument, I thought, and getting ready to transfix the silence and the darkness. A little later, a man and boy came up the lane. I asked them if that was the nightingale singing; they listened, and assured me it was none other. "Now she's on, sir; now she's on. Ah! but she don't stick. In May, sir, they makes the woods all heccho about here. Now she's on again: that's her, sir; now she's off; she won't stick." And stick she would not. I could hear a hoarse wheezing and clucking sound beneath her notes, when I listened intently. The man and boy moved away. I stood mutely invoking all the gentle divinities to spur the bird on. Just then a bird like our hermit thrush came quickly over the hedge a few yards below me, swept close past my face, and back into the thicket. I had been caught listening; the offended bird had found me taking notes of her dry and worn-out pipe there behind the hedge, and the concert abruptly ended; not another note; not a whisper. I waited a long time and then moved off; then came back, implored the outraged bird to resume; then rushed off, and slammed the door, or rather the gate, indignantly behind me. I paused by other shrines, but not a sound. The cottager had told me of a little village three miles beyond, where there were three inns, and where I could probably get lodgings for the night. I walked rapidly in that direction; committed myself to a footpath; lost the trail, and brought up at a little cottage in a wide xpanse of field or common, and by the good woman, with a babe in her arms, was set right again. I soon struck the highway by the bridge, as I had been told, and a few paces brought me to the first inn. It was ten o'clock, and the lights were just about to be put out, as the law or custom is in country inns. The landlady said she could not give me a bed; she had only one spare room, and that was not in order, and she should not set about putting it in shape at that hour; and she was short and sharp about it, too. I hastened on to the next one. The landlady said she had no sheets, and the bed was damp and unfit to sleep in. I protested that I thought an inn was an inn, and for the accommodation of travelers. But she referred me to the next house. Here were more people, and more the look and air of a public house. But the wife (the man does not show himself on such occasions) said her daughter had just got married and come home, and she had much company and could not keep me. In vain I urged my extremity; there was no room.

Could I have something to eat, then? This seemed doubtful, and led to consultations in the kitchen; but, finally, some bread and cold meat were produced. The nearest hotel was Godalming, seven miles distant, and I knew all the inns would be shut up before I could get there. So I munched my bread and meat, consoling myself with the thought that perhaps this was just the ill wind that would blow me the good I was in quest of. I saw no alternative but to spend a night under the trees with the nightingales; and I might surprise them at their revels in the small hours of the morning. Just as I was ready to congratulate myself on the richness of my experience, the landlady came in and said there was a young man there going with a "trap " to Godalming, and he had offered to take me in. I feared I should pass for an escaped lunatic if I declined the offer; so I reluctantly assented, and we were presently whirling through the darkness, along a smooth, winding road, toward town. The young man was a drummer, was from Lincolnshire, and said I spoke like a Lincolnshire man. I could believe it, for I told him he talked more like an American than any native I had met. The hotels in the larger towns close at eleven, and I was set down in front of one just as the clock was striking that hour. I asked to be conducted to a room at once. As I was about getting in bed there was a rap at the door, and a waiter presented me my bill on a tray. "Gentlemen as have no luggage, etc.," he explained; and pretend to be looking for nightingales, too! Three-and-sixpence; two shillings for the bed and one-and-six for service.

I was out at five in the morning, before any one inside was astir. After much trying of bars and doors, I made my exit into a paved court, from which a covered way led into the street. A man opened a window and directed me how to undo the great door, and forth I started, still hoping to catch my bird at her matins. I took the route of the day before. On the edge of the beautiful plowed field, looking down through the trees and bushes into the gleam of the river twenty rods below, I was arrested by the note I longed to hear. It came up from near the water, and made my ears tingle. I folded up my rubber coat and sat down upon it, saying, Now we will take our fill. But—the bird ceased, and, tarry though I did for an hour, not another note reached me. The prize seemed destined to elude me each time just as I thought it mine. Still, I treasured what little I had heard.

It was enough to convince me of the superior quality of the song, and make me more desirous than ever to hear the complete strain. I continued my rambles, and in the early morning once more hung about the Shackerford copses and loitered along the highways. Two schoolboys pointed out a tree to me in which they had heard the nightingale, on their way for milk, two hours before. But I could only repeat Emerson's lines

> Right good-will my sinews strung,
> But no speed of mine avails
> To hunt up their shining trails.

At nine o'clock I gave over the pursuit and returned to Easing in quest of breakfast. Bringing up in front of the large and comfortable-looking inn, I found the mistress of the house with her daughter engaged in washing windows. Perched upon their step-ladders, they treated my request for breakfast very coldly; in fact, finally refused to listen to it at all. The fires were out, and I could not be served. So I must continue my walk back to Godalming; and, in doing so, I found that one may walk three miles on indignation quite as easily as upon bread.

In the afternoon I returned to my lodgings at Shotter Mill, and made ready for a walk to Selborne, twelve miles distant, part of the way to be accomplished that night in the gloaming, and the rest early in the following morning, to give the nightingales a chance to make any reparation they might feel inclined to for the neglect with which they had treated me. There was a footpath over the hill and through Leechmere bottom to Liphook, and to this, with the sun half an hour high, I committed myself. The feature in this hill scenery of Surrey and Sussex that is new to American eyes is given by the furze and heather, broad black or dark brown patches of which sweep over the high rolling surfaces, like sable mantles. Tennyson's house stands amid this dusky scenery, a few miles east of Hazlemere. The path led through a large common, partly covered with grass and partly grown up to furze—another un-American feature. Doubly precious is land in England, and yet so much of it given to parks and pleasure-grounds, and so much of it left unreclaimed in commons! These commons are frequently met with; about Selborne they are miles in extent, and embrace the Hanger and other woods. No one can inclose them, or appropriate them to his own use. The landed proprietor of whose estates they form a part cannot; they belong to the people, to the lease-holders. The villagers and others who own houses on leased land pasture their cows upon them, gather the furze, and cut the wood. In some places the commons belong to the crown and are crown lands. These large uninclosed spaces often give a free-and-easy air to the landscape that is very welcome. Near the top of the hill I met a little old man nearly hidden beneath a burden of furze. He was backing it home for fuel and other uses. He paused obsequious, and listened to my inquiries. A dwarfish sort of man, whose ugliness was redolent of the humblest chimney-corner. Bent beneath his bulky burden, and grinning upon me, he was a visible embodiment of the poverty, ignorance, and, I may say, th domesticity of the lowliest peasant home. I felt as if I had encountered a walking superstition, fostered beside a hearth lighted by furze fagots and by branches dropped by the nesting rooks and ravens—a figure half repulsive and half alluring. On the border of Leechmere bottom I sat down above a straggling copse, aflame as usual with the foxglove, and gave eye and ear to the scene. While sitting here, I saw and heard for the first time the black-capped warbler. I recognized the note at once by its brightness and strength, and a faint suggestion in it of the nightingale's. But it was disappointing; I had expected a nearer approach to its great rival. The bird was very shy, but did finally show herself fairly several times, as she did also near Selborne, where I heard the song oft repeated and prolonged. It is a ringing, animated strain, but as a whole seemed to me crude, not smoothly and finely modulated. I could name several of our own birds that surpass it in pure music. Like its congeners, the garden warbler and the whitethroat, it sings with great emphasis and strength, but its song is silvern, not golden. "Little birds with big voices," one says to himself after having heard most of the British songsters.

My path led me an adventurous course through the copses and bottoms and open commons, in the long twilight. At one point I came upon three young men standing together and watching a dog that was working a near field—one of them probably the squire's son, and the other two habited like laborers. In a little thicket near by there was a brilliant chorus of bird voices, the robin, the song-thrush, and the blackbird, all vying with each other. To my inquiry, put to test the reliability of the young countrymen's ears, they replied that one of the birds I heard was the nightingale, and, after a moment's attention, singled out the robin as the bird in question. This incident so impressed me that I paid little attention to the report of the next man I met, who said he had heard a nightingale just around a bend in the road, a few minutes' walk in advance of me. At ten o'clock I reached Liphook. I expected and half hoped the inn would turn its back upon me again, in which case I proposed to make for Wolmer Forest, a few miles distant, but it did not. Before going to bed, I took a short and hasty walk down a promising-looking lane, and again met a couple who had heard nightingales. "It was a nightingale, was it not, Charley?"

If all the people of whom I inquired for nightingales in England could have been together and compared notes, they probably would not have been long in deciding that there was at least one crazy American abroad.

I proposed to be up and off at five o'clock in the morning, which seemed greatly to puzzle mine host. At first he thought it could not be done, but finally saw his way out of the dilemma, and said he would get up and undo the door for me himself. The morning was cloudy and misty, though the previous night had been of the fairest. There is one thing they do not have in England that we can boast of at home, and that is a good masculine type of weather: it is not even feminine; it is childish and puerile, though I am told that occasionally there is a full-grown storm. But I saw nothing but petulant little showers and prolonged juvenile sulks. The clouds have no reserve, no dignity; if there is a drop of water in them (and there generally are several drops), out it comes. The prettiest little showers march across the country in summer, scarcely bigger than a street watering-cart; sometimes by getting over the fence one can avoid them, but they keep the haymakers in a perpetual flurry. There is no cloud scenery, as with us, no mass and so-lidity, no height nor depth. The clouds seem low, vague, and vapory—immature, indefinite, inconsequential, like youth.

The walk to Selborne was through mist and light rain. Few bird voices, save the cries of the lapwing and the curlew, were heard. Shortly after leaving Liphook the road takes a straight cut for three or four miles through a level, black, barren, peaty stretch of country, with Wolmer Forest a short distance on the right. Under the low-hanging clouds the scene was a dismal one—a black earth beneath and a gloomy sky above. For miles the only sign of life was a baker's cart rattling along the smooth, white road. At the end of this solitude I came to cultivated fields, and a little hamlet and an inn. At this inn (for a wonder!) I got some breakfast. The family had not yet had theirs, and I sat with them at the table, and had substantial fare.

From this point I followed a footpath a couple of miles through fields and parks. The highways for the most part seemed so narrow and exclusive, or inclusive, such penalties seemed to attach to a view over the high walls and hedges that shut me in, that a footpath was always a welcome escape to me. I opened the wicket or mounted the stile without much concern as to whether it would further me on my way or not. It was like turning the flank of an enemy. These well-kept fields and lawns, these cozy nooks, these stately and exclusive houses that had taken such pains to shut out the public gaze—from the footpath one had them at an advantage, and could pluck out their mystery.

On striking the highway again, I met the postmistress, stepping briskly along with the morning mail. Her husband had died, and she had taken his place as mail-carrier. England is so densely populated, the country is so like a great city suburb, that your mail is brought to your door everywhere, the same as in town. I walked a distance with a boy driving a little old white horse with a cart-load of brick. He lived at Hedleigh, six miles distant; he had left there at five o'clock in the morning, and had heard a nightingale. He was sure; as I pressed him, he described the place minutely. "She was in the large fir-tree by Tom Anthony's gate, at the south end of the village."

Then, I said, doubtless I shall find one in some of Gilbert White's haunts; but I did not. I spent two rainy days at Selborne; I passed many chilly and cheerless hours loitering along those wet lanes and dells and dripping hangers, wooing both my bird and the spirit of the gentle parson, but apparently without getting very near to either. When I think of the place now, I see its hurrying and anxious haymakers in the field of mown grass, and hear the cry of a child that sat in the hay back of the old church, and cried by the hour while its mother was busy with her rake not far off. The rain had ceased, the hay had dried off a little, and scores of men, women, and children, but mostly women, had flocked to the fields to rake it up. The hay is got together inch by inch, and every inch is fought for. They first rake it up into narrow swaths, each person taking a strip about a yard wide. If they hold the ground thus gained, when the hay dries an hour or two longer, they take another hitch, and thus on till they get it into the cock or "carry" it from the windrow. It is usually nearly worn out with handling before they get it into the rick.

From Selborne I went to Alton, along a road that was one prolonged rifle-pit, but smooth and hard as a rock; thence by train back to London. To leave no ground for self-accusation in future, on the score of not having made a thorough effort to hear my songster, I the next day made a trip north toward Cambridge, leaving the train at Hitchin, a large picturesque old town, and thought myself in just the right place at last. I found a road between the station and the town proper called Nightingale Lane, famous for its songsters. A man who kept a thrifty-looking inn on the corner (where, by the way, I was again refused both bed and board) said they sang night and morning in the trees opposite. He had heard them the night before, but had not noticed them that morning. He often sat at night with his friends, with open windows, listening to the strain. He said he had tried several times to hold his breath as long as the bird did in uttering certain notes, but could not do it. This, I knew, was an exaggeration; but I waited eagerly for nightfall, and, when it came, paced the street like a patrolman, and paced other streets, and lingered about other likely localities, but caught nothing but neuralgic pains in my shoulder. I had no better success in the morning, and here gave over the pursuit, saying to myself, It matters little, after all; I have seen the country and had some object for a walk, and that is sufficient.

Altogether I heard the bird less than five minutes, and only a few bars of its song, but enough to satisfy me of the surprising quality of the strain. It had the master tone as clearly as Tennyson or any great prima donna or famous orator has it. Indeed, it was just the same. Here is the complete artist, of whom all these other birds are but hints and studies. Bright, startling, assured, of great compass and power, it easily dominates all other notes; the harsher *chur-r-r-rg* notes serve as foil to her surpassing brilliancy. Wordsworth, among the poets, has hit off the song nearest:

> Those notes of thine—they pierce and pierce;
> Tumultuous harmony and fierce!

I could easily understand that this bird might keep people awake at night by singing near their houses, as I was assured it frequently does; there is something in the strain so startling and awakening. Its start is a vivid flash of sound. On the whole, a high-bred, courtly, chivalrous song; a song for ladies to hear leaning from embowered windows on moonlight nights; a song for royal parks and groves—and easeful but impassioned life. We have no bird-voice so piercing and loud, with such flexibility and compass, such full-throated harmony and long-drawn cadences; though we have songs of more melody, tenderness, and plaintiveness. None but the nightingale could have inspired Keats's ode—that longing for self-forgetfulness and for the oblivion of the world, to escape the fret and fever of life.

"And with thee fade away into the forest dim."

Part Four

Science and Field Study

The Grist of the Gods

ABOUT ALL WE HAVE IN MIND when we think of the earth is this thin pellicle of soil with which the granite framework of the globe is clothed—a red-and-brown film of pulverized and oxidized rock, scarcely thicker, relatively, than the paint or enamel which some women put on their cheeks, and which the rains often wash away as a tear washes off the paint and powder. But it is the main thing to us. Out of it we came and unto it we return. "Earth to earth, and dust to dust." The dust becomes warm and animated for a little while, takes on form and color, stalks about recuperating itself from its parent dust underfoot, and then fades and is resolved into the original earth elements. We are built up out of the ground quite as literally as the trees are, but not quite so immediately. The vegetable is between us and the soil, but our dependence is none the less real. "As common as dust" is one of our sayings, but the common, the universal, is always our mainstay in this world. When we see the dust turned into fruit and flowers and grain by that intangible thing called vegetable life, or into the bodies of men and women by the equally mysterious agency of animal life, we think better of it. The trembling gold of the pond-lily's heart and its petals like carved snow are no more a transformation of a little black muck and ooze by the chemistry of the sunbeam than our bodies and minds, too, are a transformation of the soil underfoot.

We are rooted to the air through our lungs and to the soil through our stomachs. We are walking trees and floating plants. The soil which in one form we spurn with our feet, and in another take into our mouths and into our blood—what a composite product it is! It is the grist out of which our bread of life is made, the grist which the mills of the gods, the slow patient gods of Erosion, have been so long grinding—grinding probably more millions of years than we have any idea of. The original stuff, the pulverized granite, was probably not very nourishing, but the fruitful hand of time has

From *Leaf and Tendril,* 1908.

made it so. It is the kind of grist that improves with the keeping, and the more the meal-worms have worked in it, the better the bread. Indeed, until it has been eaten and digested by our faithful servitors the vegetables, it does not make the loaf that is our staff of life. The more death has gone into it, the more life comes out of it; the more it is a cemetery, the more it becomes a nursery; the more the rocks perish, the more the fields flourish.

This story of the soil appeals to the imagination. To have a bit of earth to plant, to hoe, to delve in, is a rare privilege. If one stops to consider, one cannot turn it with his spade without emotion. We look back with the mind's eye through the vista of geologic time, and we see islands and continents of barren, jagged rocks, not a grain of soil anywhere. We look again and behold a world of rounded hills and fertile valleys and plains, depth of soil where before were frowning rocks. The hand of time with its potent fingers of heat, frost, cloud, and air has passed slowly over the scene, and the miracle is done. The rocks turn to herbage, the fetid gases to the breath of flowers. The mountain melts down into a harvest field; volcanic scoria

John Burroughs with magnifying glass. Courtesy of the American Museum of Natural History.

changes into garden mould; where towered a cliff now basks a green slope; where the strata yawned now bubbles a fountain; where the earth trembled, verdure now undulates. Your lawn and your meadow are built up of the ruins of the foreworld. The leanness of granite and gneiss has become the fat of the land. What transformation and promotion!—the decrepitude of the hills becoming the strength of the plains, the decay of the heights resulting in the renewal of the valleys!

Many of our hills are but the stumps of mountains which the hand of time has cut down. Hence we may say that if God made the mountains, time made the hills.

What adds to the wonder of the earth's grist is that the millstones that did the work and are still doing it are the gentle forces that career above our heads—the sunbeam, the cloud, the air, the frost. The rain's gentle fall, the air's velvet touch, the sun's noiseless rays, the frost's exquisite crystals, these combined are the agents that crush the rocks and pulverize the mountains, and transform continents of sterile granite into a world of fertile soils. It is as if baby fingers did the work of giant powder and dynamite. Give the clouds and the sunbeams time enough, and the Alps and the Andes disappear before them, or are transformed into plains where corn may grow and cattle graze. The snow falls as softly as down and lies almost as lightly, yet the crags crumble beneath it; compacted by gravity, out of it grew the tremendous ice sheet that ground off the mountain summits, that scooped out lakes and valleys, and modeled our northern landscapes as the sculptor his clay image.

Not only are the mills of the gods grinding here, but the great cosmic mill in the sidereal heavens is grinding also, and some of its dust reaches our planet. Cosmic dust is apparently falling on the earth at all times. It is found in the heart of hailstones and in Alpine snows, and helps make up the mud of the ocean floors.

During the unthinkable time of the revolution of the earth around the sun, the amount of cosmic matter that has fallen upon its surface from out the depths of space must be enormous. It certainly must enter largely into the composition of the soil and of the sedimentary rocks. Celestial dirt we may truly call it, star dust, in which we plant our potatoes and grain and out of which Adam was made, and every son of man since Adam—the divine soil in very fact, the garden of the Eternal, contributed to by the heavens above and all the vital forces below, incorruptible, forever purifying itself, clothing the rocky framework of the globe as with flesh and blood, making the earth truly a mother with a teeming fruitful womb, and her hills veritable mammary glands. The iron in the fruit and vegetables we eat, which thence goes into our blood, may, not very long ago, have formed a part of the cosmic dust that drifted for untold ages along the highways of planets and suns.

The soil underfoot, or that we turn with our plow, how it thrills with life or the potencies of life! What a fresh, good odor it exhales when we turn it with our spade or plow in spring! It is good. No wonder children and horses like to eat it! How inert and dead it looks, yet what silent, potent fermentations are going on there—millions and trillions of minute organisms ready to further your scheme of agriculture or horticulture. Plant your wheat or your corn in it, and behold the miracle of a birth of a plant or a tree. How it pushes up, fed and stimulated by the soil, through the agency of heat and moisture! It makes visible to the eye the life that is latent or held in suspense there in the cool, impassive ground. The acorn, the chestnut, the maple keys, have but to lie on the surface of the moist earth to feel its power and send down rootlets to meet it.

From one point of view, what a ruin the globe is!—worn and crumbled and effaced beyond recognition, had we known it in its youth. Where once towered mountains are now only their stumps—low, fertile hills or plains. Shake down your great city with its skyscrapers till most of its buildings are heaps of ruins with grass and herbage growing upon them, and you have a hint of what has happened to the earth. Again, one cannot but reflect what a sucked orange the earth will be in the course of a few more centuries. Our civilization is terribly expensive to all its natural resources; one hundred years of modern life doubtless exhausts its stores more than a millennium of the life of antiquity. Its coal and oil will be about used up, all its mineral wealth greatly depleted, the fertility of its soil will have been washed into the sea through the drainage of its cities, its wild game will be nearly extinct, its primitive forests gone, and soon how nearly bankrupt the planet will be!

There is no better illustration of the way decay and death play into the hands of life than the soil underfoot. The earth dies daily and has done so through countless ages. But life and youth spring forever from its decay—indeed, could not spring at all till the decay began. All the soil was once rock, perhaps many times rock, as the water that flows by may have been many times ice.

The soft, slow, aerial forces, how long and patiently they have worked! Oxygen has played its part in the way of oxidation and dioxidation of minerals. Carbon or carbonic acid has played its part, hydrogen has played its.

Even granite yields slowly but surely to the action of rain-water. The sun is of course the great dynamo that runs the earth machinery and, through moisture and the air currents, reduces the rocks to soil. Without solar heat we should have no rain, and without rain we should have no soil. The decay of a mountain makes a hill of fertile fields. The soil, as we know it, is the product of three great processes—mechanical, chemical, and vital—which have been going on for untold ages. The mechanical we see in the friction of winds and waves and the grinding of glaciers, and in the destructive effects of heat and cold upon the rocks; the chemical in the solvent power of rain-water and of water charged with various acids and gases. The soil is rarely the color of the underlying rock from which it came, by reason of the action of the various gases of the atmosphere. Iron is black, but when turned into rust by the oxygen of the air, it is red.

The vital processes that have contributed to the soil we see going on about us in the decay of animal and vegetable matter. It is this process that gives the humus to the soil, in fact, almost humanizes it, making it tender and full of sentiment and memories, as it were, so that it responds more quickly to our needs and to our culture. The elements of the soil remember all those forms of animal and vegetable life of which they once made a part, and they take them on again the more readily. Hence the quick action of wood ashes upon vegetable life. Iron and lime and phosphorus that have once been taken up by growing plants and trees seem to have acquired new properties, and are the more readily taken up again.

The soil, like mankind, profits by experience, and grows deep and mellow with age. Turn up the cruder subsoil to the sun and air and to vegetable life, and after a time its character is changed; it becomes more gentle and kindly and more fertile.

All things are alike or under the same laws—the rocks, the soil, the soul of man, the trees in the forest, the stars in the sky. We have fertility, depth, geniality, in the ground underfoot, on the same terms upon which we have these things in human life and character.

We hardly realize how life itself has stored up life in the soil, how the organic has wedded and blended with the inorganic in the ground we walk upon. Many if not all of the sedimentary rocks that were laid down in the abysms of the old ocean, out of which our soil has been produced, and that are being laid down now, out of which future soils will be produced, were and are largely of organic origin, the leavings of untold myriads of minute marine animals that lived millions of years ago. Our limestone rocks, thousands of feet thick in places, the decomposition of which furnishes some of our most fertile soils, are mainly of plant and animal origin. The chalk hills of England, so smooth and plump, so domestic and mutton-suggesting, as Huxley says, are the leavings of minute creatures called *Globigerinae* that lived and died in the ancient seas in the remote past. Other similar creatures, *Radiolaria* and diatoms, have played an equally important part in contributing the foundation of our soils. Diatom earth is found in places in Virginia forty feet thick. The coral insects have also contributed their share to the soil-making rocks. Our marl-beds, our phosphatic and carbonaceous rocks, are all largely of animal origin. So that much of our soil has lived and died many times, and has been charged more and more during the geologic ages or eternities with the potencies of life.

Indeed, Huxley, after examining the discoveries of the *Challenger* expedition, says there are good grounds for the belief "that all the chief known constituents of the crust of the earth may have formed part of living bodies; that they may be the 'ash' of protoplasm."

This implies that life first appeared in the sea, and gave rise to untold myriads of minute organisms, that built themselves shells out of the mineral matter held in solution by the water. As these organisms perished, their shells fell to the bottom and formed the sedimentary rocks. In the course of ages these rocks were lifted up above the sea, and their decay and disintegration under the action of the elements formed our soil — our clays, our marls, our green sand — and out of this soil man himself is built up. I do not wonder that the Creator found the dust of the earth the right stuff to make Adam of. It was half man already. I can easily believe that his spirit was evoked from the same stuff, that it was latent there, and in due time, under the brooding warmth of the creative energy, awoke to life.

If matter is eternal, as science leads us to believe, and creation and re-creation a never-ending process, then the present world, with all its myriad forms of the organic and the inorganic, is only one of the infinite number of forms that matter must have assumed in past aeons. The whole substance of the globe must have gone to the making of other globes such a number of times as no array of figures could express. Every one of the sixty or more primary elements that make up our own bodies and the solid earth beneath us must have played the same part in the drama of life and death, growth and decay, organic and inorganic, that it is playing now, and will continue to play through an unending future.

This gross matter seems ever ready to vanish into the transcendental. When the new physics is done with it, what is there left but spirit, or something akin to it? When the physicist has followed matter through all its transformations, its final disguise seems to be electricity. The solid earth is resolvable into electricity, which comes as near to spirit as anything we can find in the universe.

Our senses are too dull and coarse to apprehend the subtle and incessant play of forces about us—the finer play and emanations of matter that go on all about us and through us. From a lighted candle, or gas-jet, or glowing metal shoot corpuscles or electrons, the basic constituents of matter, of inconceivable smallness—a thousand times smaller than an atom of hydrogen—and at the inconceivable speed of 10,000 to 90,000 miles a second. Think how we are bombarded by these bullets as we sit around the lamp or under the gas-jet at night, and are all unconscious of them! We are immersed in a sea of forces and potentialities of which we hardly dream. Of the scale of temperatures, from absolute zero to the heat of the sun, human life knows only a minute fraction. So of the elemental play of forces about us and over us, terrestrial and celestial—too fine for our apprehension on the one hand, and too large on the other—we know but a fraction.

The quivering and the throbbing of the earth under our feet in changes of temperature, the bendings and oscillations of the crust under the tread of the great atmospheric waves, the vital fermentations and oxidations in the soil—are all beyond the reach of our dull senses. We hear the wind in the treetops, but we do not hear the humming of the sap in the trees. We feel the pull of gravity, but we do not feel the medium through which it works. During the solar storms and disturbances all our magnetic and electrical instruments are agitated, but you and I are all unconscious of the agitation.

There are no doubt vibrations from out the depths of space that might reach our ears as sound were they attuned to the ether as the eye is when it receives a ray of light. We might hear the rush of the planets along their orbits; we might hear the explosions and uprushes in the sun; we might hear the wild whirl and dance of the nebulae, where suns and systems are being formed; we might hear the "wreck of matter and the crush of worlds" that evidently takes place now and then in the abysms of space, because all these things must send through the ether impulses and tremblings that reach our planet. But if we felt or heard or saw or were conscious of all that was going on in the universe, what a state of agitation we should be in! Our scale of apprehension is wisely limited, mainly to things that concern our well-being.

But let not care and humdrum deaden us to the wonders and the mysteries amid which we live, nor to the splendors and the glories. We need not translate ourselves in imagination to some other sphere or state of being to find the marvelous, the divine, the transcendent; we need not postpone our day of wonder and appreciation to some future time and condition. The true inwardness of this gross visible world, hanging like an apple on the bough of the great cosmic tree, and swelling with all the juices and potencies of life, transcends anything we have dreamed of super-terrestrial abodes. It is because of these things, because of the vitality, spirituality, oneness, and immanence of the universe as revealed by science, its condition of transcending time and space, without youth and without age, neither beginning nor ending, neither material nor spiritual, but forever passing from one into the other, that I was early and deeply impressed by Walt Whitman's lines:

> There was never any more inception than there is now,
> Nor any more youth or time than there is now;
> And will never be any more perfection than there is now,
> Nor any more heaven or hell than there is now.

And I may add, nor any more creation than there is now, nor any more miracles, or glories, or wonders, or immortality, or judgment days, than there are now. And we shall never be nearer God and spiritual and transcendent things than we are now. The babe in its mother's womb is not nearer its mother than we are to the invisible sustaining and mothering powers of the universe, and to its spiritual entities, every moment of our lives.

The doors and windows of the universe are all open; the screens are all transparent. We are not barred or shut off; there is nothing foreign or unlike; we find our own in the stars as in the ground underfoot; this clod may become a man; yon shooting star may help redden his blood.

Whatever is upon the earth is of the earth; it came out of the divine soil, beamed upon by the fructifying heavens, the soul of man not less than his body.

I never see the spring flowers rising from the mould, or the pond-lilies born of the black ooze, that matter does not become transparent and reveal to me the working of the same celestial powers that fashioned the first man from the common dust.

Man's mind is no more a stranger to the earth than is his body. Is not the clod wise? Is not the chemistry underfoot intelligent? Do not the roots of the trees find their way? Do not the birds know their times and seasons? Are not all things about us filled to overflowing with mind-stuff? The cosmic mind is the earth mind, and the earth mind is man's mind, freed but narrowed, with vision but with erring reason, conscious but troubled — and shall we say? — human but immortal.

From "The Animal and the Puzzle-Box"

II

PROBABLY ONE REASON why the laboratory investigator finds so little of what we call intelligence in his subjects is that he takes them out of the animal sphere and puts them in the human sphere. The problems he sets before them are human problems and not animal problems—they imply a knowledge of mechanical and artificial conditions; this places the dog, the cat, the monkey, the coon in situations entirely foreign to those in which Nature places them, and to which their lives have been shaped. Ideas from the human plane are introduced into the animal plane. The way the cat and the dog deal with these might be a test of their human intelligence, but not of their native intelligence. An animal out of its proper sphere is likely to prove very stupid, while in its sphere, confronted by its own life-needs, it may surprise us by its resourcefulness. We know this to be true of men; why not, in a lesser degree, of course, of animals?

One need only note the misdirected fury of a robin dashing at a supposed rival—its own reflected image on the window-pane of a darkened room—to appreciate what witless machines the birds are under certain conditions; or watch the raccoon seriously engaged in the farce of washing its food in the sand or the straw on the bottom of its cage, to reach the same conclusion. Yet in the field of their normal free activity, away from conditions imposed by man, how clever these creatures are! The animals show little wit in dealing with human problems, but their own natural problems they are fitted, both by organization and by instinct, to solve.

Birds in nesting will often avail themselves of human handiwork and shelter, as when they build in our barns, or on our porches, or in our chimneys; but in so doing they are solving their own problems, and not ours. I heard of a well-authenticated case of a pair of robins building their nest

---

From *The Summit of the Years,* 1913.

under the box on the running-gear of a farmer's wagon which stood under a shed, and with which the farmer was in the habit of making two trips to the village, two miles away, each week. The robins followed him on these trips, and the mother bird went forward with her incubation while the farmer did his errands, and the birds returned with him when he drove home. And, strange to say, the brood was duly hatched and reared. But in this case the bird's primary problem, that of nest-building, was her own; human agency came in only accidentally, furnishing the nest's support. The incident only shows what a hustler and true American the robin is, and that he could have gone west with the farmers on a prairie schooner, and reared a family, or several of them, on the way.

I know it is hard for us to grasp the idea of a qualitative difference in intelligence, yet we seem almost forced to admit such a difference. A plant shows intelligence in getting on in life, in its many devices for scattering its seed, in securing cross-fertilization, in adapting itself to its environment; yet how this differs from human intelligence! When the curving canes of the black raspberry bend down to the earth at a certain time and take root at the end, do they act as wisely and apparently as voluntarily as do some animals? Yet this intelligence differs in kind from that of man. The same may be said of the intelligence that pervades all Nature. Man's intelligence has arisen out of this cosmic mind through a process of creative evolution, but it is of a different order; it does not go with Nature as does that of the lower orders, so much as it bends and guides, or thwarts, Nature. An animal on the animal plane is one thing; on the human plane it is quite another. It is reasonable to suppose that it will show more wit in solving its own life-problems than it will show in solving those which man, in the fever of his scientific curiosity, sets for it. What could the indoor investigator learn of the cunning of the crow or fox, of the sagacity of the dog, of the art and skill of the bird in building its nest and caring for its young?

The laboratory investigator has animal behavior more in a nutshell, and for that very reason is cut off from all perspective, all total effects. He cannot reconstruct a complete dog or cat or monkey out of his laboratory analyses without aid from free observation outside. He could learn very little about a collie dog, or a setter dog, in his laboratory that would enable him to infer all the capacities of those creatures, any more than he could of a man. Indeed, he would fare better with a man, because he could probe his mentality, his power of thought, though not his power of action. The animal acts, it does not think; and to test its power of action is harder than to test a man's thinking capacity.

In leading their own unrestrained lives there often is, among both wild and domesticated animals, something, some resourcefulness in meeting a new condition, some change of habit, some adaptation of new means to an old end, or old means to a new end, that looks, at least, like a gleam of free intelligence, or an attribute of true mind: as when a chipmunk cuts a groove in the side of a hole he is digging, so as to get out a stone he has struck, and then fills up the groove; or when a monkey selects a straw from the floor of his cage to poke an insect out of a crack in the side; or when wolves combine to run down a deer or a hare by relays; or a pointer dog, of his own accord, runs round a bevy of quail that will not sit, but keep moving off, and places them between himself and the sportsman; or when gulls carry shellfish high in the air and drop them on the rocks to break their shells; or when, in Africa, a bird called the honey-guide leads the hunter to stores of wild honey—a fact which Roosevelt verified. We have no ways in the laboratory, or out, to assay such incidents and discover how much, if any, of the gold of real thought they contain. They may contain none, but may be only phases of the animal's instinctive activities, yet they are phases which the laboratory investigator is powerless to bring out. If there are degrees in instinct, as in judgment, then in the cases just cited we have the higher degrees.

III

The laboratory naturalist is hampered by the narrowness of his field: he has but one string to his bow, he has to do with only one phase or motive of animal life—the desire for food; the mainspring of the behavior of all his subjects is their hunger. Spurred on by the sight or smell of food, they attack the problems he sets before them. All the rest of their varied and picturesque activities in field and wood, their multiplex life-problems for which Nature has equipped them, both physically and mentally, their loves, their wars, their home-making and nest-building, their migrations, their herdings, their flockings, their rivalries, eluding their enemies, hunting their prey, their social instincts, their cooperation—in fact, all their relations with one another, and with their natural environment—from all this the indoor investigator is cut off; only the stimulus of food or the fear of punishment remains for him to work upon. His animals act only under the incentive of appetite. The greater the hunger, the greater the wit. The experimenters at times starve their subjects till they become abnormally eager and active. The food question certainly enters very largely into an animal's life, and its resourcefulness in obtaining food may well serve as one measure of its intelligence. But it has other life-problems, several of them, which are just as important, and about which it is just as keen, but which the experimenter cannot bring to bear.

His laboratory is too narrow a field for these activities, as is even the large zoological park. He cannot study the migratory instinct, the flocking or herding or hunting instinct, nor, with the wild creatures, the mating and breeding instinct. He can throw no light on an animal's life habits. He can find out how it will act under given strange conditions, but not how it behaves under its natural conditions. Hence the little interest the natural-historians feel in his inferences and conclusions.

It is true that the laboratory student of animal psychology can reach his results more rapidly than can the field naturalist; he takes a short cut, he gets the bare fact, shorn of its picturesque details. But how much he misses! I sometimes think of him under the parable of a man dining on capsules that contain the chemical equivalents of the food we eat—a short cut, surely, but the pleasure and satisfaction of the dinner table, social and gustatory, the taste of fruit and milk and meat and grain, are not his. Live natural history in the field and woods and on the shore, the uncontrolled animal going its free, picturesque ways, solving its life-problems as they come to it in the revolving seasons, using such mind as it has, without constraint or arbitrary direction, threading only the labyrinth which Nature prepares for it, stimulated only by the sights and sounds and odors of its natural habitat, perplexed with no puzzles but how to get its food, avoid its enemies, rear its young, hide its nest or den, and get out of life what there is in it—how much more engaging and stimulating an animal under such conditions than the same creature being put through its paces under controlled conditions in the laboratory.

So far as an exact science of animal conduct is possible, the experimentalist has the advantage over the free observer; so far as natural history is a joy, and of educational value, and an introduction to the whole field of animal life, he is not to be named the same day with the outdoor observer. Welcome, thrice welcome, all the light the laboratory method of inquiry can throw upon the puzzle of animal mentality and its relation to our own; it is engaging the attention of some serious-minded men, and I would not undervalue its contributions to our knowledge of the springs of animal psychology. At the same time I am bound to say that I think it can take us but a little way into the great field of animal life. The true perspective of such life can only be given by the student of the uncontrolled behavior of our dumb friends.

The low valuation I set upon animal experimentation does not, as some of my readers seem to think, apply with the same force to all experimental science. Experimental science has given us our material civilization; what has animal experimentation given us? The inorganic elements and forces behave the same in the laboratory and out. But a live animal does not. You cannot control life as you can chemical reactions. Sound, heat, light, electricity are the same everywhere, but an animal has nerves and instincts and associative memory. The dog with the puzzle-box is quite a different creature from the dog with the woodchuck.

Anything like an exact science of animal behavior is, it seems to me, as impossible in the laboratory as out of it. If animals were perfect automata, then we might have the science of animal behavior that the experimentalists dream of. . . .

IV

The university psychologist has little confidence in the ability of the field naturalist to interpret correctly "what he supposes himself to have seen," even if it be only the doings of a downy woodpecker excavating his chamber in an old post. What, he asks in substance, does one know about a downy woodpecker, which one has observed from one's front porch, excavating a cavity for a winter home in the top of a chestnut post? What does he know in detail of the bird's past experience, what of its age, what of its various sense-powers, such as its seeing, smelling, and hearing powers, what of the way its various powers have been developed, what of the number of times it has tried the same act and failed, what of the circumstances that may have enabled it to invent a new plan of action, whether it is an average bird of the species, or an unusual one, etc.? What indeed and how better off in this respect would the experimentalist be? The naturalist is probably familiar with the life and habits of the bird, he may have seen it excavating its winter chamber many times—not this same individual bird, but its duplicate in other specimens—and he knows that each one of these shows exactly the same characteristics, though it is undoubtedly true that under pressure, in confinement, and in unnatural conditions, different birds would show different traits and aptitudes. Yet neither the naturalist nor the experimentalist could get at all the facts in the woodpecker's past life—its age, its failures, its stupidities, its rate of development, its sense-powers, and the like.

The experimentalist referred to would seem to imply that if he had the bird in his laboratory, he could settle all these points; whereas it seems to me that the field observer knows just as much about these things as the laboratory experimenter could know. Neither can get at all the exact facts in the bird's past history, while it is extremely doubtful if, in confinement, the bird would even attempt to excavate a chamber in a post, or exhibit any of its natural aptitudes, or give any clues to its real life history. The acuteness of its various senses can surely be better tested in the open air than in the laboratory, because in the open it is leading a free, natural life, while in the cage it is leading a constrained, unnatural life. It might be trained to run the maze, or to pull a string to open a puzzle-box; but of its real life what would or could the bird disclose to you in rigid experiments? If the free bird is endowed with any sense-powers of which the "mere observer" can gain no firsthand knowledge, what chance has the laboratory observer of gaining a firsthand knowledge of them?

The field observer sees the woodpecker excavating a cavity in a dry limb or stub in the autumn; he sees that all birds of this species proceed in exactly the same way, because they all have the same organization, and hence the same needs. He sees how carefully the bird usually places its entrance where it will be more or less shielded from driving storms; he sees that it rarely or never selects a limb that is too rotten, or insecure; he sees where it makes many beginnings and then abandons the limb because, apparently, it is too soft or too hard; he sees the bird cautiously resorting to these retreats as night comes on; he sees him living alone in there, little hermit that he is; he sees how he is often dispossessed of his cabin by the hairy woodpecker, or by the flying squirrel or the English sparrow. He sees him selecting a dry resonant limb for a drum in the spring, on which to drum up a mate; he sees his changed demeanor when the female appears, the curious, mincing flight, as if on the tiptoe of his wings, with which he follows her about—he sees, in short, a long series of interesting facts which reveal the real psychology of the bird, and of which the laboratory naturalist could get no inkling.

The laboratory study of the animal mind is within its proper limits worthy of all respect, but you can no more get at a complete animal psychology by this method than you can get at the beauty and character and natural history of a tree by studying a cross section of its trunk or of one of its branches. You may get at the anatomy and cell structure of the tree by this means, but will not the real tree escape you? A little may be learned of the science of animal behavior in the laboratory, but the main, the illuminating things can be learned only from observation of the free animal. . . .

ᴧ* ᴧ* ᴧ*

We cannot make Darwins in the laboratory, though the laboratory may give Darwin a fact or a hint now and then that will be of service to him.

V

. . . In the absence of language and reason, how do the animals over a wide extent of country become possessed of the same knowledge and the same impulse at the same time, and begin their movements simultaneously? The vast moving armies of the passenger pigeons in the old days, the migrating crowds of the lemmings in Norway, or reindeer in Siberia, and of caribou in Labrador, every spring—how do these all act in such concert? Hunted animals suddenly become wild—even those which have had no individual experience with the hunter—as if the tribe were a unit, and what one knew, they all knew at the same time. One would like such problems cleared up. I have no doubt at all that the higher animals have some means of communication which the race of man, since it came into the gift of language and of reason, has lost, or nearly lost, and that our fitful and exceptional experience of becoming aware of what our friend or companion is thinking about, that experience which we call telepathy, is a survival of the lost power. There is something like a community of mind or of emotional states among the lower orders, to which we are strangers, except when, under extraordinary conditions—as in the frenzy of mobs and like unreasoning bodies—we relapse into a state of savage nature, and behave as the wild creatures do. In such cases there is really a community of mind and purpose. But birds in a flock possess this oneness of mental states as a normal and everyday condition. Fish and insects in vast numbers often show a like unity of instantaneous action.

There is so much in animal behavior that is interesting, and that throws light on our own psychology and its origin, that one begrudges the time spent in learning that dancing mice are deaf, or the numerous data as to the tactual sensations of the white rat, or "the relative strength of stimulus to rate of learning in the chick," or the psychic reactions of the crayfish, or cockroach, or angleworm, or grasshopper, unless they yield the key to some large problem. We do not want elaborate experiments to prove that frogs can hear—does not every schoolboy know that they can, and see, too? Though he may not know "that there is some evidence that the influence of auditory stimuli is most marked when the drum is half-submerged in water," or that "the influence upon tactual reactions is evident when the frog is submerged in water to a depth of four centimeters," or that "sounds varying in pitch from those of fifty to ten thousand vibrations a second affect the frog." But what of it? Who is really the wiser for this discovery? I know there is no reason why I should quarrel with men who prefer to dine on the concentrated equivalents of our meals and viands. Rather should I wish them a good appetite for their capsules. At the same time I can see no good reason why I should not extol the pleasure and the profit of taking our natural-history manna of field and wood as Nature provides it for us, and with a relish that only the open air can give.

From *Under the Apple Trees*

THERE ARE FEW PLACES on the farm where there is so much live natural history to be gathered as in the orchard. All the wild creatures seem to feel the friendly and congenial atmosphere of the orchard. The trees bear a crop of birds, if not of apples, every season. Few are the winged visitors from distant climes that do not, sooner or later, tarry a bit in the orchard. Many birds, such as the robin, the chippy, the hummingbird, the cedarbird, the goldfinch, and some of the flycatchers nest there. The great crested flycatcher loves the old hollow limbs, and the little red owl often lives in a cavity in the trunk. The jays visit the orchard on their practical excursions in quest of birds' eggs, and now and then they discover the owl in his retreat and set up a great hue and cry over their discovery. On such occasions they will take turns in looking into the dim cavity and crying, "Thief, thief!" most vociferously, the culprit, meanwhile, sitting wrapped in utter oblivion.

In May and June the cuckoo comes to the orchard for tent caterpillars, and the woodpeckers come at all seasons — the downy and the hairy to the good of the trees, the yellow-bellied often to their injury. The two former search for the eggs and the larvae of the insects that infest the trees, as do the nuthatches and the chickadees, which come quite as regularly; but the yellow-bellied comes for the life-blood of the trees themselves. He is popularly known as the "sapsucker," and a sapsucker he is. Many apple trees in every orchard are pock-marked by his bill, and occasionally a branch is evidently killed by his many and broad drillings. As I write these lines, on September the 26th, in my bush tent in one of the home orchards, a sapsucker is busy on a veteran apple tree whose fruit has often gone to school with me in my pockets during my boyhood days on the farm. He goes about his work systematically, visiting now one of the large branches and then a portion of the trunk, and drilling his holes in rows about a quarter of an inch

---

From *Under the Apple Trees*, 1916.

apart. Every square foot of the trunk contains from three hundred to four hundred holes, new and old, cut through into the inner, vital cambium layer. The holes are about the size of the end of a rye-straw, and run in rings around the tree, the rings being about a half an inch apart. The newly cut ones quickly fill with sap, which, to my tongue, has a rather insipid taste, but which is evidently relished by the woodpecker. He drills two or three holes, then pauses a moment, and when they are filled, sips his apple tree tipple leisurely. The drain upon the vitality of the tree at any one time, by this tapping, cannot be very serious, but in the course of years must certainly affect its vigor considerably. I have seen it stated in print, by a writer who evidently draws upon his fancy for his facts, that in making these holes the bird is setting a trap for insects, and that these are what it feeds upon. But the bird is a sapsucker; there are no insects at his wells today; he visits them very regularly, and is constantly drilling new ones.

His mate, or at least a female, comes, and I overhear the two in soft, gentle conversation. When I appear upon the scene, the female scurries away in alarm, calling as she retreats, as if for the male to follow; but he does not. He eyes me for a moment, and then sidles round behind the trunk of the tree, and as I go back to my table, I hear his hammer again. Very soon the female is back, and I hear their conversation going on as before. Day after day the male is here tapping the trees. His blows are soft and can be heard only a few yards away. He evidently has his favorites. In this orchard of twenty or more trees, only two are worked now, and only three have ever been worked much. The two favorites bear hard, sour fruit. The bark of a sweet apple tree does not show a single hole. A grafted tree shows no holes in the original stock, but many punctures on the graft. One day I saw the bird frequently leave his drilling on one tree and go to another, drilling into a small red apple which had lodged among some twigs on a horizontal branch; he ate the pulp, and had made quite a large hole in the apple tree, when it became dislodged and fell to the ground. It is plain, therefore, that the sapsucker likes the juice of the apple, and of the tree that bears the apple. He is the only orchard bird who is a tippler. Among the forests, he sucks the sap of the sugar maples in spring, and I have seen evidence of his having drilled into small white pines, cutting out an oblong section from the bark, apparently to get at the soft cambium layer.

It is a pleasant experience to sit in my orchard camp of a still morning and hear an apple drop here and there—"indolent ripe," as Whitman says, in the fullness of time, or prematurely ripe from a worm at its heart. The worm finds its account in getting down to the ground where it can pupate, and in both cases the tree has finished a bit of its work and is getting ready for its winter sleep; and in both cases the squirrels and the woodchucks profit by the fall. But September woodchucks are few; most of them retire to their holes for the long winter sleep during this month; the harvest apples that fall in August hit them at the right moment; but the red squirrels are alert for the apple-seeds during both months, and they chip up many apples for these delicate morsels. They also love the hollow branches and trunks of the trees, in which they make their homes.

Little currents of wild life hourly flow about me. Yesterday, amid the slow rain and mist and general obscurity, there was suddenly an influx of birds in all the old apple trees about me. Robins appeared by twos and threes in some choke-cherry bushes a few yards below me, and with much cackling and fluttering helped themselves to the fruit. A hermit thrush perched on a dry limb in front of my tent and in many different postures surveyed me in my canvas cavern, uttering a low note which I took to be his comments upon me. You may always know the hermit thrush from the other thrushes by that peculiar, soft, breathing motion of its tail. A male redstart came and flitted and flashed about the apple branches without heeding me at all. Whitman asks:

> Do you take it I would astonish?
> Does the daylight astonish? does the early redstart twittering through the
> woods?
> Do I astonish more than they?

The redstart, with his black-and-orange suit, and his quick, lively motions, does not astonish, but few birds give the eye more pleasure. How gay and festive he looks, darting and flashing amid the gnarled and scaly branches of the decaying apple trees! It seems as if all his motions were designed to show off his plumage to the best advantage.

With tail slightly raised and spread, and wings a little drooping, he springs and swoops here and there in the trees—a bit of black holding and momentarily revealing a flame of orange. Redstart is a good name for him, as we see his colors only when he is in motion. Note our other black-and-orange bird, the Baltimore oriole; its color is conspicuous while the bird is at rest. Another brilliantly colored bird, the scarlet tanager, is seen from afar when quietly perched. He shows amid the green leaves like a burning coal; and his motions are all slow and deliberate when contrasted with those of the redstart. The latter is a flycatcher, or insect-catcher, and his movements are necessarily sudden and rapid.

The birds are quite likely to go in troops in late summer or early fall, different species apparently being drawn along by a common impulse.

While the robins and the hermit thrush are among the choke-cherries, a family of indigo-birds, five or six of them, all of the brown color of the mother bird, are grouped around the mother on a flat stone for half a minute, being fed. It is a pretty little tableau. The father bird with his bright plumage is not in evidence. In one of the trees another warbler which I cannot identify, with an olive back and a yellow front, is in a great hurry about its own business. One little olive-green warbler, doubtless a young bird, comes and perches on the edge of my table, and, quite oblivious of my presence, looks my papers and books over for the insect tidbit which he does not find. How round and brilliant and eager are his eyes! If he is looking for a bookworm, he fails to find it.

A phoebe-bird perches here and there and makes sudden swoops to the ground for the insects which she cannot find on the wing. Phoebe hunts by sight at long range. Her eye seems telescopic, rather than microscopic like the warbler's. She explores the air and the ground and sees her game from afar. At all hours of the day she perches on the brown dead branches of the apple trees, and waits for her prey to appear, her straight, stiff tail hingeing up and down at her rump.

At present my favorite denizen of the orchard is the chipmunk. He, too, likes the apple-seeds, but he is not given to chipping up the apples as much as is the red squirrel. He waits till the apples are ripe and then nibbles the pulp. He also likes the orchard because it veils his movements; when making his trips to and fro, if danger threatens, the trunk of every tree is a house of refuge.

As I write these lines in my leafy tent, a chipmunk comes in, foraging for his winter supplies. I have brought him cherry-pits and peach-pits and cracked wheat, from time to time, and now he calls on me several times a day. His den is in the orchard but a few yards from me, and I enjoy having him for so near a neighbor. He has at last become so familiar that he climbs to my lap, then to the table, then to my shoulder and head, looking for the kernels of popcorn that he is convinced have some perennial source of supply near me or about me. He clears up every kernel, and then on his return, in a few minutes, there they are again! I might think him a good deal puzzled by the prompt renewal of the supply if I were to read my own thoughts into his little noddle, but I see he is only eager to gather his harvest while it is plentiful and so near at hand. No, he is not influenced even by that consideration; he does not consider at all, in fact, but just goes for the corn in nervous eagerness and haste. Yet, if he does not reflect, he certainly has a wisdom and foresight of his own. This morning I mixed kernels of fresh-cut green corn with a handful of the dry, hard popcorn upon the floor. At first he began to eat the soft sweet corn, but, finding the small, dry kernels, of the popcorn, he at once began to stuff his cheek pockets with them, and when they were full he hastened off to his den. Back he came in about three minutes, and he kept on doing this till the popcorn was all gone; then he proceeded to make his breakfast off the green corn. When this was exhausted, he began to strip some choke-cherries (which I had also placed among the corn) of their skins and pulp, and to fill his pockets with the pits, thus carrying no perishable food to his den. He acted exactly as if he knew that the green corn and the choke-cherries would spoil in his underground retreat, and that the hard, dry kind, and the cherry-pits, would keep. He did know it, but not as you and I know it, by experience; he knew it, as all the wild creatures know how to get on in the world, by the wisdom that pervades nature, and is much older than we or they are.

My chipmunk knows corn, cherry wheat, beech-nuts, apple-seeds, and probably several other foods, at sight; but peach-pits, hickory-nuts, dried sweet corn he at first passed by, and peanuts I could not tempt him to touch at all. He was at first indifferent to the rice, but, on nibbling at it and finding it toothsome, he began to fill his pockets with it. Amid the rice I scattered puffed wheat. This he repeatedly took up and chipped into, attracted probably by the odor, but, finding it hollow, or at least very spongy and unsubstantial in its interior, he quickly dropped it. It was not solid enough to get into his winter stores. After I had cracked a few hickory-nuts he became very eager for them, and it was amusing to see him, as he sat on my table, struggle to force the larger ones into his pockets, supplementing the contractile power of his cheek muscles with his paws. When he failed to pocket one, he would take it in his teeth and make off. I offered him some peach-pits also, but he only carried one of them up on the stone wall and handled it awhile, then looked it over and left it. But after I had cracked a few of them and had thus given him a taste of what was in them, he began to carry them to his den.

It is interesting to see how well these wild creatures are groomed—every hair in its place and shining as if it had just been polished. The tail of my chipmunk is perfect—not a hair missing or soiled or worn. In fact, the whole animal looks as new and fresh as a coin just minted, or a flower just opened. His underground habits leave no mark or stain upon him, and his daily labors do not ruffle a hair. This is true of nearly all the wild creatures. Domestication changes all this; domestic animals become dirty and unkempt. The half-tame gray squirrels in the parks have little of the wild grace and beauty of the squirrels in the woods. Especially do their tails deteriorate, and their sylvan airiness and delicacy disappear.

The whole character of the squirrel culminates and finds expression in its tail—all its nervous restlessness and wild beauty, all its jauntiness, archness, and suspicion, and every change of emotion seem to ripple out along this appendage.

How furtive and nervous my chipmunk is, rushing about by little jerks incessantly, not stopping for anything! His bright, unwinking eyes, his palpitating body, his sudden spasmodic movements, his eagerness, his industry, his sleekness and cleanliness—what a picture he makes! Apparently he does not know me from a stump or a clothes-horse. His cold paws on my warm hand, on my arm, or on my head give him no hint of danger; no odors from my body, or look from my eyes, disturb him; the sound of my voice does not alarm him; but any movement on my part, and he is off. It is *moving* things—cats, weasels, hawks, foxes—that mean danger to him. In the little circuit of his life—gathering his winter stores and his daily subsistence, spinning along the fences, threading the woods and bushes, his eye and his ear are evidently his main dependence; odors and still objects concern him little, but moving things very much. I once saw a chipmunk rush to his den in the side of a bank with great precipitation, and in a moment, like a flash, a shrike darted down and hovered over the entrance.

I can talk to my chipmunk in low, slow tones and he heeds me not, but any unusual sound outside the camp, and he is alertness itself. One day when he was on my table, a crow flew over and called sharply and loudly; the squirrel sat up and took notice instantly; with his paws upon his breast he listened and looked intently for a few seconds, and then resumed his foraging. At another time the sharp call of a red squirrel in a tree near by made him still more nervous. With one raised paw he looked and listened for two or three minutes. The red squirrel hazes him on all occasions, and, I think, often robs him of his stores.

No doubt the chipmunk has many narrow escapes from hawks. A hunter told me recently of a hawk-and-chipmunk incident that he had witnessed the day before in the woods on the mountain. He was standing still listening to the baying of his hound on the trail of a fox. Suddenly there was a rush and clatter of wings in the maple-trees near him, and he saw a large hawk in pursuit of a chipmunk coming down, close to the trunk of a tree, like a thunderbolt. As the hawk struck the ground, the hunter shot him dead. He had the squirrel in his claw as in a trap, and the hunter had to pry the talon open to free the victim, which was alive and able to run away. From the description I guessed the hawk to be a goshawk. What the chipmunk was doing up that tree is a mystery to me, since he seldom ventures far from the ground; but the truth of the incident is unquestioned.

When the chipmunk is in the open, the sense of danger is never absent from him. He is always on the alert. In his excursions along the fences to collect wild buckwheat, wild cherries, and various grains, he is watchfulness itself. In every trip to his den with his supplies, his manner is like that of the baseball-player in running the bases—he makes a dash from my study, leaping high over the grass and weeds, to an apple tree ten yards away; here he pauses a few seconds and nervously surveys his course ahead; then he makes another sprint to a second apple tree, and pauses as before, quickly glancing round; then in a few leaps he is at home, and in his den. Returning, he usually pursues the same course. He leaves no trail, and is never off his guard. No baseball runner was ever more watchful. Apparently while in the open he does not draw one breath free from a keen sense of danger.

I have tempted him to search my coat pockets for the nuts or cherry-pits that I have placed there, and, when he does so, he seems to appreciate at what a disadvantage his enemy might find him—his eyes are for the moment covered, his rear is exposed, his whole situation is very insecure; hence he seizes a nut and reverses his position in a twinkling; his body palpitates; his eyes bulge; then he dives in again and seizes another nut as before, acting as if he thought each moment might be his last. When he goes into the tin cocoa-box for the cherry-pits, he does it with the hurry of fear; his eyes are above the rim every second or two; he does not stop to clean the pits as he does when on my table, but scoops them up with the greatest precipitation, as if he feared I might clap on the lid at any moment and make him prisoner. In all the hundred and one trips he has made from my camp to his den he has not for one moment forgotten himself; he runs all the bases with the same alertness and precaution. Coming back, he emerges from his hole, sits up, washes his face, then looks swiftly about, and is off for the base of supplies.

One day I went by a roundabout course and stood three paces from his hole. In the mean time he had loaded up, and he came running over the course in his usual style, but before he left the second base he saw me, or an apparition that was not there before, and became very nervous. He jumped about; he sat up on his haunches and looked; crouched by a woodchuck's hole and eyed me, his cheeks protruding; changed his attitude a dozen times; then, as the apparition changed not, he started and came one-third of the way; then his heart failed him and he rushed back. More posing and scrutinizing, when he made a second dash that brought him two-thirds of the way; then his fears overcame him again, and he again rushed to cover. Repeating his former behavior for a few moments, he made a third dash and reached the home base in safety. How carefully he seems to carry his tail on entering his hole, so as not to let it touch the sides!

He is out again in less than a minute, and, erect upon his haunches, looks me squarely in the eye. He is greatly agitated; he has not had that experience before. What does it mean? Erect on his hind legs, he stands almost motionless and eyes me. I stand motionless, too, with a half-eaten apple in my hand. I wink and breathe; so does he. For ten minutes we confront each other in this fashion, then he turns his back upon me and drops down. He looks toward the camp; he remembers the nuts and corn awaiting him there; he stirs uneasily; he changes his position; he looks at my motionless figure again, then toward the source of supplies, and is off, leaving me at his threshold. In two minutes he is back again with protruding pockets, and now makes the home run without a pause. He emerges again from his den, washes his face three times, his mouth first, then his nose and cheeks, then is off for another load. I return to my chair, and soon he is again on my lap and table, or sitting in the hollow of my hand, loading up as before. The apparition in the chair has no terrors for him.

I would not say that he is burdened with a conscious sense of danger; rather is his fear instinctive and unconscious. It is in his blood—born with him and a part of his life. His race has been the prey of various animals and birds for untold ages, and it has survived by reason of an instinctive watchfulness that has been pushed to the highest degree of development. He is on the lookout for danger as constantly as he is on the lookout for food, and he takes no more thought about the one than about the other. His life is keyed to the fear pitch all the time. His heart beats as fast as the ticking of a watch, and all his movements are as abrupt and spasmodic as if they were born of alarm. His behavior is an excellent illustration of the unconscious fear that pervades a large part of the animal kingdom.

All creatures that are preyed upon by others lead this life of fear. I don't know that the crow is ever preyed upon by any other creature, so he apparently has a pretty good time. He is social and noisy and in the picnicking mood all the day long. Hawks apparently are afraid of man only. Hence their lives must be comparatively free from harassing fear. Even fish in the streams are not exempt from fear. They are preyed upon by large fish, and by minks and otters, and by the fish hawk. If the weasel has a natural enemy, I don't know what it is. He is the boldest of the bold. He might be captured by a hawk or an eagle, but such occurrences are probably very rare, as a weasel can dodge almost anything but a gun.

Of all our wild creatures the rabbit has the most enemies; weasels, minks, foxes, wildcats, and owls are hovering about poor Bunnie at all times. No wonder she never closes her eyes, even in sleep. To compensate in a meas-ure for all this, nature has made her very fleet of foot and very prolific, so that the race of rabbits is in full tide, notwithstanding its many enemies.

Such animals as the skunk and the porcupine show little fear, because their natural enemies, if they have any, would go by on the other side. There is evidence that the skunk is sometimes preyed upon by the fox and the eagle and the horned owl, and the porcupine by the lynx and the wolf, but these must be exceptional occurrences. The lion probably fears nothing but man. Little wonder that he looks calm and majestic and always at his ease! But I am getting away from my apple trees.

The arch-enemy of the chipmunk is the small red weasel, and I wonder if it is to hide from him that he usually digs his den away from the fences and other cover, in clean open ground, leaving no clue whatever as to its whereabouts. He carries away all the soil, and either makes a pile of it some feet away, or else hides it completely. The den of my little neighbor is in the open grassy space between the rows of apple trees, thirty or more yards from either fence. All that is visible of it is a small round hole in the ground nearly concealed by the overhanging grass. I had to watch him in order to find it.

His chamber is about three feet below the surface of the ground, and has but one entrance, through a long crooked passage eight or ten feet long. If his arch-enemy were to find it, there would be no escape. There is no back door, and there are no secret passages. Probably many a tragedy is enacted in those little earth-chambers. The weasel himself fears nothing; he is the incarnation of bloodthirstiness, and his victims seem so horrified at the dis-covery that he is pursuing them that they become paralyzed. Even the fleet-footed rabbit in the open woods or fields falls an easy prey.

One day last summer as I sat at the table in my hay-barn study, there boldly entered through the open door this arch-enemy of our small rodents, brown of back and white of belly. He rushed in as if on very hurrying busi-ness, and all my efforts to detain him, by squeaking like a mouse, and chirping like a bird, proved unavailing. He thrust out his impudent snake-like head and neck from an opening in the wall, and fixed his intense, beady eyes upon me for a moment, and was gone. I feared he was on the trail of the chipmunk that had just carried away the cherry-pits I had placed for him on a stone near by; but the little rodent appeared a half-hour later, as sleek as ever, but with a touch of something suspicious and anxious in his manner, as if he had at least had tidings that his deadly enemy was in the neighborhood.

After I had cracked some hickory-nuts for my little friend this morning, and he had got a taste of the sweet morsel inside, he quickly began to stuff the whole nuts into his pockets and carry them to his storehouse. It was amusing to see him struggle with the larger nuts, first moistening them with his tongue, to force them into those secret and apparently inadequate pockets. The smooth, trim cheeks would suddenly assume the appearance of enormous wens, extending well down on the sides of the neck. The pouches are not merely passive receptacles; they evidently possess some power of muscular action, like the throat muscles, which enables them to force the grain and nuts along their whole course. As the little squirrel picks the corn from the floor you can see the pouches swell, first on the one side, then on the other. He seems to pick up the kernels and swallow them. What part the tongue plays in the process, one cannot see. In forcing a whole or a half hickory-nut into them, the chipmunk uses his paws. The pouches are doubtless emptied by muscular movements similar to those by which they were filled—a self-acting piece of machinery, a pocket that can fill and empty itself.

I see my little hermit making frequent visits to my study in the morning before I am seated there, exploring the floor, the chair, the table, to see if the miracle of the corn manna has not again happened. He is anxious to be on hand as soon as it occurs. He is no discriminator of persons. One morning a woman friend took her seat in my chair with corn in her lap and under her arched hand on the table, and waited. Presently the little forager appeared and climbed to her lap, and pushed under her hand, as he had under mine. Another woman sat on the cot a few feet away, and the two conversed in low tones. The squirrel gave little heed to them, but any movement of their hands or feet startled him. One day I shifted my position from the table to near the cot, with my extended feet near the entrance. The squirrel was in the act of coming in when I made some slight movement. With that characteristic chippering of his, he retreated hastily to the first apple tree twenty feet away, and, perched upon its leaning trunk, sounded his little alarm, *Chuck, chuck,* for fifteen minutes or more. Apparently he had but just discovered me. After a time he came slyly back and resumed his foraging.

The activity of the chipmunk when he is out of his den is almost incessant. Like the honey-bee, he seems filled with a raging impulse to lay up his winter stores. When he finds an ever-renewed supply, as in my orchard camp, his eagerness and industry are delightful to see. The more nuts I place for him, the more eager he becomes, as most of us do when we strike a rich lead of the things we are in quest of. Will his greed carry him to the point of filling his den so full that there remains no room for himself in it? Will he let the god of plenty turn him out of doors? Last summer I had seen a chipmunk's hole filled up with choke-cherries to within three inches of the top. ("Naturally, being choke-cherries," says a friend, looking over my shoulder.)

From previous experience I calculated the capacity of his chamber to be not more than four or five quarts. One day I gave him all I thought he could manage — enough, I fancied, to fill his chamber full — two quarts of hickory-nuts and some corn. How he responded to the invitation! How he flew over the course from my den to his! He fairly panted. The day might prove too short for him, or some other chipmunk might discover the pile of treasures. Three, and often four, nuts at a time, went into his pockets. If one of them was too large to go in readily, he would take it between his teeth. He would first bite off the sharp point from the nut to keep it from pricking or irritating his pouches. I do not think he feared a puncture. I renewed the pile of nuts from time to time, and looked on with interest.

The day was cloudy and wet, but he ran his express train all day. His feet soon became muddy, and it was amusing to see him wash his face with those soiled paws every time he emerged from his hole. It was striking to see how much like a machine he behaved, going through the same motions at the same points, as regularly as a clock. He disappeared into his hole each time with a peculiarly graceful movement which seemed to find expression in the sweep of his tail. It was to the eye what melodious sounds are to the ear, and contrasted strangely with the sudden impulsive movements of his usual behavior. When he emerged, the top of his head and eyes first appeared, then a moment's pause, then the head and neck arose, then the whole body shot up in the erect posture with the paws folded and hanging down on the white breast. The face-washing was the next move, first the mouth, then the nose and cheeks. Then, after a swift glance around, off he goes, with tail well up in the air, for another load.

As the day declined, and the pile of nuts was ever renewed, I thought I saw signs that he was either getting discouraged or else that his den was getting too full. At five o'clock he began to carry the nuts out from my camp and conceal them here and there under the leaves and dry grass. His manner seemed undecided. He did not return to his den again while I waited near it. After some delay I saw him go to the stone wall and follow it till he was lost from sight under the hill. I concluded that his greed had at last really turned him out of doors and that he had gone off to spend the night with a neighbor. But my inference was wrong. The next day he was back again, carrying away a fresh supply of nuts as eagerly as ever. Two more quarts disappeared before night. The next day was rainy, and though other chipmunks were hurrying about, my little miser rested from his labors. A day later a fresh supply of nuts arrived—two quarts of chestnuts and one of hickory-nuts, and the greed of the little squirrel rose to the occasion. He made his trips as frequently as ever.

My enforced absence for a few days prevented me from witnessing all that happened, but a friend took notes for me. He tried to fool the chipmunk with a light-colored marble placed among the nuts. The squirrel picked it up, but quickly dropped it. Watching his opportunity, my friend rubbed the marble with the meat of a hickory-nut. The chipmunk smelled it; then put it in his pocket; then took it out, held it in his paws a moment and looked at it, and returned it to his pocket. Three times he did this before rejecting it. Evidently his sense of taste discredited his sense of smell.

On my return at the end of the week, the enthusiasm of the chipmunk had greatly abated. He was seldom out of his den. A nut or two placed at its entrance disappeared, but he visited me no more in my camp. Other chipmunks were active on all sides, but his solicitude about the winter had passed, or rather his hoarding instinct had been sated. His cellar was full. The rumor that right here was a land of plenty seemed to have gone abroad upon the air, and other chipmunks appeared upon the scene. Red squirrels and gray squirrels came, but we wasted no nuts upon them. A female chipmunk that came and occupied an old den at my doorstep was encouraged, however. She soon became as familiar as my first acquaintance, climbing to my table, taking nuts from my hand, and nipping my fingers spitefully when I held on to the nuts. Her behavior was as nearly like that of the other as two peas are alike. I gave her a fair supply of winter stores, but did not put her greed to the test.

So far as I have observed, the two sexes do not winter together, and there seems to be no sort of *camaraderie* between them. One day, earlier in this history, I saw my male neighbor chase a smaller chipmunk, which I have little doubt was this female, out of the camp and off into the stone wall, with great spitefulness. All-the-year-round love among the wild creatures is very rare, if it occurs at all. Love is seasonal and brief among most of them. My little recluse has ample supplies for quite a family, but I am certain he will spend the winter alone there in the darkness of his subterranean dwelling. He must have at least a peck of nuts that we gave him, besides all the supplies that he carried in from his foraging about the orchard and the fields earlier in the season. The temptation to dig down and uncover his treasures is very great, but my curiosity might lead to his undoing, at least to his serious discomfort, so I shall forbear, resting content in the thought that at least one fellow mortal has got all that his heart desires.

As our lives have touched here at my writing table, each working out his life-problems, I have thought of what a gulf divides my little friend and me; yet he is as earnestly solving his problems as I am mine; though, of course, he does not worry over them, or take thought of them, as I do. I cannot even say that something not himself takes thought for him; there is no thought in the matter; there is what we have to call impulse, instinct, inherited habit, and the like, though these are only terms for mysteries. He, too, shares in this wonderful something we call life. The evolutionary struggle and unfolding was for him as well as for me. He, too, is a tiny bubble on the vast current of animate nature, whose beginning is beyond our ken in the dim past, and whose ending is equally beyond our ken in the dim future. He goes his pretty ways, gathers his precarious harvest, has his adventures, his hairbreadth escapes, his summer activity, his autumn plenty, his winter solitude and gloom, and his spring awakening and gladness. He has made himself a home here in the old orchard; he knows how deep to go into the ground to get beyond the frost-line; he is a pensioner upon the great bounty upon which we all draw, and probably lives up to the standard of the chipmunk life more nearly than most of us live up to the best standards of human life. May he so continue to live, and may we yet meet for many summers under the apple-boughs.

[Here ends part 1 of this two-part essay. Part 2 can be found in *Under the Apple Trees*, Houghton Mifflin, 1916.]

Reading the Book of Nature

IN STUDYING NATURE, the important thing is not so much what we see as how we interpret what we see. Do we get at the true meaning of the facts? Do we draw the right inference? The fossils in the rocks were long observed before men drew the right inference from them. So with a hundred other things in nature and life.

During May and a part of June of 1903, a drouth of unusual severity prevailed throughout the land. The pools and marshes nearly all dried up. Late in June the rains came again and filled them up. Then an unusual thing happened: suddenly, for two or three days and nights, the marshes about me were again vocal with the many voices of the hyla, the "peepers" of early spring. That is the fact. Now, what is the interpretation? With me the peepers become silent in early May, and, I suppose, leave the marshes for their life in the woods. Did the drouth destroy all their eggs and young, and did they know this and so come back to try again? How else shall one explain their second appearance in the marshes? But how did they know of the destruction of their young, and how can we account for their concerted action? These are difficulties not easily overcome. A more rational explanation to me is this, namely, that the extreme dryness of the woods — nearly two months without rain — drove the little frogs to seek for moisture in their spring haunts, where in places a little water would be pretty certain to be found. Here they were holding out, probably hibernating again, as such creatures do in the tropics during the dry season, when the rains came, and here again they sent up their spring chorus of voices, and, for aught I know, once more deposited their eggs. This to me is much more like the ways of Nature with her creatures than is the theory of the frogs' voluntary return to the swamps and pools to start the season over again.

The birds at least show little or no wit when a new problem is presented to them. They have no power of initiative. Instinct runs in a groove, and

From *Ways of Nature*, 1905.

cannot take a step outside of it. One May day we started a meadowlark from her nest. There were three just hatched young in the nest, and one egg lying on the ground about two inches from the nest. I suspected that this egg was infertile and that the bird had had the sense to throw it out, but on examination it was found to contain a nearly grown bird. The inference was, then, that the egg had been accidentally carried out of the nest some time when the sitting bird had taken a sudden flight, and that she did not have the sense to roll or carry it back to its place.

There is another view of the case which no doubt the sentimental "School of Nature Study" would eagerly adopt: a very severe drouth reigned throughout the land; food was probably scarce, and was becoming scarcer; the bird foresaw her inability to care for four young ones, and so reduced the possible number by ejecting one of the eggs from the nest. This sounds pretty and plausible, and so credits the bird with the wisdom that the public is so fond of believing it possesses. Something like this wisdom often occurs among the hive bees in seasons of scarcity; they will destroy the unhatched queens. But birds have no such foresight, and make no such calculations. In cold, backward seasons, I think, birds lay fewer eggs than when the season is early and warm, but that is not a matter of calculation on their part; it is the result of outward conditions.

A great many observers and nature students at the present time are possessed of the notion that the birds and beasts instruct their young, train them and tutor them, much after the human manner. In the familiar sight of a pair of crows foraging with their young about a field in summer, one of our nature writers sees the old birds giving their young a lesson in flying. She says that the most important thing that the elders had to do was to teach the youngsters how to fly. This they did by circling about the pasture, giving a peculiar call while they were followed by their flock—all but one. This was a bobtailed crow, and he did not obey the word of command. His mother took note of his disobedience and proceeded to discipline him. He stood upon a big stone, and she came down upon him and knocked him off his perch. "He squawked and fluttered his wings to keep from failing, but the blow came so suddenly that he had not time to save himself, and he fell flat on the ground. In a minute he clambered back upon his stone, and I watched him closely. The next time the call came to fly he did not linger, but went with the rest, and so long as I could watch him he never disobeyed again." I should interpret this fact of the old and young crows flying about a field in summer quite differently. The young are fully fledged, and are already strong flyers when this occurs. They do not leave the nest until they can fly well and need no tutoring. What the writer really saw was what any-one may see on the farm in June and July: she saw the parent crows foraging with their young in a field. The old birds flew about followed by their brood, clamorous for the food which their parents found. The bobtailed bird, which had probably met with some accident, did not follow, and the mother returned to feed it; the young crow lifted its wings and flapped them, and in its eagerness probably fell off its perch; then when its parent flew away, it followed.

I think it highly probable that the sense or faculty by which animals find their way home over long stretches of country, and which keeps them from ever being lost as man so often is, is a faculty entirely unlike anything man now possesses. The same may be said of the faculty that guides the birds back a thousand miles or more to their old breeding-haunts. In caged or housed animals I fancy this faculty soon becomes blunted. President Roo-sevelt tells in his "Ranch Life" of a horse he owned that ran away two hun-dred miles across the plains, swimming rivers on the way to its old home. It is very certain, I think, that this homing feat is not accomplished by the aid of either sight or scent, for usually the returning animal seems to follow a comparatively straight line. It is, or seems to be, a consciousness of direction that is as unerring as the magnetic needle. Reason, calculation, and judg-ment err, but these primary instincts of the animal seem almost infallible.

In Bronx Park in New York a grebe and a loon lived together in an inclo-sure in which was a large pool of water. The two birds became much at-tached to each other and were never long separated. One winter day on which the pool was frozen over, except a small opening in one end of it, the grebe dived under the ice and made its way to the far end of the pool, where it remained swimming about aimlessly for some moments. Presently the loon missed its companion, and with an apparent look of concern dived under the ice and joined it at the closed end of the pool. The grebe seemed to be in distress for want of air. Then the loon settled upon the bottom, and with lifted beak sprang up with much force against the ice, piercing it with its daggerlike bill, but not breaking it. Down to the bottom it went again, and again hurled itself up against the ice, this time shattering it and rising to the surface, where the grebe was quick to follow.

Now it looked as if the loon had gone under the ice to rescue its friend from a dangerous situation, for had not the grebe soon found the air, it must have perished, and persons who witnessed the incident interpreted it in this way. It is in such cases that we are so apt to read our human motives and emotions into the acts of the lower animals. I do not suppose the loon realized the danger of its companion, nor went under the ice to rescue it. It followed the grebe because it wanted to be with it, or to share in any food that might be detaining it there, and then, finding no air-hole, it proceeded to make one, as it and its ancestors must often have done before. All our northern divers must be more or less acquainted with ice, and must know how to break it. The grebe itself could doubtless have broken the ice had it desired to. The birds and the beasts often show much intelligence, or what looks like intelligence, but, as Hamerton says, "the moment we think of them as *human,* we are lost."

A farmer had a yearling that sucked the cows. To prevent this, he put on the yearling a muzzle set full of sharpened nails. These of course pricked the cows, and they would not stand to be drained of their milk. The next day the farmer saw the yearling rubbing the nails against a rock in order, as he thought, to dull them so they would not prick the cows! How much easier

John Burroughs and child with magnifying glass. Courtesy of the American Museum of Natural History.

to believe that the beast was simply trying to get rid of the awkward incumbrance upon its nose. What can a calf or a cow know about sharpened nails, and the use of a rock to dull them? This is a kind of outside knowledge—outside of their needs and experiences—that they could not possess.

An Arizona friend of mine lately told me this interesting incident about the gophers that infested his cabin when he was a miner. The gophers ate up his bread. He could not hide it from them or put it beyond their reach. Finally, he bethought him to stick his loaf on the end of a long iron poker that he had, and then stand up the poker in the middle of his floor. Still, when he came back to his cabin, he would find his loaf eaten full of holes. One day, having nothing to do, he concluded to watch and see how the gophers reached the bread, and this was what he saw: the animals climbed up the side of his log cabin, ran along one of the logs to a point opposite the bread, and then sprang out sidewise toward the loaf, which each one struck—but upon which only one seemed able to effect a lodgment. Then this one would cling to the loaf and act as a stop to his fellows when they tried a second time, his body affording them the barrier they required. My friend felt sure that this leader deliberately and consciously aided the others in securing a footing on the loaf. But I read the incident differently. This successful jumper aided his fellows without designing it. The exigencies of the situation compelled him to the course he pursued. Having effected a lodgment upon the impaled loaf, he would of course cling to it when the others jumped so as not to be dislodged, thereby, willy nilly, helping them to secure a foothold. The cooperation was inevitable, and not the result of design.

The power to see straight is the rarest of gifts; to see no more and no less than is actually before you; to be able to detach yourself and see the thing as it actually is, uncolored or unmodified by your own sentiments or prepossessions. In short, to see with your reason as well as with your perceptions, that is to be an observer and to read the book of nature aright.

Part Five

Conservation and
Environmental Concerns

✳

The Spring Bird Procession

O NE OF THE NEW PLEASURES of country life when one has made the acquaintance of the birds is to witness the northward bird procession as it passes or tarries with us in the spring—a procession which lasts from April till June and has some new feature daily.

The migrating wild creatures, whether birds or beasts, always arrest the attention. They seem to link up animal life with the great currents of the globe. It is moving day on a continental scale. It is the call of the primal in-stinct to increase and multiply, suddenly setting in motion whole tribes and races. The first phoebe-bird, the first song sparrow, the first robin or bluebird in March or early April is like the first ripple of the rising tide on the shore.

In my boyhood the vast armies of the passenger pigeons were one of the most notable spring tokens. Often late in March, or early in April, the naked beechwoods would suddenly become blue with them, and vocal with their soft, childlike calls; or all day the sky would be streaked with the long lines or dense masses of the moving armies. The last great flight of them that I ever beheld was on the 10th of April, 1875, when, for the greater part of the day, one could not at any moment look skyward above the Hudson River Valley without seeing several flocks, great and small, of the migrating birds. But that spectacle was never repeated as it had been for generations before. The pigeons never came back. Death and destruction, in the shape of the greed and cupidity of man, were on their trail. The hosts were pur-sued from State to State by professional pot-hunters and netters, and the numbers so reduced, and their flocking instinct so disorganized, that their vast migrating bands disappeared, and they were seen only in loosely scat-tered and diminishing flocks in different parts of the West during the

From *Field and Study,* 1919.

remainder of the century. A friend of mine shot a few in Indiana in the early eighties, and scattered bands of them have occasionally been reported, here and there, up to within a few years. The last time that my eyes beheld a passenger pigeon was in the fall of 1876 when I was out for grouse. I saw a solitary cock sitting in a tree. I killed it, little dreaming that, so far as I was concerned, I was killing the last pigeon. What man now in his old age who witnessed in youth that spring or fall festival and migration of the passenger pigeons would not hail it as one of the gladdest hours of his life if he could be permitted to witness it once more? It was such a spectacle of bounty, of joyous, copious animal life, of fertility in the air and in the wilderness, as to make the heart glad. I have seen the fields and woods fairly inundated for a day or two with these fluttering, piping, blue-and-white hosts. The very air at times seemed suddenly to turn to pigeons.

One May evening recently, near sundown, as I sat in my summer-house here in the Hudson Valley, I saw a long, curved line of migrating fowl high in the air, moving with great speed northward, and for a moment I felt the old thrill that I used to experience on beholding the pigeons. Fifty years ago I should have felt sure that they were pigeons; but they were only ducks. A more intense scrutiny failed to reveal the sharp, arrowlike effect of a swiftly moving flock of pigeons. The rounder, bottle-shaped bodies of the ducks also became apparent. But migrating ducks are a pleasing spectacle, and when, a little later, a line of geese came into my field of vision, and re-formed and trimmed their ranks there against the rosy sky above me, and drove northward with their masterly flight, there was no suggestion of the barnyard or farm pond up there.

> Whither, midst falling dew.
> While glow the heavens with the last steps of day,
> Far, through their rosy depths, dost thou pursue
> Thy solitary way?

Bryant, by the way, handled natural subjects in a large, free, simple way, which our younger poets never attained. When one is fortunate enough to see a line of swans etched upon the sky near sunset, a mile or more high, as has been my luck but twice in my life, one has seen something he will not soon forget.

The northward movement of the smaller bodies—the warblers and finches and thrushes—gives one pleasure of a different kind, the pleasure of rare and distinguished visitors who tarry for a few hours or a few days, enlivening the groves and orchards and garden borders, and then pass on.

Delicacy of color, grace of form, animation of movement, and often snatches of song, and elusive notes and calls, advise the bird-lover that the fairy procession is arriving. Tiny guests from Central and South America drop out of the sky like flowers borne by the night winds, and give unwonted interest to our tree-tops and roadside hedges. The ruby-crowned kinglet heralds the approach of the procession, morning after morning, by sounding his elfin bugle in the evergreens.

The migrating thrushes in passing are much more chary of their songs, although the hermit, the veery, and the olive-backed may occasionally be heard. I have even heard the northern water-thrush sing briefly in my currant-patch. The bobolink begins to burst out in sudden snatches of song, high in air, as he nears his northern haunts. I have often in May heard the black-poll warbler deliver his fine strain, like that of some ticking insect, but have never heard the bay-breasted nor the speckled Canada during migration. None of these birds sing or nest in the tropical countries where they pass more than half the year. They are like exiles there; the joy and color fade out of their lives in the land of color and luxuriance. The brilliant tints come to their plumage, and the songs to their hearts, only when the breeding impulse sends them to their brief northern homes. Tennyson makes his swallow say,

I do but wanton in the South . . .

That birds of a feather flock together, even in migration, is evident enough every spring. When in the morning you see one of a kind, you may confidently look for many more. When, in early May, I see one myrtle warbler, I presently see dozens of them in the trees and bushes all about me; or, if I see one yellow red-poll on the ground, with its sharp chirp and nervous behavior, I look for more. Yesterday, out of the kitchen window, I saw three speckled Canada warblers on the ground in the garden. How choice and rare they looked on the dull surface! In my neighbor's garden or dooryard I should probably have seen more of them, and in his trees and shrubbery as many magnolia and bay-breasted and black-throated blue warblers as in my own; and about his neighbor's place, and his, and his, throughout the township, and on west throughout the county, and throughout the State, and the adjoining State, on west to the Mississippi and beyond, I should have found in every bushy tangle and roadside and orchard and grove and wood and brookside, the same advancing line of migrating birds—warblers, flycatchers, finches, thrushes, sparrows, and so on—that I found here. I should have found high-holes calling and drumming, robins and phoebes nesting, swallows skimming, orioles piping, oven-birds demurely tripping over the leaves in the woods, tanagers and grosbeaks in the ploughed fields, purple finches in the cherry-trees, and white-throats and white-crowned sparrows in the hedges.

One sees the passing bird procession in his own grounds and neighborhood without pausing to think that in every man's grounds and in every neighborhood throughout the State, and throughout a long, broad belt of States, about several millions of homes, and over several millions of farms, the same flood-tide of bird-life is creeping and eddying or sweeping over the land. When the mating or nesting high-holes are awakening you in the early morning by their insistent calling and drumming on your metal roof or gutters or ridge-boards, they are doing the same to your neighbors near by, and to your fellow countrymen fifty, a hundred, a thousand miles away. Think of the myriads of dooryards where the "chippies" are just arriving; of the blooming orchards where the passing many-colored warblers are eagerly inspecting the buds and leaves; of the woods and woody streams where the oven-birds and water-thrushes are searching out their old haunts; of the secluded bushy fields and tangles where the chewinks, the brown thrashers, the chats, the catbirds, are once more preparing to begin life anew—think of all this and more, and you may get some idea of the extent and importance of our bird-life.

I fancy that on almost any day in mid-May the flickers are drilling their holes into a million or more decayed trees between the Hudson and the Mississippi; that any day a month earlier the phoebes are starting their nests under a million or more woodsheds or bridges or overhanging rocks; that several millions of robins are carrying mud and straws to sheltered projections about buildings, or to the big forked branches in the orchards.

When in my walk one day in April, through an old cedar lane, I found a mourning dove's nest on the top of an old stone wall—the only one I ever found in such a position—I wondered how many mourning doves throughout the breadth and length of the land had built or were then building their nests on stone walls or on rocks.

Considering the enormous number of birds of all species that flood the continent at this season, as if some dike or barrier south of us had suddenly given way, one wonders where they could all have been pent up during the winter. Mexico and Central and South America have their own bird populations the seasons through; and with the addition of the hosts from this country, it seems as if those lands must have literally swarmed with birds, and that the food question (as with us) must have been pressing. Of course, a great many of our birds such as sparrows, robins, blackbirds, meadow-larks, jays, and chewinks spend the winter in the Southern States, but many more—warblers, swallows, swifts, hummers, orioles, tanagers, cuckoos, fly-catchers, vireos, and others—seek out the equatorial region.

The ever-memorable war spring of 1917 was very backward—about two weeks later than the average—very cold, and very wet. Few fruit-trees bloomed before the 9th of May; then they all bloomed together: cherry, pear, peach, apple, all held back till they could stand it no longer. Pink peach-orchards and white apple-orchards at the same time and place made an unusual spectacle.

The cold, wet weather, of course, held up the bird procession also. The warblers and other migrants lingered and accumulated. The question of food became a very serious one with all the insect-eaters. The insects did not hatch, or, if they did, they kept very close to cover. The warblers, driven from the trees, took to the ground. It was an unusual spectacle to see these delicate and many-colored spirits of the air and of the tree-tops hopping about amid the clods and the rubbish, searching for something they could eat. They were like jewels in the gutter, or flowers on the sidewalk.

For several days in succession I saw several speckled Canada warblers hopping about my newly planted garden, evidently with poor results; then it was two or more Blackburnian warblers looking over the same ground, their new black-and-white and vivid orange plumage fairly illuminating the dull surface. The redstarts flashed along the ground and about the low bushes and around the outbuildings, delighting the eye in the same way. Bay-breasted warblers tarried and tarried, now on the ground, now in the lower branches of the trees or in bushes. I sat by a rapid rocky stream one afternoon and watched for half an hour a score or more of myrtle warblers snapping up the gauzy-winged insects that hovered above the water in the fitful sunshine. What loops and lines of color they made, now perched on the stones, now on the twigs of the overhanging trees, now hovering, now swooping! What an animated scene they presented! They had struck a rare find and were making the most of it.

On other occasions I saw the magnolia and Cape May and chestnut-sided warblers under the same stress of food-shortage, searching in un-wonted places. One bedraggled and half-starved female magnolia warbler lingered eight or ten days in a row of Japanese barberry-bushes under my window, where she seemed to find some minute and, to me, invisible insect on the leaves and in the blossoms that seemed worth her while.

This row of barberry-bushes was the haunt for a week or more of two or three male ruby-throated hummingbirds. Not one female did we see, but two males were often there at the same time, and sometimes three. They came at all hours and probed the clusters of small greenish-yellow blossoms, and perched on the twigs of intermingled lilacs, often remaining at rest five or six minutes at a time. They chased away the big queen bumblebees which also reaped a harvest there, and occasionally darted spitefully at each other. The first day I saw them, they appeared to be greatly fatigued, as if they had just made the long journey from Central America. Never before had I seen this bird-jewel of omnipotent wing take so kindly and so habituatedly to the perch.

The unseasonable season, no doubt, caused the death of vast numbers of warblers. We picked up two about the paths on my place, and the neighbors found dead birds about their grounds. Often live birds were so reduced in vitality that they allowed the passer-by to pick them up. Where one dead bird was seen, no doubt hundreds escaped notice in the fields and groves. A bird lives so intensely—rapid breathing and high temperature—that its need for food is always pressing. These adventurous little aviators had come all the way from South and Central America; the fuel-supply of their tiny engines was very low, and they suffered accordingly.

A friend writing me from Maine at this time had the same story of famishing warblers to tell. Certain of our more robust birds suffered. A male oriole came under my window one morning and pecked a long time at a dry crust of bread—a food, I dare say, it had never tasted before. The robins alone were in high feather. The crop of angleworms was one hundred per cent, and one could see the robins "snaking" them out of the ground at all hours.

Emerson is happy in his epithet "the punctual birds." They are nearly always here on time—always, considering the stage of the season; but the inflexible calendar often finds them late or early.

There is one bird, however, that keeps pretty close to the calendar. I refer to the white-crowned sparrow, the most distinguished looking of all our sparrows. Year after year, be the season early or late, I am on the lookout for him between the 12th and the 16th of May. This year, on the 13th, I looked out of my kitchen window and saw two males hopping along side by side in the garden. Unhurriedly they moved about, unconscious of their shapely forms and fine bearing. Their black-and-white crowns, their finely penciled backs, their pure ashen-gray breasts, and their pretty carriage give them a decided look of distinction. Such a contrast to our nervous and fidgety song sparrow, bless her little heart! And how different from the more chunky and plebeian-looking white-throats—bless their hearts also for their longer tarrying and their sweet, quavering ribbon of song! The fox sparrow, the most brilliant singer of all our sparrows, is an uncertain visitor in the Hudson River Valley, and seasons pass without one glimpse of him.

The spring of 1917 was remarkable for the number of migrating blue jays. For many days in May I beheld the unusual spectacle of processions of jays streaming northward. Considering the numbers I saw during the short time in the morning that I was in the open, if the numbers I did not see were in like proportion, many thousands of them must have passed my outlook northward. The jay is evidently more or less a migrant. I saw not one here during the winter, which is unusual. As one goes south in winter, the number of jays greatly increases, till in Georgia they are nearly as abundant as robins are here in summer.

The waves of bird migrants roll on through the States into Canada and beyond, breaking like waves on the shore, and spreading their contents over large areas. The warbler wave spends itself largely in the forests and mountains of the northern tier of States and of Canada, its utmost range, in the shape of the pileolated warbler (the western form of Wilson's black-cap) and a few others, reaching beyond the Arctic Circle, while its content of ground warblers, in the shape of the Maryland yellow-throat and the Kentucky and the hooded warblers, begins to drop out south of the Potomac and in Ohio.

The robins cover a very wide area, as do the song sparrows, the kingbirds, the vireos, the flickers, the orioles, the catbirds, and others. The area covered by the bobolinks is fast becoming less and less, or at least it is moving farther and farther north. Bobolinks in New York State meadows are becoming rare birds, but in Canadian meadows they appear to be on the increase. The mowing-machine and the earlier gathering of the hay-crop by ten or fourteen days than fifty years ago probably account for it. As the birds begin to arrive from the south in the spring, the birds that have come down from the north to spend the winter with us—the crossbills, the pine grosbeaks, the pine linnets, the red-breasted nuthatches, the juncos, and the snow buntings begin to withdraw. The ebb of one species follows the flow of another. One winter, in December, a solitary red-breasted nuthatch took up his abode with me, attracted by the suet and nuts I had placed on a maple-tree-trunk in front of my study window for the downy woodpecker, the chickadees, and the native nuthatches. Red-breast evidently said to himself, "Needless to look farther." He took lodgings in a wren-box on a post near by, and at night and during windy, stormy days was securely housed there. He tarried till April, and his constancy, his pretty form, and his engaging ways greatly endeared him to us. The pair of white-breasted nuthatches that fed at the same table looked coarse and common beside this little delicate waif from the far north. He could not stand to see lying about a superabundance of cracked hickory-nuts, any more than his larger relatives could, and would work industriously, carrying them away and hiding them in the woodpile and summer-house near by. The other nuthatches bossed him, as they in turn were bossed by Downy, and as he in turn bossed the brown creeper and the chickadees. In early April my little redbreast disappeared, and I fancied him turning his face northward, urged by a stronger impulse than that for food and shelter merely. He was my tiny guest from unknown lands, my baby bird, and he left a vacancy that none of the others could fill.

The nuthatches are much more pleasing than the woodpeckers. Soft-voiced, soft-colored, gentle-mannered, they glide over the rough branches and the tree-trunks with their boat-shaped bodies, going up and down and around, with apparently an extra joint in their necks that enables them, head-downward, to look straight out from the tree-trunk; their motions seem far less mechanical and angular than those of the woodpeckers and the creepers. Downy can back down a tree by short hitches, but he never ventures to do it headfirst, nor does the creeper; but the universal joint in the nuthatch's body and its rounded keel enable it to move head on indifferently in all directions. Its soft nasal call in the spring woods is one of the most welcome of sounds. It is like the voice of children, plaintive but contented, a soft interrogation in the ear of the sylvan gods. What a contrast to the sharp, steely note of the woodpeckers—the hairy's like the metallic sounds of the tinsmith and Downy's a minor key of the same!

But the woodpeckers have their drums which make the dry limbs vocal, and hint the universal spring awakening in a very agreeable manner. The two sounds together, the childish *Yank, yank,* of the nuthatch, and the resonant *Rat-tat-tat* of Downy, are coincident with the stirring sap in the maple trees. The robin, the bluebird, the song sparrow, and the phoebe have already loosened the fetters of winter in the open. It is interesting to note how differently the woodpeckers and the nuthatches use their beaks in procuring their food. Downy's head is a trip-hammer, and he drives his beak into the wood by short, sharp blows, making the chips fly, while the nuthatch strikes more softly, using his whole body in the movement. He delivers a kind of feathered blow on the fragment of nut which he has placed in the vise of the tree's bark. My little redbreast, previously referred to, came down on a nut in the same way, with a pretty extra touch of the flash of his wings at each stroke, as the woodchopper says "Hah!" when sending his axe home. If this does not add force to his blows, it certainly emphasizes them in a very pretty manner.

Each species of wild creature has its own individual ways and idiosyncrasies which one likes to note. As I write these lines, a male kingbird flies by the apple tree in which his mate is building a nest, with that peculiar mincing and affected flight which none other of the flycatchers, so far as I know, ever assumes. The olive-sided flycatcher has his own little trick, too, which the others do not have: I have seen his whole appearance suddenly change while sitting on a limb, by the exhibition of a band of white feathers like a broad chalk-mark outlining his body. Apparently the white feathers under the wings could be projected at will, completely transforming the appearance of the bird. He would change in a twinkling from a dark, motionless object to one surrounded by a broad band of white.

It occasionally happens that a familiar bird develops an unfamiliar trait. The purple finch is one of our sweetest songsters and best-behaved birds, but one that escapes the attention of most country people. But the past season he made himself conspicuous with us by covering the ground beneath the cherry-trees with cherry-blossoms. Being hard put to it for food, a flock of the birds must have discovered that every cherry blossom held a tidbit in the shape of its ovary. At once the birds began to cut out these ovaries, soon making the ground white beneath the trees. I grew alarmed for the safety of my crop of Windsors, and tried to "shoo" the birds away. They looked down upon me as if they considered it a good joke. Even when we shot one, to make sure of the identity of the bird, the flock only flew to the next tree and went on with the snipping. Beneath two cherry trees that stood beside the highway, the blossoms drifted into the wagon tracks like snowflakes. I concluded that the birds had taken very heavy toll of my cherries, but it turned out that they had only done a little of the much-needed *thinning*.

Out of a cluster of six or eight blossoms they seldom took more than two or three, as if they knew precisely what they were about, and were intent on rendering me a service. When the robins and the cedar-birds come for the cherries, they are not so considerate, but make a clean sweep. The finches could teach them manners—and morals.

The Ways of Sportsmen

I HAVE OFTEN HAD OCCASION to notice how much more intelligence the bird carries in its eye than do any of the quadrupeds. The animal will see you, too, if you are moving, but if you stand quite still, even the wary fox will pass within a few yards of you and not know you from a stump, unless the wind brings him your scent. But a crow or a hawk will discern you when you think yourself quite hidden. His eye is as keen as the fox's sense of smell, and seems fairly to penetrate veils and screens. Most of the water-fowl are equally sharp-eyed. The chief reliance of the animals for their safety, as well as for their food, is upon the keenness of their scent, while the fowls of the air depend mainly upon the eye.

A hunter out in Missouri relates how closely a deer approached him one day in the woods. The hunter was standing on the top of a log, about four feet from the ground, when the deer bounded playfully into a glade in the forest, a couple of hundred yards away. The animal began to feed and to move slowly toward the hunter. He was on the alert, but did not see or scent his enemy. He never took a bite of grass, says the sportsman, without first putting his nose to it, and then instantly raising his head and looking about.

In about ten minutes the deer had approached within fifty yards of the gunner; then the murderous instinct of the latter began to assert itself. His gun was loaded with fine shot, but he dared not make a move to change his shells lest the deer see him. He had one shell loaded with No. 4 shot in his pocket. Oh! if he could only get that shell into his gun.

The unsuspecting deer kept approaching; presently he passed behind a big tree, and his head was for a moment hidden. The hunter sprang to his work; he took one of the No. 8 shells out of his gun, got his hand into his pocket, and grasped the No. 4. Then the shining eyes of the deer were in

---

From *Riverby*, 1894.

view again. The hunter stood in this attitude five minutes. How we wish he had been compelled to stand for five hundred!

Then another tree shut off the buck's gaze for a moment; in went the No. 4 shell into the barrel, and the gun was closed quickly, but there was no time to bring it to the shoulder. The animal was now only thirty yards away. His hair was smooth and glossy, and every movement was full of grace and beauty. Time after time he seemed to look straight at the hunter, and once or twice a look of suspicion seemed to cross his face.

The man began to realize how painful it was to stand perfectly still on the top of a log for fifteen minutes. Every muscle ached and seemed about to rebel against his will. If the buck held to his course, he would pass not more than fifteen feet to one side of the gun, and the man that held it thought he might almost blow his heart out.

There was one more tree for him to pass behind, when the gun could be raised. He approached the tree, rubbed his nose against it, and for a moment was half hidden behind it. When his head appeared on the other side, the gun was pointed straight at his eye—and with only No. 4 shot, which could only wound him, but could not kill him.

The deer stops; he does not expose his body back of the fore leg, as the hunter had wished. The latter begins to be ashamed of himself, and has about made up his mind to let the beautiful creature pass unharmed, when the buck suddenly gets his scent, his head goes up, his nostrils expand, and a look of terror comes over his face. This is too much for the good resolutions of the hunter. Bang! goes the gun, the deer leaps into the air, wheels around a couple of times, recovers himself, and is off in a twinkling, no doubt carrying, the narrator says, a hundred No. 4 shot in his face and neck. The man says: "I've always regretted shooting at him."

I should think he would. But a man in the woods with a gun in his hand is no longer a man—he is a brute. The devil is in the gun to make brutes of us all.

If the game on this occasion had been, say, a wild turkey or a grouse, its discriminating eye would have figured out the hunter there on that log very quickly. This manly exploit of the western hunter reminds me of an exploit of a Brooklyn man, who last winter killed a bull moose in Maine. It was a more sportsmanlike proceeding, but my sympathies were entirely with the moose. The hero tells his story in a New York paper. With his guides, all armed with Winchester rifles, he penetrated far into the wilderness till he found a moose yard. It was near the top of a mountain. They started one of the animals and then took up its trail. As soon as the moose found it was being followed, it led right off in hopes of outwalking its enemies. But they had snow-shoes and he did not; they had food and he did not. On they went, pursued and pursuers, through the snow-clogged wilderness, day after day. The moose led them the most difficult route he could find.

At night the men would make camp, build a fire, eat and smoke, and roll themselves in their blankets and sleep. In the morning they would soon come up to the camping-place of the poor moose, where the imprint of his great body showed in the snow, and where he had passed a cold, supperless night.

On the fifth day the moose began to show signs of fatigue; he rested often, he also tried to get around and behind his pursuers and let them pass on. Think how inadequate his wit was to cope with the problem — he thought they would pass by him if he went to one side.

On the morning of the sixth day he had made up his mind to travel no farther, but to face his enemies and have it out with them. As he heard them approach, he rose up from his couch of snow, mane erect, his look fierce and determined. Poor creature, he did not know how unequal the contest was. How I wish he could at that moment have had a Winchester rifle, too, and known how to use it. There would have been fair play then. With such weapons as God had given him he had determined to meet the foe, and if they had had only such weapons as God had given them, he would have been safe. But they had weapons which the devil had given them, and their deadly bullets soon cut him down, and now probably his noble antlers decorate the hall of his murderer.

Keeping the Iron from Our Souls

PITTSBURGH IS A CITY that sits with its feet in or very near the lake of brimstone and fire, and its head in the sweet country air of the hill-tops. I think I got nearer the infernal regions there than I ever did in any other city in this country. One is fairly suffocated at times driving along the public highway on a bright, breezy August day. It might well be the devil's laboratory. Out of such blackening and blasting fumes comes our civilization. That weapons of war and of destructiveness should come out of such pits and abysses of hellfire seemed fit and natural, but much more comes out of them—much that suggests the pond-lily rising out of the black slime and muck of the lake bottoms.

We live in an age of iron and have all we can do to keep the iron from entering our souls. Our vast industries have their root in the geologic history of the globe as in no other past age. We delve for our power, and it is all barbarous and unhandsome. When the coal and oil are all gone and we come to the surface and above the surface for the white coal, for the smokeless oil, for the winds and the sunshine, how much more attractive life will be! Our very minds ought to be cleaner. We may never hitch our wagons to the stars, but we can hitch them to the mountain streams, and make the summer breezes lift our burdens. Then the silver age will displace the iron age.

From "A Strenuous Holiday," in *Under the Maples,* 1921.

Part Six

On Writers and Writing

Emerson and the Pine Tree

B UT THE REAL WHITE PINE among our poets is Emerson. Against that
rustling deciduous background of the New England poets he shows
dark and aspiring. Emerson seems to have a closer fellowship with the pine
than with any other tree, and it recurs again and again in his poems. In his
"Garden" the pine is the principal vegetable, "the snow-loving pines," as he
so aptly says, and "the hemlocks tall, untamable." It is perhaps from the
pine that he gets the idea that "Nature loves the number five"; its leaves are
in fives, and its whorl of branches is composed of five. His warbler is the
"pine warbler," and he sees "the pigeons in the pines," where they are seldom to be seen. He even puts a "pine state-house" in his "Boston Hymn."

But, more than that, his "Woodnotes," one of his longest poems, is
mainly the notes of the pine. Theodore Parker said that a tree that talked
like Emerson's pine ought to be cut down; but if the pine were to find a
tongue, I should sooner expect to hear the Emersonian dialect from it than
almost any other. It would be pretty high up, certainly, and go over the
heads of most of the other trees. It were sure to be pointed, though the
point few could see. And it would not be garrulous and loudmouthed,
though it might talk on and on. Whether it would preach or not is a question, but I have no doubt it would be a fragrant healing gospel if it did. I
think its sentences would be short ones with long pauses between them,
and that they would sprout out of the subject independently and not con-
nect or interlock very much. There would be breaks and chasms or maybe
some darkness between the lines, but I should expect from it a lofty, cheerful, and all-the-year-round philosophy. The temptation to be oracular
would no doubt be great, and could be more readily overlooked in this tree
than in any other. Then, the pine being the oldest tree, great wisdom and
penetration might be expected of it.

From "A Spray of Pine," in *Signs and Seasons,* 1886.

Though Emerson's pine boasts

> My garden is the cloven rock,
> And my manure the snow;
> And drifting sand-heaps feed my stock,
> In summer's scorching glow,

yet the great white pine loves a strong deep soil. How it throve along our river bottom and pointed out the best land to the early settlers! Remnants of its stumps are still occasionally seen in land that has been given to the plow these seventy or eighty years. In Pennsylvania the stumps are wrenched from the ground by machinery and used largely for fencing. Laid upon their side, with their wide branching roots in the air, they form a barrier before which even the hound-pursued deer may well pause.

This aboriginal tree is fast disappearing from the country. Its second growth seems to be a degenerate race, what the carpenters contemptuously call pumpkin pine, on account of its softness. All the large tracts and provinces of the original tree have been invaded and ravished by the lumbermen, so that only isolated bands and straggling specimens, like the remnants of a defeated and disorganized army, are now found scattered up and down the country. The spring floods on our northern rivers have for decades of years been moving seething walls of pine logs, sweeping down out of the wilderness. I remember pausing beside a mammoth pine in the Adirondack woods, standing a little to one side of the destroyer's track, that must have carried its green crown near one hundred and fifty feet above the earth. How such a tree impresses one! How it swells at the base and grows rigid as if with muscular effort in its determined grip of the earth! How it lays hold of the rocks, or rends them asunder to secure its hold! Nearly all trunk, it seems to have shed its limbs like youthful follies as it went skyward, or as the builders pull down their scaffoldings and carry them higher as the temple mounts; nothing superfluous, no waste of time or energy, the one purpose to cleave the empyrean steadily held to.

Thoreau's Wildness

D OUBTLESS THE WILDEST MAN New England has turned out since the
red aborigines vacated her territory was Henry Thoreau—a man in
whom the Indian reappeared on the plane of taste and morals. One is
tempted to apply to him his own lines on "Elisha Dugan," as it is very certain they fit himself much more closely than they ever did his neighbor:

> O man of wild habits,
> Partridges and rabbits,
> Who hast no cares,
> Only to set snares,
> Who liv'st all alone
> Close to the bone,
> And where life is sweetest
> Constantly eatest.

His whole life was a search for the wild, not only in nature but in literature, in life, in morals. The shyest and most elusive thoughts and impressions were the ones that fascinated him most, not only in his own mind,
but in the minds of others. His startling paradoxes are only one form his
wildness took. He cared little for science, except as it escaped the rules and
technicalities, and put him on the trail of the ideal, the transcendental.
Thoreau was of French extraction; and every drop of his blood seems to
have turned toward the aboriginal, as the French blood has so often done
in other ways in this country. He, for the most part, despised the white
man; but his enthusiasm kindled at the mention of the Indian. He envied
the Indian; he coveted his knowledge, his arts, his woodcraft. He accredited
him with a more "practical and vital science" than was contained in the
books. "The Indian stood nearer to wild Nature than we." "It was a new
light when my guide gave me Indian names for things for which I had only
scientific ones before. In proportion as I understood the language, I saw

---

From *Literary Values,* 1902.

them from a new point of view." And again, "The Indian's earthly life was as far off from us as Heaven is."

In his "Week" he complains that our poetry is only white man's poetry. "If we could listen but for an instant to the chant of the Indian muse, we should understand why he will not exchange his savageness for civilization." Speaking of himself, he says, "I am convinced that my genius dates from an older era than the agricultural. I would at least strike my spade into the earth with such careless freedom, but accuracy, as the woodpecker his bill into a tree. There is in my nature, methinks, a singular yearning toward all wildness." Again and again he returns to the Indian:

> We talk of civilizing the Indian, but that is not the name for his improvement. By the wary independence and aloofness of his dim forest life he preserves his intercourse with his native gods, and is admitted from time to time to a rare and peculiar society with Nature. He has glances of starry recognition, to which our saloons are strangers. The steady illumination of his genius, dim only because distant, is like the faint but satisfying light of the stars compared with the dazzling but ineffectual and short-lived blaze of candles.

> We would not always be soothing and taming nature, breaking the horse and the ox, but sometimes ride the horse wild, and chase the buffalo.

The only relics that interest him are Indian relics. One of his regular spring recreations or occupations is the hunting of arrow-heads. He goes looking for arrow-heads as other people go berrying or botanizing. In his published journal he makes a long entry under date of March 28, 1859, about his pursuit of arrow-heads. "I spend many hours every spring," he says,

> gathering the crop which the melting snow and rain have washed bare. When, at length, some island in the meadow or some sandy field elsewhere has been plowed, perhaps for rye, in the fall, I take note of it, and do not fail to repair thither as soon as the earth begins to be dry in the spring. If the spot chances never to have been cultivated before, I am the first to gather a crop from it. The farmer little thinks that another reaps a harvest which is the fruit of his toil.

He probably picked up thousands of arrow-heads. He had an eye for them. The Indian in him recognized its Own.

His genius itself is arrowlike, and typical of the wild weapon he so loved—hard, flinty, fine-grained, penetrating, winged, a flying shaft, bringing down its game with marvelous sureness. His literary art was to let fly with a kind of quick inspiration; and though his arrows sometimes go wide, yet it is always a pleasure to watch their aerial course. Indeed, Thoreau was a kind of Emersonian or transcendental red man, going about with a pocket-glass and an herbarium, instead of with a bow and a tomahawk. He appears to have been as stoical and indifferent and unsympathetic as a veritable Indian; and how he hunted without trap or gun, and fished without hook or snare!

Everywhere the wild drew him. He liked the telegraph because it was a kind of aeolian harp; the wind blowing upon it made wild, sweet music. He liked the railroad through his native town, because it was the wildest road he knew of: it only made deep cuts into and through the hills. "On it are no houses nor foot-travelers. The travel on it does not disturb me. The woods are left to hang over it. Though straight, it is wild in its accompaniments, keeping all its raw edges. Even the laborers on it are not like other laborers." One day he passed a little boy in the street who had on a home-made cap of woodchuck's skin, and it completely filled his eye. He makes a delightful note about it in his journal. That was the kind of cap to have—"a perfect little idyl, as they say." Any wild trait unexpectedly cropping out in any of the domestic animals pleased him immensely. The crab-apple was his favorite apple, because of its beauty and perfume. He perhaps never tried to ride a wild horse, but such an exploit was in keeping with his genius.

Thoreau hesitated to call himself a naturalist. That was too tame; he would perhaps have been content to have been an Indian naturalist. He says in his journal, and with much truth and force, "Man cannot afford to be a naturalist, to look at Nature directly, but only with the side of his eye. He must look through and beyond her. To look at her is as fatal as to look at the head of Medusa. It turns the man of science to stone."

When he was applied to by the secretary of the Association for the Advancement of Science, at Washington, for information as to the particular branch of science he was most interested in, he confesses he was ashamed to answer for fear of exciting ridicule. But he says, "If it had been the secretary of an association of which Plato or Aristotle was the president, I should not have hesitated to describe my studies at once and particularly." "The fact is, I am a mystic, a transcendentalist, and a natural philosopher to boot." Indeed, what Thoreau was finally after in nature was something ulterior to science, something ulterior to poetry, something ulterior to philosophy; it was that vague something which he calls "the higher law," and which eludes all direct statement. He went to Nature as to an oracle; and though he sometimes, indeed very often, questioned her as a naturalist and a poet, yet there was always another question in his mind. He ransacked the country about Concord in all seasons and weathers, and at all times of the day and night he delved into the ground, he probed the swamps, he searched the waters, he dug into woodchuck holes, into muskrats' dens, into the retreats of the mice and squirrels; he saw every bird, heard every sound, found every wildflower, and brought home many a fresh bit of natural history; but he was always searching for something he did not find. This search of his for the transcendental, the unfindable, the wild that will not be caught, he has set forth in a beautiful parable in Walden:

> I long ago lost a hound, a bay horse, and a turtle-dove, and am still on their trail. Many are the travelers I have spoken concerning them, describing their tracks, and what calls they answered to. I have met one or two who had heard the hound, and the tramp of the horse, and even seen the dove disappear behind a cloud; and they seemed as anxious to recover them as if they had lost them themselves.

From *Whitman: A Study*

Preliminary

T HE WRITING OF THIS PRELIMINARY CHAPTER, and the final survey
and revision of my Whitman essay, I am making at a rustic house I
have built at a wild place a mile or more from my home upon the river.
I call this place Whitman Land, because in many ways it is typical of my
poet—an amphitheatre of precipitous rock, slightly veiled with a delicate
growth of verdure, enclosing a few acres of prairielike land, once the site of
an ancient lake, now a garden of unknown depth and fertility. Elemental
ruggedness, savageness, and grandeur, combined with wonderful tenderness, modernness, and geniality. There rise the gray scarred cliffs, crowned
here and there with a dead hemlock or pine, where, morning after morning,
I have seen the bald-eagle perch, and here at their feet this level area of tender humus, with three perennial springs of delicious cold water flowing in
its margin; a huge granite bowl filled with the elements and potencies of
life. The scene has a strange fascination for me, and holds me here day after
day. From the highest point of rocks I can overlook a long stretch of the
river and of the farming country beyond; I can hear owls hoot, hawks
scream, and roosters crow. Birds of the garden and orchard meet birds of
the forest upon the shaggy cedar posts that uphold my porch. At dusk the
call of the whip-poor-will mingles with the chorus of the pickerel frogs, and
in the morning I hear through the robins' cheerful burst the somber plaint
of the mourning-dove. When I tire of my manuscript, I walk in the woods,
or climb the rocks, or help the men clear up the ground, piling and burning
the stumps and rubbish.

This scene and situation, so primitive and secluded, yet so touched with
and adapted to civilization, responding to the moods of both sides of the

Published in 1896. These selections from Burroughs's second book on Whitman are intended to convey enough of the substance of this pioneering work to encourage readers to
seek out the whole.

life of imagination of a modern man, seems, I repeat, typical in many ways of my poet, and is a veritable Whitman land. Whitman does not to me suggest the wild and unkempt as he seems to do to many; he suggests the cosmic and the elemental, and this is one of the dominant thoughts that run through my dissertation. Scenes of power and savagery in nature were more welcome to him, probably more stimulating to him, than the scenes of the pretty and placid, and he cherished the hope that he had put into his *Leaves* some of the tonic and fortifying quality of Nature in her more grand and primitive aspects.

His wildness is only the wildness of the great primary forces from which we draw our health and strength. Underneath all his unloosedness, or free launching forth of himself, is the sanity and repose of nature. . . .

II

. . . My absorption of Emerson had prepared me in a measure for Whitman's philosophy of life, but not for the ideals of character and conduct which he held up to me, nor for the standards in art to which the poet perpetually appealed. Whitman was Emerson translated from the abstract into the concrete. There was no privacy with Whitman; he never sat me down in a corner with a cozy, comfortable shut-in feeling, but he set me upon a hill or started me upon an endless journey. Wordsworth had been my poet of nature, of the sequestered and the idyllic; but I saw that here was a poet of a larger, more fundamental nature, indeed of the Cosmos itself. Not a poet of dells and fells, but of the earth and the orbs. This much soon appeared to me, but I was troubled by the poet's apparent "colossal egotism," by his attitude towards evil, declaring himself "to be the poet of wickedness also"; by his seeming attraction toward the turbulent and the disorderly; and, at times, by what the critics had called his cataloguing style of treatment.

When I came to meet the poet himself, which was in the fall of 1863, I felt less concern about these features of his work; he was so sound and sweet and gentle and attractive as a man, and withal so wise and tolerant, that I soon came to feel the same confidence in the book that I at once placed in its author, even in the parts which I did not understand. I saw that the work and the man were one, and that the former must be good as the latter was good. There was something in the manner in which both the book and its author carried themselves under the sun, and in the way they confronted America and the present time, that convinced beyond the power of logic or criticism.

John Burroughs and dog at waterfall. Courtesy of the American Museum of
Natural History.

The more I saw of Whitman, and the more I studied his *Leaves,* the more
significance I found in both, and the clearer it became to me that a new
type of a man and a new departure in poetic literature were here foreshad-
owed. There was something forbidding, but there was something vital and
grand back of it. I found to be true what the poet said of himself:

> Bearded, sunburnt, gray-neck'd, forbidding, I have arrived,
> To be wrestled with as I pass for the solid prizes of the universe,
> For such I afford whoever can persevere to win them,—

I have persevered in my study of the poet, though balked many times,
and the effect upon my own mental and spiritual nature has been great; no
such "solid prizes" in the way of a broader outlook upon life and nature,

and, I may say, upon art, has any poet of my time afforded me. There are passages or whole poems in the *Leaves* which I do not yet understand ("Sleep-Chasings" is one of them), though the language is as clear as daylight; they are simply too subtle or elusive for me; but my confidence in the logical soundness of the book is so complete that I do not trouble myself at all about these things. . . .

VIII

The much that I have said in the following pages about Whitman's radical differences from other poets — his changed attitude towards the universe, his unwonted methods and aims etc. — might seem to place him upon a ground so unique and individual as to contradict my claims for his breadth and universality. The great poets stand upon common ground; they excel along familiar lines, they touch us, and touch us deeply, at many points. What always saves Whitman is his enormous endowment of what is "commonest, nearest, easiest," — his atmosphere of the common day, the common life, and his fund of human sympathy and love. He is strange because he gives us the familiar in such a direct, unexpected manner. His *Leaves* are like some new fruit that we have never before tasted. It is the product of another clime, another hemisphere. The same old rains and dews, the same old sun and soil nursed it, yet in so many ways how novel and strange! We certainly have to serve a certain apprenticeship to this poet, familiarize ourselves with his point of view and with his democratic spirit, before we can make much of him. The spirit in which we come to him from the other poets — the poets of art and culture — is for the most part unfriendly to him.

There is something rude, strange, and unpoetic about him at first sight that is sure to give most readers of poetry a shock. I think one might come to him from the Greek poets, or the old Hebrew or Oriental bards, with less shock than from our modern delicate and refined singers, because the old poets were more simple and elemental, and aimed less at the distilled dainties of poetry, than the modern. They were full of action, too, and volition — of that which begets and sustains life. Whitman's poetry is almost entirely the expression of will and personality, and runs very little to intellectual subtleties and refinements. It fulfills itself in our wills and character, rather than in our taste.

IX

Whitman will always be a strange and unwonted figure among his country's poets, and among English poets generally—a cropping out again, after so many centuries, of the old bardic prophetic strain. Had he dropped upon us from some other sphere, he could hardly have been a greater surprise and puzzle to the average reader or critic. Into a literature that was timid, imitative, conventional, he fell like leviathan into a duck-pond, and the commotion and consternation he created there have not yet subsided. All the reigning poets in this country except Emerson denied him, and many of our minor poets still keep up a hostile sissing and cackling. He will probably always be more or less a stumbling-block to the minor poet, because of his indifference to the things which to the minor poet are all in all. He was a poet without what is called artistic form, and without technique, as that word is commonly understood. His method was analogous to the dynamic method of organic nature, rather than to the mechanical or constructive method of the popular poets. . . .

X

I make no claim that my essay is a dispassionate, disinterested view of Whitman. It will doubtless appear to many as a one-sided view, or as colored by my love for the man himself. And I shall not be disturbed if such turns out to be the case. A dispassionate view of a man like Whitman is probably out of the question in our time, or in any near time. His appeal is so personal and direct that readers are apt to be either violently for him or violently against, and it will require the perspective of more than one generation to bring out his true significance. Still, for any partiality for its subject which my book may show, let me take shelter behind a dictum of Goethe. "I am more and more convinced," says the great critic, "that whenever one has to vent an opinion on the actions or on the writings of others, unless this be done from a certain one-sided enthusiasm, or from a loving interest in the person and the work, the result is hardly worth gathering up. Sympathy and enjoyment in what we see is in fact the only reality, and, from such reality, reality as a natural product follows. All else is vanity."

To a loving interest in Whitman and his work, which may indeed amount to one-sided enthusiasm, I plead guilty. This at least is real with me, and not affected; and, if the reality which Goethe predicts in such cases only follows, I shall be more than content. . . .

XVII

Call his work poetry or prose, or what you will: that it is an inspired utterance of some sort, any competent person ought to be able to see. And what else do we finally demand of any work than that it be inspired? How all questions of form and art, and all other questions, sink into insignificance beside that! The exaltation of mind and spirit shown in the main body of Whitman's work, the genuine, prophetic fervor, the intensification and amplification of the simple ego, and the resultant raising of all human values seem to me as plain as daylight.

Whitman is to be classed among the great names by the breadth and all-inclusiveness of his theme and by his irrepressible personality. I think it highly probable that future scholars and critics will find his work fully as significant and era-marking as that of any of the few supreme names of the past. It is the culmination of an age of individualism, and, as opposites meet, it is also the best lesson in nationalism and universal charity that this century has seen.

Biographical and Personal

Few men were so deeply impressed by our Civil War as Whitman. It aroused all his patriotism, all his sympathies, and, as a poet, tested his power to deal with great contemporary events and scenes. He was first drawn to the seat of war on behalf of his brother, Lieutenant-Colonel George W. Whitman, 51st New York Volunteers, who was wounded by the fragment of a shell at Fredericksburg. This was in the fall of 1862. This brought him in contact with the sick and wounded soldiers, and henceforth, as long as the war lasts and longer, he devoted his time and substance to ministering to them. The first two or three years of his life in Washington he supported himself by correspondence with Northern newspapers, mainly with the *New York Times.* These letters, as well as the weekly letters to his mother during the same period, form an intensely pathetic and interesting record.

They contain such revelations of himself and such pictures of the scenes he moved among that I shall here quote freely from them. . . .

> December 22 to 31. Am among the regimental, brigade, and division hospitals somewhat. Few at home realize that these are merely tents, and sometimes very poor ones, the wounded lying on the ground, lucky if their blanket is spread on a layer of pine or hemlock twigs, or some leaves. No cots; seldom

even a mattress on the ground. It is pretty cold. I go around from one case to another. I do not see that I can do any good, but I cannot leave them. Once in a while some youngster holds on to me convulsively, and I do what I can for him; at any rate, stop with him and sit near him for hours, if he wishes it.

Besides the hospitals, I also go occasionally on long tours through the camps, talking with the men, etc.; sometimes at night among the groups around the fires, in their shebang enclosures of bushes. I soon get acquainted anywhere in camp, with officers or men, and am always well used. Sometimes I go down on picket with the regiments I know best.

After continuing in front through the winter, he returns to Washington, where the wounded and sick have mainly been concentrated. The capital city, truly, is now one huge hospital; and there Whitman establishes himself, and thenceforward, for several years, has but one daily and nightly avocation.

He alludes to writing letters by the bedside, and says:

I do a good deal of this, of course, writing all kinds, including love-letters. Many sick and wounded soldiers have not written home to parents, brothers, sisters, and even wives, for one reason or another, for a long, long time. Some are poor writers, some cannot get paper and envelopes; many have an aversion to writing, because they dread to worry the folks at home — the facts about them are so sad to tell. I always encourage the men to write, and promptly write for them. . . .

In a letter to his mother in 1863 he says, in reference to his hospital services,

I have got in the way, after going lightly, as it were, all through the wards of a hospital, and trying to give a word of cheer, if nothing else, to every one, then confining my special attention to the few where the investment seems to tell best, and who want it most. . . . Mother, I have real pride in telling you that I have the consciousness of saving quite a number of lives by keeping the men from giving up, and being a good deal with them. The men say it is so, and the doctors say it is so; and I will candidly confess I can see it is true, though I say it myself. I know you will like to hear it, mother, so I tell you.

. . . During the war and after, I used to see a good deal of Whitman in Washington. Summer and winter he was a conspicuous figure on Pennsylvania Avenue, where he was wont to walk for exercise and to feed his hunger for faces. One would see him afar off, in the crowd but not of it — a large, slow-moving figure, clad in gray, with broad-brimmed hat and gray beard — or, quite as frequently, on the front platform of the street horse-cars with the driver. My eye used to single him out many blocks away.

There were times during this period when his aspect was rather forbidding—the physical man was too pronounced on first glance; the other man was hidden beneath the broad-brimmed hat. One needed to see the superbly domed head and classic brow crowning the rank physical man.

In his middle manhood, judging from the photos, he had a hirsute, kindly look, but very far removed from the finely cut traditional poet's face. . . .

※　※　※

I have often heard Whitman say that he inherited most excellent blood from his mother—the old Dutch Van Velser strain, Long Island blood filtered and vitalized through generations by the breath of the sea. He was his mother's child unmistakably. With all his rank masculinity, there was a curious feminine undertone in him which revealed itself in the quality of his voice, the delicate texture of his skin, the gentleness of his touch and ways, the attraction he had for children and the common people. A lady in the West, writing to me about him, spoke of his "great mother-nature." He was receptive, sympathetic, tender, and met you not in a positive, aggressive manner, but more or less in a passive or neutral mood. He did not give his friends merely his mind, he gave them himself. It is not merely his mind or intellect that he has put into his poems, it is himself. Indeed, this feminine mood or attitude might be dwelt upon at much length in considering his poems—their solvent, absorbing power, and the way they yield themselves to diverse interpretations.

The sea, too, had laid its hand upon him, as I have already suggested. He never appeared so striking and impressive as when seen upon the beach. His large and tall gray figure looked at home, and was at home, upon the shore. The simple, strong, flowing lines of his face, his always clean fresh air, his blue absorbing eye, his commanding presence, and something pristine and elemental in his whole expression, seemed at once to put him *en rapport* with the sea. No phase of nature seems to have impressed him so deeply as the sea, or recurs so often in his poems. . . .

※　※　※

Whitman was of large mould in every way, and of bold, far-reaching schemes, and is very sure to fare better at the hands of large men than of small. The first and last impression which his personal presence always made upon one was of a nature wonderfully gentle, tender, and benignant.

His culture, his intellect, was completely suffused and dominated by his humanity, so that the impression you got from him was not that of a learned or a literary person, but of fresh, strong, sympathetic human nature—such an impression, I fancy, only fuller, as one might have got from Walter Scott.

This was perhaps the secret of the attraction he had for the common, unlettered people and for children. I think that even his literary friends often sought his presence less for conversation than to bask in his physical or psychical sunshine, and to rest upon his boundless charity. The great service he rendered to the wounded and homesick soldiers in the hospitals during the war came from his copious endowment of this broad, sweet, tender democratic nature. He brought father and mother to them, and the tonic and cheering atmosphere of simple, affectionate home life.

In person Whitman was large and tall, above six feet, with a breezy, open-air look. His temperament was sanguine; his voice was a tender baritone. The dominant impression he made was that of something fresh and clean. I remember the first time I met him, which was in Washington, in the fall of 1863. I was impressed by the fine grain and clean, fresh quality of the man. Some passages in his poems had led me to expect something different. He always had the look of a man who had just taken a bath. The skin was light and clear, and the blood well to the surface. His body, as I once noticed when we were bathing in the surf, had a peculiar fresh bloom and fineness and delicacy of texture. His physiology was undoubtedly remarkable, unique. The full beauty of his face and head did not appear till he was past sixty. After that, I have little doubt, it was the finest head this age or country has seen. Every artist who saw him was instantly filled with a keen desire to sketch him. The lines were so simple, so free, and so strong. High, arching brows; straight, clear-cut nose; heavy-lidded blue-gray eyes; forehead not thrust out and emphasized, but a vital part of a symmetrical, dome-shaped head; ear large, and the most delicately carved I have ever seen; the mouth and chin hidden by a soft, long, white beard. It seems to me his face steadily refined and strengthened with age. Time depleted him in just the right way—softened his beard and took away the too florid look; subdued the carnal man, and brought out more fully the spiritual man. When I last saw him (December 26, 1891), though he had been very near death for many days, I am sure I had never seen his face so beautiful. There was no breaking-down of the features, or the least sign of decrepitude, such as we usually note in old men. The expression was full of pathos, but it was as grand as that of a god. I could not think of him as near death, he looked so unconquered.

In Washington I knew Whitman intimately from the fall of 1863 to the time he left in 1873. In Camden I visited him yearly after that date, usually in the late summer or fall. I will give one glimpse of him from my diary, under date of August 18, 1887. I reached his house in the morning, before he was up. Presently he came slowly down stairs and greeted me:

> Find him pretty well—looking better than last year. With his light-gray suit, and white hair, and fresh pink face, he made a fine picture. Among other things, we talked of the Swinburne attack [then recently published]. W. did not show the least feeling on the subject, and, I clearly saw, was absolutely undisturbed by the article. I told him I had always been more disturbed by S.'s admiration for him than I was now by his condemnation. By and by W. had his horse hitched up, and we started for Glendale, ten miles distant, to see young Gilchrist, the artist. A fine drive through a level farming and truck-gardening country; warm, but breezy. W. drives briskly, and salutes every person we meet, little and big, black and white, male and female. Nearly all return his salute cordially. He said he knew but few of those he spoke to, but that, as he grew older, the old Long Island custom of his people, to speak to every one on the road, was strong upon him. One tipsy man in a buggy responded, "Why, pap, how d' ye do, pap?" etc. We talked of many things. . . . We returned to Camden before dark, W. apparently not fatigued by the drive of twenty miles.

In death what struck me most about the face was its perfect symmetry. It was such a face, said Mr. Conway, as Rembrandt would have selected from a million. "It is the face of an aged loving child. As I looked, it was with the reflection that, during an acquaintance of thirty-six years, I never heard from those lips a word of irritation, or depreciation of any being. I do not believe that Buddha, of whom he appeared an avatar, was more gentle to all men, women, children, and living things." . . .

₃ℓ ₃ℓ ₃ℓ

I predict a great future for Whitman, because the world is so unmistakably going his way. The three or four great currents of the century—the democratic current, the scientific current, the humanitarian current, the new religious current, and what flows out of them—are underneath all Whitman has written. They shape all and make all. They do not appear in him as mere dicta, or intellectual propositions, but as impulses, will, character, flesh-and-blood reality. We get these things, not as sentiments or yet theories, but as a man. We see life and the world as they appear to the inevitable democrat, the inevitable lover, the inevitable believer in God and immortality, the inevitable acceptor of absolute science.

We are all going his way. We are more impatient of formalities, cere-
monies, and make-believe; we more and more crave the essential, the real.
More and more we want to see the thing as in itself it is; more and more is
science opening our eyes to see the divine, the illustrious, the universal in
the common, the near at hand; more and more do we tire of words and
crave things; deeper and deeper sinks the conviction that personal qualities
alone tell—that the man is all in all, that the brotherhood of the race is not
a dream, that love covers all and atones for all.

Everything in our modern life and culture that tends to broaden, liberal-
ize, free; that tends to make hardy, self-reliant, virile; that tends to widen
charity, deepen affection between man and man, to foster sanity and self-
reliance; that tends to kindle our appreciation of the divinity of all things;
that heightens our rational enjoyment of life; that inspires hope in the future and faith in the unseen [is] on Whitman's side. All these things prepare
the way for him.

On the other hand, the strain and strife and hoggishness of our civilization, our trading politics, our worship of conventions, our millionaire
ideals, our high-pressure lives, our pruriency, our sordidness, our perver-
sions of nature, our scoffing caricaturing tendencies are against him. He an-
tagonizes all these things.

The more democratic we become, the more we are prepared for Whitman; the more tolerant, fraternal, sympathetic we become, the more we are
ready for Whitman; the more we inure ourselves to the open air and to real
things, the more we value and understand our own bodies, the more the
woman becomes the mate and equal of the man, the more social equality
prevails—the sooner will come to Whitman fullness and fruition. . . .

⁊＊ ⁊＊ ⁊＊

Whitman's democracy is the breath of his nostrils, the light of his eyes, the
blood in his veins. The reader does not feel that here is some fine scholar,
some fine poet singing the praises of democracy; he feels that here is a democrat, probably, as Thoreau surmised, the greatest the world has yet seen,
turning the light of a great love, a great intellect, a great soul, upon America, upon contemporary life and events, and upon the universe, and reading
new lessons, new meanings, therein. He is a great poet and prophet, speaking through the average man, speaking as one of the people, and interpreting life from the point of view of absolute democracy. . . .

⁊＊　⁊＊　⁊＊

Whitman is a projection into literature of the cosmic sense and conscience of the people, and their participation in the forces that are shaping the world in our century. Much comes to a head in him. Much comes to joyous speech and song that heretofore had only come to thought and speculation. A towering, audacious personality has appeared which is strictly the fruit of the democratic spirit, and which has voiced itself in an impassioned utterance touching the whole problem of national and individual life. . . .

His Relation to Science

I

The stupendous disclosures of modern science, and what they mean when translated into the language of man's ethical and aesthetic nature, have not yet furnished to any considerable extent the inspiration of poems. That all things are alike divine, that this earth is a star in the heavens, that the celestial laws and processes are here underfoot, that size is only relative, that good and bad are only relative, that forces are convertible and interchangeable, that matter is indestructible, that death is the law of life, that man is of animal origin, that the sum of forces is constant, that the universe is a complexus of powers inconceivably subtle and vital, that motion is the law of all things—in fact, that we have got rid of the notions of the absolute, the fixed, the arbitrary, and the notion of origins and of the dualism of the world—to what extent will these and kindred ideas modify art and all aesthetic production? The idea of the divine right of kings and the divine authority of priests is gone; that, in some other time or some other place God was nearer man than now and here—this idea is gone. Indeed, the whole of man's spiritual and religious belief which forms the background of literature has changed—a change as great as if the sky were to change from blue to red or to orange. The light of day is different.

But literature deals with life, and the essential conditions of life, you say, always remain the same. Yes, but the expression of their artistic values is forever changing. If we ask where is the modern imaginative work that is based upon these revelations of science, the work in which they are the blood and vital juices, I answer, *Leaves of Grass,* and no other. The work is the outgrowth of science and modern ideas, just as truly as Dante is the outgrowth of mediaeval ideas and superstitions; and the imagination, the creative spirit, is just as unhampered in Whitman as in Dante or in Shakespeare.

The poet finds the universe just as plastic and ductile, just as obedient to his will, and just as ready to take the impress of his spirit, as did these supreme artists. Science has not hardened it at all. The poet opposes himself to it, and masters it and rises superior. He is not balked or oppressed for a moment. He knows from the start what science can bring him, what it can give, and what it can take away; he knows the universe is not orphaned; he finds more grounds than ever for a paean of thanksgiving and praise. His conviction of the identity of soul and body, matter and spirit, does not shake his faith in immortality in the least. His faith arises not from half views, but from whole views. In him the idea of the soul, of humanity, of identity, easily balanced the idea of the material universe. Man was more than a match for nature. It was all for him, and not for itself. His enormous egotism, or hold upon the central thought or instinct of human worth and import, was an anchor that never gave way.

Science sees man as the ephemeron of an hour, an iridescent bubble on a seething, whirling torrent, an accident in a world of incalculable and clashing forces. Whitman sees him as inevitable and as immortal as God himself. Indeed, he is quite as egotistical and anthropomorphic, though in an entirely different way, as were the old bards and prophets before the advent of science. The whole import of the universe is directed to one man — to you. His anthropomorphism is not a projection of himself into nature, but an absorption of nature in himself. The tables are turned. It is not alien or superhuman beings that he sees and hears in nature, but his own that he finds everywhere. All gods are merged in himself.

Not the least fear, not the least doubt or dismay, in this book. Not one moment's hesitation or losing of the way. And it is not merely an intellectual triumph, but the triumph of soul and personality. The iron knots are not untied; they are melted. Indeed, the poet's contentment and triumph in view of the fullest recognition of all the sin and sorrow of the world, and of all that baffles and dwarfs, is not the least of the remarkable features of the book.

II

Whitman's relation to science is fundamental and vital. It is the soil under his feet. He comes into a world from which all childish fear and illusion has been expelled. He exhibits the religious and poetic faculties perfectly adjusted to a scientific, industrial, democratic age, and exhibits them more fervent and buoyant than ever before. We have gained more than we have lost. The world is anew created by science and democracy, and he pronounces it good with the joy and fervor of the old faith.

⁂   ⁂   ⁂

. . . Let me give a page or two from the "Song of Myself," illustrative of his attitude in this respect:

> I find I incorporate gneiss, coal, long-threaded moss, fruits, grains, esculent
> roots
> And am stuccoed with quadrupeds and birds all over,
> And have distanced what is behind me for good reasons,
> And call anything close again, when I desire it.
>
> In vain the speeding or shyness,
> In vain the plutonic rocks send their old heat against any approach,
> In vain the mastodon retreats beneath its own powdered bones,
> In vain objects stand leagues off, and assume manifold shapes,
> In vain the ocean settling in hollows, and the great monsters lying low,
> In vain the buzzard houses herself with the sky,
> In vain the snake slides through the creepers and logs,
> In vain the elk takes to the inner passes of the woods,
> In vain the razor-billed auk sails far north to Labrador,
> I follow quickly, I ascend to the nest in the fissure of the cliff.

His Relation to Religion

Whitman, as I have elsewhere said, was swayed by two or three great passions, and the chief of these was doubtless his religious passion. He thrilled to the thought of the mystery and destiny of the soul. . . .

⁂   ⁂   ⁂

It is hardly necessary to say that the religion which Whitman celebrates is not any form of ecclesiasticism. It was larger than any creed that has yet been formulated. It was the conviction of the man of science touched and vivified by the emotion of the prophet and poet. As exemplified in his life, its chief elements were faith, hope, charity. Its object was to prepare you to live, not to die, and to "earn for the body and the mind what adheres and goes forward, and is not dropped by death."

The old religion, the religion of our fathers, was founded upon a curse. Sin, repentance, Satan, hell, play important parts. Creation had resulted in a tragedy in which the very elemental forces were implicated. The grand scheme of an infinite Being failed through the machinations of the Devil. Salvation was an escape from wrath to come. The way was through agony and tears. Heaven was only gained by denying earth. The great mass of the human race was doomed to endless perdition. Now there is no trace of this religion in Whitman, and it does not seem to have left any shadow upon him. Ecclesiasticism is dead; he clears the ground for a new growth. To the priests he says, "Your day is done."

He sings a new song; he tastes a new joy in life. The earth is as divine as heaven, and there is no god more sacred than yourself. It is as if the world had been anew created, and Adam had once more been placed in the garden—the world, with all consequences of the fall purged from him.

Hence we have in Whitman the whole human attitude towards the universe, towards God, towards life and death, towards good and evil, completely changed. We have absolute faith and acceptance in place of the fear and repentance of the old creeds; we have death welcomed as joyously as life, we have political and social equality as motifs and impulses, and not merely as sentiments. He would show us the muse of poetry, as impartial, as sweeping in its vision, as modern, as real, as free from the morbid and make-believe as the muse of science. He sees good in all, beauty in all. It is not the old piety, it is the new faith; it is not the old worship, it is the new acceptance; not the old corroding religious pessimism, but the new scientific optimism.

He does not deny, he affirms; he does not criticize, he celebrates; his is not a call to repentance, it is a call to triumph:

I say no man has ever yet been half devout enough,
None has ever yet adored or worship'd half enough,
None has begun to think how divine he himself is, or how certain the future is.

He accepted science absolutely, yet science was not an end in itself: it was not his dwelling; he but entered by it to an area of his dwelling.

The flower of science was religion. Without this religion, or something akin to it—without some spiritual, emotional life that centred about an ideal—Whitman urged that there could be no permanent national or individual development. In the past this ideal was found in the supernatural; for us and the future democratic ages, it must be found in the natural, in the now and the here.

The aristocratic tradition not only largely shaped the literature of the past, it shaped the religion. Man was a culprit, his life a rebellion; his proper attitude toward the unseen powers was that of a subject to his offended sovereign—one of prostration and supplication. Heaven was a select circle reserved for the few—the aristocracy of the pure and just. The religion of a democratic and scientific era, as voiced by Whitman and as exemplified in his life, is of quite another character—not veneration, but joy and triumph; not fear, but love; not self-abasement, but self-exaltation; not sacrifice, but service: in fact, not religion at all in the old sense of the spiritual at war with the natural, the divine with the human, this world a vale of tears, and mundane things but filth and ashes, heaven for the good and hell for the bad; but in the new sense of the divinity of all things, of the equality of gods and men, of the brotherhood of the race, of the identity of the material and the spiritual, of the beneficence of death and the perfection of the universe.

The poet turns his face to earth and not to heaven; he finds the miraculous, the spiritual, in the things about him, and gods and goddesses in the men and women he meets. He effaces the old distinctions; he establishes a sort of universal suffrage in spiritual matters; there are no select circles, no privileged persons. Is this the democracy of religion?—liberty, fraternity, and equality carried out in the spiritual sphere? Death is the right hand of God, and evil plays a necessary part also. Nothing is discriminated against; there are no reprisals or postponements, no dualism or devilism. Everything is in its place; man's life and all the things of his life are well considered.

Carried out in practice, this democratic religion will not beget priests, or churches, or creeds, or rituals, but a life cheerful and full on all sides, helpful, loving, unworldly, tolerant, open-souled, temperate, fearless, free, and contemplating with pleasure, rather than alarm, "the exquisite transition of death."

An Egotistical Chapter

A FEW YEARS AGO the editor of a popular magazine inveigled a good many people, myself among the number, into writing about themselves and their experiences in life. None of us, I imagine, needed very much persuading, for as a rule there is no subject which a man or a woman is more ready or willing to talk about than himself or herself. One's ailments are always a favorite subject; next to that, one's good luck or ill luck in his last undertaking; then one's experiences, one's likes and dislikes; and lastly, self-analysis and criticism. And it has been said that a man "is never so sure to please as when he writes of himself with good faith, and without affectation." Ay, there's the rub; to write of one's self without affectation! A false note of this kind is fatal to the interest and value of the criticism.

In a certain sense, a man of the literary or artistic temperament never portrays or writes of anything but himself; that is, he gives us things as seen through the intimate personal medium which he himself is. All things reflect his line and quality. This is the bane of science, but it is the life of literature. I have probably unwittingly written myself in my books more fully and frankly than I ever can by any direct confession and criticism; but the latter may throw some side light at least, and, on looking over what I wrote for the editor above referred to, I find that portions of it possess a certain interest and value to myself, and therefore I trust may not seem entirely amiss to my reader.

If a man is not born into the environment best suited to him, he, as a rule, casts about him until he finds such environment. My own surroundings and connections have been mainly of the unliterary kind. I was born of and among people who neither read books nor cared for them, and my closest associations since have been with those whose minds have been alien to literature and art. My unliterary environment has doubtless been best suited to me. Probably what little freshness and primal sweetness my books

From *Indoor Studies,* 1889.

contain is owing to this circumstance. Constant intercourse with bookish men and literary circles I think would have dwarfed or killed my literary faculty. This perpetual rubbing of heads together, as in the literary clubs, seems to result in literary sterility. In my own case, at least, what I most needed was what I had—a few books and plenty of real things. I never had any aptitude for scholarly attainments; my verbal or artificial memory, so to speak, was poor, but my mind always had a certain magnetic or adhesive quality for things that were proper to it and that belonged to me.

I early took pleasure in trying to express myself on paper, probably in my sixteenth or seventeenth year. In my reading I was attracted by everything of the essay kind. In the libraries and bookstores I was on the lookout for books of essays. And I wanted the essay to start not in a casual arid inconsequential way, but the first sentence must be a formal enunciation of a principle. I bought the whole of Dr. Johnson's works at a secondhand bookstore in New York, because, on looking into them, I found his essays appeared to be of solid essay-stuff from beginning to end. I passed by Montaigne's Essays at the same time, because they had a personal and gossipy look. Almost my first literary attempts were moral reflections, somewhat in the Johnsonian style. I lived on the *Rambler* and the *Idler* all one year, and tried to produce something of my own in similar form. As a youth I was a philosopher, as a young man I was an Emersonian; as a middle-aged man I am a literary naturalist—but always have I been an essayist.

It was while I was at school, in my nineteenth year, that I saw my first author; and I distinctly remember with what emotion I gazed upon him, and followed him in the twilight, keeping on the other side of the street. He was of little account—a man who had failed as a lawyer, and then had written a history of Poland, which I have never heard of since that time; but to me he was the embodiment of the August spirit of authorship, and I looked upon him with more reverence and enthusiasm than I had ever looked before upon any man. I do not think I could have approached and spoken to him on any consideration. I cannot at this date divine why I should have stood in such worshipful fear and awe of this obscure individual, but I suppose it was the instinctive tribute of a timid and imaginative youth to a power which he was just beginning vaguely to see—the power of letters.

It was at about this time that I first saw my own thoughts in print—a communication of some kind to a little country paper published in an adjoining town. In my twenty-second or twenty-third year, I began to send rude and crude essays to the magazines and to certain New York weekly papers, but they came back again pretty promptly. I wrote on such subjects as

"Revolutions," "A Man and his Times," "Genius," "Individuality." At this period of my life I was much indebted to Whipple—whose style, as it appears in his earlier essays and in the thin volume of lectures published by Ticknor, Reed & Fields about 1853, is, in my judgment, much better than in his later writings. It was never a good style, not at all magnetic or penetrating, but it was clear and direct, and, to my mind at that period, stimulating. Higginson had just begun to publish his polished essays in the *Atlantic,* and I found much help in them also. They were a little cold, but they had the quality which belongs to the work of a man who looks upon literature as a fine art. My mind had already begun to turn to outdoor themes, and Higginson gave me a good send-off in this direction.

But the master-enchanter of this period of my life and of many following years was Emerson. While at school, in my nineteenth year, in my search for essays I had carried to my room one volume of his, but I could do nothing with it. What, indeed, could a Johnsonian youth make of Emerson? A year or so later I again opened one of his books in a Chicago bookstore, and was so taken with the first taste of it that I then and there purchased the three volumes—the *Essays* and the *Miscellanies.* All that summer I fed upon them and steeped myself in them: so that when, a year or two afterwards, I wrote an essay on "Expression" and sent it to the *Atlantic,* it was so Emersonian that the editor thought someone was trying to palm off on him an early essay of Emerson's which he had not seen. Satisfying himself that Emerson had published no such paper, he printed it in the November number of 1860. It had not much merit. I remember this sentence, which may contain some truth aptly put: "Dr. Johnson's periods act like a lever of the third kind: the power applied always exceeds the weight raised."

It was mainly to break the spell of Emerson's influence and to get upon ground of my own that I took to writing upon outdoor themes. I wrote half a dozen or more sketches upon all sorts of open-air subjects, which were published in the New York *Leader.* The woods, the soil, the waters helped to draw out the pungent Emersonian flavor and restore me to my proper atmosphere. But to this day I am aware that a suggestion of Emerson's manner often crops out in my writings. His mind was the firmer, harder substance, and was bound to leave its mark upon my own. But, in any case, my debt to him is great. He helped me to better literary expression, he quickened my perception of the beautiful, he stimulated and fertilized my religious nature. Unless one is naturally more or less both of a religious and of a poetic turn, the writings of such men as Emerson and Carlyle are mainly lost upon him. Two-thirds of the force of these writers, at least, is directed into these channels. It is the quality of their genius, rather than the scope and push of their minds, that endears them to us. They quicken the conscience and stimulate the character as well as correct the taste. They are not the spokesmen of science or of the reason, but of the soul.

About this period I fell in with Thoreau's *Walden,* but I am not conscious of any great debt to Thoreau: I had begun to write upon outdoor themes before his books fell into my hand; but he undoubtedly helped confirm me in my own direction. He was the intellectual child of Emerson, but added a certain crispness and pungency, as of wild roots and herbs, to the urbane philosophy of his great neighbor. But Thoreau had one trait which I always envied him, namely his indifference to human beings. He seems to have been as insensible to people as he was open and hospitable to nature. It probably gave him more pleasure to open his door to a woodchuck than to a man.

Let me confess that I am too conscious of persons—feel them too much, defer to them too much, and try too hard to adapt myself to them. Emerson says, "A great man is coming to dine with me: I do not wish to please him, I wish that he should wish to please me." I should be sure to overdo the matter in trying to please the great man: more than that, his presence would probably take away my appetite for my dinner.

In speaking of the men who have influenced me or to whom I owe the greatest debt, let me finish the list here. I was not born out of time, but in good time. The men I seemed to need most were nearly all my contemporaries, the ideas and influences which address themselves to me the most directly and forcibly have been abundantly current in my time. Hence I owe, or seem to owe, more to contemporary authors than to the men of the past. I have lived in the present time, in the present hour, and have invested myself in the objects nearest at hand. Besides the writers I have mentioned, I am conscious of owing a debt to Whitman, Ruskin, Arnold, Wordsworth, Coleridge, and Tennyson. To Whitman I owe a certain liberalizing influence, as well as a lesson in patriotism which I could have got in the same measure from no other source. Whitman opens the doors, and opens them wide. He pours a flood of human sympathy which sets the whole world afloat. He is a great humanizing power. There is no other personality in literature that gives me such a sense of breadth and magnitude in the purely human and personal qualities. His poems are dominated by a sense of a living, breathing man as no other poems are. This would not recommend them to some readers, but it recommends them to such as I, who value in books perennial human qualities above all things. To put a great personality in poetry is to establish a living fountain of power, where the jaded and exhausted race can refresh and renew itself.

To a man in many ways the opposite of Whitman, who stands for an entirely different, almost antagonistic, order of ideas—to wit, Matthew Arnold—I am indebted for a lesson in clear thinking and clean expression such as I have got from no other. Arnold's style is probably the most lucid, the least embarrassed by anything false or foreign, of that of any writer living. His page is as clear as science and as vital and flexible as poetry. Indeed, he affords a notable instance of the cool, impartial scientific spirit wedded to, or working through, the finest poetic delicacy and sensibility.

I have not been deeply touched or moved by any English poet of this century save Wordsworth. Nearly all other poetry of nature is tame and insincere compared with his. But my poetic sympathies are probably pretty narrow. I cannot, for instance, read Robert Browning, except here and there a poem. The sheer mechanical effort of reading him, of leaping and dodging and turning sharp corners to overtake his meaning, is too much for me. It makes my mental bones ache. It is not that he is so subtle and profound, for he is less in both these respects than Shakespeare, but that he is so abrupt and elliptical and plays such fantastic tricks with syntax. His verse is like a springless wagon on a rough road. He is full of bounce and vigor, but it is of the kind that bruises the flesh and makes one bite his tongue. Swinburne has lilt and flow enough, certainly, and yet I cannot read him. He sickens me from the opposite cause: I am adrift in a sea of melodious words, with never an idea to cling to. There is to me something gruesome and uncanny about Swinburne's poetry, like the clammy and rapidly-growing fungi in nature. . . . Words, words, words! and all struck with the leprosy of alliteration. Such poetry would turn my blood to water. "Wan skies and waste white light,"—are there ever any other skies or any other lights in Swinburne?

But this last is an ill wind which I fear can blow no good to anyone. I have lived long enough to know that my own private likes and dislikes do not always turn out to be the decrees of the Eternal. Some writers confirm one and brace him where he stands; others give him a lift forward. I am not aware that more than two American writers have been of the latter service to me—Emerson and Whitman. Such a spirit as Bryant is confirmatory. I may say the same of Whittier and Longfellow. I owe to these men solace and encouragement, but no new territory.

Still, the influences that shape one's life are often so subtle and remote and of such small beginning that it will not do to be too positive about these matters. At any rate, self-analysis is a sort of back-handed work, and one is lucky if he comes at all near the truth.

As such a paper must of necessity be egotistical, let me not flinch in any part of my task on that account.

What little merit my style has is the result of much study and discipline. I have taught myself always to get down to the quick of my mind at once, and not fumble about amid the husks at the surface. Unless one can give the sense of vitality in his pages, no mere verbal brightness or scholarly attainments will save him. In the best writing, every sentence is filled with the writer's living, breathing quality, just as in the perfected honeycomb every cell is filled with honey. But how much empty comb there is even in the best books! I wish to give an account of a bird, or a flower, or of any open-air scene or incident. My whole effort is to see the thing just as it was. I ask myself, "Exactly how did this thing strike my mind? What was prominent? What was subordinated? I have been accused of romancing at times. But it is not true. I set down the thing exactly as it fell out. People say, "I do not see what you do when I take a walk." But for the most part they do, but the fact as it lies there in nature is crude and raw: it needs to be brought out, to be passed through the heart and mind and presented in appropriate words. This humanizes it and gives it an added charm and significance. This, I take it, is what is meant by idealizing and interpreting nature. We do not add to or falsely color the facts: we disentangle them and invest them with the magic of written words.

To give anything like vitality to one's style, one must divest one's self of any false or accidental or factitious mood or feeling, and get down to his real self, and speak as directly and sincerely as he does about his daily business or affairs, and with as little affectation. One may write from the outside of his mind, as it were, write and write, glibly and learnedly, and make no impression; but when one speaks from real insight and conviction of his own, men are always glad to hear him, whether they agree with him or not. So much writing or speaking is like mere machine-work, as if you turned a crank and the piece or discourse came out. It is not the man's real mind, his real experience. This, he does not know how to get at; it has no connection with his speaking or writing faculty. How rare are real poems—poems that spring from real feeling, a real throb of emotion, and not from a mere surface-itching of the mind for literary expression! The world is full of "rhyming parasites," as Milton called them. The great mass of the poetry of any age is purely artificial, and has no root in real things. It is a kind of masquerading. The stock poetic forms are masks behind which the poetlings

hide their real poverty of thought and feeling. In prose one has no such factitious aids; here he must stand upon his own merits—he has not the cloak
of Milton or Tennyson, or Spenser, to hide in.

It is, of course, the young writer who oftenest fails to speak his real mind,
or to speak from any proper basis of insight and conviction. He is carried
away by a fancy, a love of novelty, or an affectation of originality. The
strange things, the novel things, are seldom true. Look for truth under your
feet. To be original, Carlyle said, is to be sincere. When one is young, how
many discoveries he makes—real mare's-eggs which by and by turn out to
be nothing but field-pumpkins!

Men who, like myself, are deficient in self-assertion, or whose personalities are flexible and yielding, make a poor show in politics or business, but
in certain other fields these defects have their advantages. In action, Renan
says, one is weak by his best qualities—such, I suppose, as tenderness, sympathy, religiousness—and strong by his poorer, or at least his less-attractive
qualities. But in letters the reverse is probably true. How many of us owe
our success in this field to qualities which in a measure disqualified us for an
active career! A late writer upon Carlyle seeks to demonstrate that the "open
secret of his life" was his desire to take a hand in the actual affairs of English
politics; but it is quite certain that the traits and gifts which made him such
a power in literature—namely, his tremendous imagination and his burdened prophetic conscience—would have stood in his way in dealing with
the coarse affairs of this world.

In my own case, what hinders me with the world helps me with impersonal nature. I do not stand in my own light. My will, my personality offer
little resistance: they let the shy, delicate influences pass. I can surrender
myself to nature without effort, but am more or less restrained and self-
conscious in the presence of my fellows. Bird and beast take to me, and I to
them. I can look in the eye of an ugly dog and win him, but with an ugly
man I have less success.

I have unmistakably the feminine idiosyncrasy. Perhaps this is the reason
that my best and most enthusiastic readers appear to be women. In the gen-
esis of all my books, feeling goes a long way before intellection. What I feel
I can express, and only what I feel. If I had run after the birds only to write
about them, I never should have written anything that anyone would have
cared to read. I must write from sympathy and love, or not at all; I have in
no sort of measure the gift of the ready writer who can turn his pen to all
sorts of themes, or the dramatic, creative gift of the great poets, which enables them to get out of themselves and to present vividly and powerfully

things entirely beyond the circle of their own lives and experiences. I go to the woods to enjoy myself, and not to report them; and if I succeed, the expedition may by and by bear fruit at my pen. When a writer of my limited range begins to "make believe," or to go outside of his experience, he betrays himself at once. My success, such as it is, has been in putting my own personal feelings and attractions into subjects of universal interest. I have loved Nature no more than thousands upon thousands of others have, but my aim has been not to tell that love to my reader, but to tell it to the trees and the birds and to let them tell him. I think we all like this indirect way the best. It will not do in literature to compliment Nature and make love to her by open profession and declaration: you must show your love by your deeds or your spirit, and by the sincerity of your service to her.

For my part, I never can interview Nature in the reporter fashion: I must camp and tramp with her to get any good, and what I get I absorb through my emotions rather than consciously gather through my intellect. Hence the act of composition with me is a kind of self-exploration to see what hidden stores my mind holds. If I write upon a favorite author, for instance, I do not give my reader something which lay clearly defined in my mind when I began to write: I give him what I find, after closest scrutiny, in the subconscious regions—a result as unknown to me as to him when I began to write. The same with outdoor subjects. I come gradually to have a feeling that I want to write upon a given theme—rain, for instance, or snow—but what I may have to say upon it is as vague as the background of one of Millet's pictures; my hope is entirely in the feeling or attraction which draws my mind that way; the subject is congenial, it sticks to me; whenever it recurs to me, it awakens as it were a warm personal response.

Perhaps this is the experience of all other writers: their subjects find them, or bring the key to their hidden stores. Great poets, like Milton, however, cast about them and deliberately choose a theme: they are not hampered by their sympathies, nor are they prisoners of their own personalities, like writers who depend upon this pack of unconscious impressions at their back. An experience must lie in my mind a certain time before I can put it on paper—say from three to six months. If there is anything in it, it will ripen and mellow in that time. I rarely take any notes, and I have a very poor memory, but rely upon the affinity of my mind for a certain order of truths or observations. What is mine will stick to me, and what is not will drop off. When I returned from England after a three months' visit in the summer of 1882, I was conscious of having brought back with me a few observations that I might expand into two or three short essays. But when I began to open my pack, the contents grew so upon my hands that it reached many times the measure I at first proposed. Indeed, when I look back over my seven volumes, I wonder where they have all come from. I am like a boy who at the close of the day looks over his string of fish curiously, not one of which did he know of in the morning, and every one of which came to his hand from depths beyond his ken by luck and skill in fishing. I have often caught my fish when I least expected to, and as often my most determined efforts have been entirely unavailing.

It is a wise injunction, "Know thyself," but how hard to fulfill! This unconscious region in one, this unconscious setting of the currents of his life in certain directions—how hard to know that! The influences of his family, his race, his times, his environment are all deeper than the plummet of his self-knowledge can reach. Yet how we admire the ready man, the man who always has complete control of his resources, who can speak the right word instantly! My own wit is always belated. After the crisis is past, the right word or the right sentence is pretty sure to appear and mock me by its tardiness.

There is, no doubt, a great difference in men with reference to this knowledge and command of their own resources. Some writers seem to me to be like those military states wherein every man is numbered, drilled, and equipped, and ready for instant service: the whole male population is a standing army. Then there are men of another type who have no standing army. They are absorbed in mere living, and, when the occasion requires, they have to recruit their ideas slowly from the vague, uncertain masses in the background. Hence they never cut a brilliant figure upon paper, though they may be capable of doing real heartfelt work.

Part Seven
Religion and Philosophy of Life

The Faith of a Naturalist

I

To say that man is as good as God would to most persons seem like blasphemy; but to say that man is as good as Nature would disturb no one. Man is a part of Nature and shares in what we call her imperfections. But what is Nature a part of and what or who is its author? Is it not true that this earth, which is so familiar to us, is as good as yonder morning or evening star and made of the same stuff? That it is just as much in the heavens, just as truly a celestial abode? Venus seems to us like a great jewel in the crown of night or morning. The heavens seem afar off and free from all stains and impurities of the face of the Eternal, but our science reveals no body or place there so suitable for human abode and human happiness as this earth. In fact, this planet is the only desirable heaven of which we have any clue. Innumerable other worlds may exist in the abysses of space which may be the abodes of beings superior or inferior to ourselves. We place our gods afar off so as to dehumanize them, never suspecting that when we do so, we discount their divinity. The more human we are—remembering that to err is human—the nearer God we are. Of course, good and bad are human concepts and are a verdict upon created things as they stand related to us, promoting or hindering our well-being. In the councils of the Eternal there is apparently no such distinction.

Man is not only as good as God; some men are a good deal better from our point of view; they attain a degree of excellence of which there is no hint in nature—moral excellence. It is not until we treat man as a part of nature—as a product of the earth as literally as are the trees—that we can reconcile these contradictions. If we could build up a composite man out of all the peoples of the earth, he would represent fairly well the God in nature.

From *Accepting the Universe*, 1920.

Communing with God is communing with our own hearts, our own best selves, not with something foreign and accidental. Saints and devotees have gone into the wilderness to find God; of course, they took God with them and the silence and detachment enabled them to hear the still small voice of their own souls, as one hears the ticking of his own watch in the stillness of the night. We are not cut off, we are not isolated points; the great currents flow through us, over us, around us and unite us to the whole of nature. Moses saw God in the burning bush, saw him with the eyes of early man whose divinities were clothed in the extraordinary, the fearful, the terrible; we see him in the meanest weed that grows and hear him in the gentle murmur of our own heart's blood. The language of devotion and religious conviction is only the language of soberness and truth written large and aflame with emotion.

Man goes away from home searching for the gods he carries with him always. Man can know and feel and love only man. There is a deal of sound psychology in the new religion called Christian Science—in that part which emphasizes the power of the mind over the body, and the fact that the world is largely what we make it, that evil is only the shadow of good. This helps us to understand the hold it has taken upon such a large number of admirable persons. Disease is a reality, but not in the same sense that health is a reality. Positive and negative electricity are both facts, but positive and negative good belong to a different order. Christian Science will not keep the distemper out of the house if the sewer gas gets in; inoculation will do more to prevent typhoid and diphtheria than "declaring the truth," saying your prayers, or counting your beads. In its therapeutical value, experimental science is the only safe guide in dealing with human corporal ailments.

We need not fear alienation from God. I feed Him when I feed a beggar. I serve Him when I serve my neighbor. I love Him when I love my friend. I praise Him when I praise the wise and good of any race or time. I shun Him when I shun the leper. I forgive Him when I forgive my enemies. I wound Him when I wound a human being. I forget Him when I forget my duty to others. If I am cruel, unjust, resentful, envious or inhospitable toward any man, woman or child, I am guilty of all these things toward God: "Inasmuch as ye have done it unto one of the least of these my brethren, ye have done it unto me."

II

I am persuaded that a man without religion falls short of the proper human ideal. Religion, as I use the term, is a spiritual flowering, and the man who has it not is like a plant that never blooms. The mind that does not open and unfold its religious sensibilities in the sunshine of this infinite and spiritual universe is to be pitied. Men of science do well enough with no other religion than the love of truth, for this is indirectly a love of God. The astronomer, the geologist, the biologist tracing the footsteps of the Creative Energy throughout the universe—what need have they of any formal, patent-right religion? Were not Darwin, Huxley, Tyndall, and Lyall, and all other seekers and verifiers of natural truth among the most truly religious of men? Any of these men would have gone to hell for the truth—not the truth of creeds and rituals, but the truth as it exists in the councils of the Eternal and as it is written in the laws of matter and of life.

For my part I had a thousand times rather have Huxley's religion than that of the bishops who sought to discredit him, or Bruno's than that of the church that burnt him. The religion of a man that has no other aim than his own personal safety, from some real or imaginary future calamity, is of the selfish, ignoble kind.

Amid the decay of creeds, love of nature has high religious value. This has saved many persons in this world—saved them from mammon worship and from the frivolity and insincerity of the crowd. It has made their lives placid and sweet. It has given them an inexhaustible field for inquiry, enjoyment, and the exercise of all their powers—and in the end has not left them soured and dissatisfied. It has made them contented and at home wherever they are in nature—in the house not made with hands. This house is their church, the rocks and the hills are the altars, the creed is written in the leaves of the trees, in the flowers of the field and in the sands of the shore. A new creed every day, new preachers and holy days all the week through. Every walk to the woods is a religious rite, every bath in the stream is a saving ordinance. Communion service is at all hours, and the bread and wine are from the heart and marrow of Mother Earth. There are no heretics in Nature's church; all are believers, all are communicants. The beauty of natural religion is that you have it all the time; you do not have to seek it far off in myths and legends, in catacombs, garbled texts, miracles of dead saints or wine-bibbing friars. It is of today, now and here; it is everywhere. The crickets chirp it, birds sing it, breezes chant it, thunder proclaims it, streams

John Burroughs in field, looking at hawk in sky. Courtesy of Special Collections, Jones Library, Amherst, Massachusetts.

murmur it, the unaffected man lives it. Its incense rises from the plowed fields, it is on the morning breeze, it is in the forest breath and the spray of the wave. The frosts write it in exquisite characters, the dews impearl it, and the rainbow paints it in the sky. It is not an insurance policy underwritten by a bishop or priest; it is not even a faith; it is a love, an enthusiasm, a consecration to natural truth.

The God of sunshine and storms speaks a less-uncertain language than the God of revelation.

Our fathers had their religion, and their fathers had theirs. Their religions lifted them above themselves, healed their wounds; they consoled them for many of the failures and disappointments of this world; they developed character; they tempered the steel in their nature. How childish to us seems the plan of salvation as our fathers found it in the fervid and inspired utterances of Saint Paul! But it saved them, built character, made life serious. It was an heroic creed which has lost credence in our more knowing age. We see how impossible it is, but we do not see the great natural truths upon which it rests.

A man is not saved by the truth of the things he believes but by the truth of his belief—its sincerity, its harmony with his character. The absurdities of the popular religions do not matter; what matters is the lukewarm belief, the empty forms, the shallow conceptions of life and duty. We are prone to think that if the creed is false, the religion is false. Religion is an emotion, an inspiration, a feeling of the Infinite and may have its root in any creed or in no creed. What can be more unphilosophical than the doctrines of the Christian Scientists? Yet Christian Science is a good practical religion. It makes people cheerful, happy, and helpful yes, and helps make them healthy, too. Its keynote is love, and love holds the universe together. Any creed that ennobles character and opens a door or a window upon the deeper meanings of this marvelous universe is good enough to live by, and good enough to die by. The Japanese-Chinese religion of ancestor worship, sincerely and devoutly held, is better than the veneer of much of our fashionable well-dressed religion.

Guided by appearances alone, how surely we should come to look upon the sun as a mere appendage of the earth!—as much so as the moon. How near it seems at sunrise and sunset! We do not realize that this is merely a terrestrial phenomenon, and the sun knows it not.

Viewed from the sun, the earth is a mere speck in the sky, and the amount of light and heat from the sun that is received on the earth is so comparatively small the mind can hardly grasp it. Yet for all practical purposes the sun shines for us alone. Our relation to it could not be any more direct and sustaining if it were created for that purpose. It is the source of all our energy and therefore of our life. Its bounties are universal. The other planets find it is their sun also. It is as special and private to them as to us. We think the sun paints the bow in the sky, but the bow follows from the laws of optics. The sun knows it not.

It is the same with what we call God. His bounty is of the same universal impersonal kind and yet for all practical purposes it exists especially for us. There is no special Providence. Nature sends the rain upon the just and the unjust, upon the sea as upon the land. We are here and find life good because Providence is general and not special. The conditions are not too easy, the struggle has made men of us. The bitter has tempered the sweet. Evil has put us on our guard and keeps us so.

III

That wise old Roman, Marcus Aurelius, said, "Nothing is evil which is according to nature." At that moment he was thinking especially of death, which, when it comes in the course of nature, is not an evil unless life itself is also an evil. After the lamp of life is burned out, death is not an evil, rather is it a good. But premature death, death by accident or disease before a man has done his work or used up his capital of vitality, is an evil. Evil is that which is against our well-being, and good is that which promotes it. We always postulate the existence of life when we speak of good and evil. Excesses in nature are evil to us because they bring destruction and death in their train. They are disharmonies in the scheme of things because they frustrate and bring to naught. The war which Marcus Aurelius was waging when he wrote those passages was an evil in itself though good might come out of it.

Everything in organic nature—trees, grasses, flowers, insects, fishes, mammals—is beset by evil of some kind. The natural order is good because it brought us here and keeps us here, but evil has always dogged our footsteps. Leaf blight is an evil to the tree, smallpox is an evil to man, frost is an evil to insects, flood an evil to fishes.

Moral evil—hatred, envy, greed, lying, cruelty, cheating—is of another order. These vices have no existence below the human sphere. We call them evils because they are disharmonies; they are inimical to the highest standard of human happiness and well-being. They make a man less a man, they work discord and develop needless friction. Sand in the engine of your car and water in the gasoline are evils, and malice, jealousy, and selfishness in your heart are analogous evils.

In our day we read the problem of Nature and God in a new light, the light of science, of emancipated human reason — the old myths mean little to us. We accept Nature as we find it and do not crave the intervention of a God that sits behind and is superior to it. The self-activity of the cosmos suffices. We accept the tornadoes, earthquakes, and world wars and do not lose faith. We arm ourselves against them as best we can. We accept the bounty of the rain, the sunshine, the soil, the changing seasons, the vast amount of nonliving forces and from them equip or teach ourselves to escape, endure, modify, or ward off the destructive and nonhuman forces that beset our way. We draw our strength from the Nature that seems and is so regardless of us; our health and wholeness are its gifts. The biologic ages, with all their carnival of huge and monstrous forms, had our well-being at heart. The evils and dangers that beset our way have been outmatched by the good and the helpful. The deep-sea fish would burst and die if brought to the surface; the surface life would be crushed and killed in the deep sea. Life adapts itself to its environment. Winds, floods, inclement seasons have driven life around the earth; the severer the cold, the thicker the fur; compensations always abound. If Nature is not all-wise and all-merciful from our human point of view, she has placed us in a world where our own wisdom and mercy can be developed; she has sent us to a school in which we learn to see her own shortcomings and imperfections and to profit by them.

The unreasoning, unforeseeing animals suffer more from the accidents of nature — drought, flood, lightning — than man does; but man suffers more from evils of his own making — war, greed, intemperance — but development in both lines goes on, and life is still abundant.

Good and evil are inseparable. We cannot have light without shade, warmth without cold, life without death, or development without struggle. The struggle for life, of which Darwinism makes so much, is only the struggle of the chick to get out of the shell, of the flower to burst its bud, or of the root to penetrate the soil. It is not the struggle of battle and hate. It is for the most part a beneficent struggle with the environment in which the fittest of individual units of a species survive, but in which the strong and the feeble, the great and the small also survive. The lamb survives with the lion, the wren with the eagle, the Eskimo with the European — all manner of small and delicate forms survive with the great and robust. One species of carnivora, of rodents or herbivore, does not, as a rule, exterminate another species. It is true that species prey upon species, cats eat mice, hawks eat smaller birds, and man slays and eats the domestic animals. Probably man alone has exterminated species. But outside of man's doings all the rest belong to Nature's system of checks and balances and bears no analogy to human or in human wars and conquests.

Life struggles with matter, the tree struggles with the wind and with other trees. Man struggles with gravity, cold, wet, heat, and all the forces that hinder him. The tiniest plant that grows has to force its root down into the soil; earlier than that it has to burst its shell or case. The corn struggles to lift itself up after the storm has beaten it down; effort, effort everywhere in the organic world. Says Whitman:

> Urge and urge and urge,
> Always the procreant urge of the world.

IV

Every few years we have an ice storm or a snowstorm that breaks down and disfigures the trees. Some trees suffer much more than others. The storm goes its way; the laws of physical force prevail; the great world of mechanical forces is let loose upon the small world of vital forces; occasionally a tree is so crushed that it never entirely recovers; but after many years the woods and groves have repaired the damages and taken on their usual thrifty appearance. The evil was temporary; the world of trees has suffered no permanent setback. But had the trees been conscious beings, what a deal of suffering they would have experienced! An analogous visitation to human communities brings misery, but in time it too is forgotten and its scars healed. Fire, flood, war, epidemics, earthquakes are such visitations, but the race survives them and reaps good from them.

We say that Nature cares nothing for the individual, but only for the race or the species. The whole organic world is at war with the inorganic, and, as in human wars, the individuals are sacrificed that the army may live; so in the strife and competition of nature the separate units fall that the mass may prosper.

It is probably true that, in the course of the biological history of the earth, whole species have been rendered extinct by parasites or by changing outward conditions. But this has been the exception and not the rule. The chestnut blight now seems to threaten the very existence of this species of tree in this country, but I think the chances are that this fungus will meet with some natural check.

In early summer comes the June drop of apples. The trees start with more fruit than they can carry and, if they are in vigorous health, will drop the surplus. It is a striking illustration of Nature's methods. The tree does its own thinning. But if not at the top of its condition, it fails to do this. It takes health and strength simply to let go; only a living tree drops its fruit or its leaves; only a growing man drops his outgrown opinions.

If we put ourselves in the place of the dropped apples, we must look upon our fate as unmixed evil. If we put ourselves in the place of the tree and of the apples that remain on it, the June drop would appear an unmixed good—finer fruit and a healthier, longer-lived tree results. Nature does not work so much to specific as to universal ends. The individual may go, but the type must remain. The ranks may be decimated, but the army and its cause must triumph. Life in all its forms is a warfare only in the sense that it is a struggle with its outward conditions, in which the strongest force prevails. Small and weak forms prevail because at the feast of life there is a place for the small and weak. But lion against lion, man against man, mouse against mouse, the strongest will be the victor.

Man's effort is to save waste, reduce friction, take short cuts, make smooth the way, seize the advantage, economize time, but the physical forces know none of these things.

Go into the woods and behold the evil the trees have to contend with—typical of the evil we have to contend with—too crowded in places, one tree crushing another by its fall, specimens on every hand whose term of life might be lengthened by a little wise surgery; borers, blight, disease, insect pests, storm, wreckage, thunderbolt scars—evil besetting every tree and leaving its mark. A few—oaks, maples, pines, elms—reach a greater age than the others, but they fail at last and go down in a gale. But after many long years their places are filled. The new generation of trees is feeding upon the accumulations of the old. Evil is turned to good. The destruction of the cyclone, the ravages of fire, the wreckage of the ice storm are all obliterated, and the forest spirit is rank and full again.

There is no exemption from this rule of waste and struggle in this world, nor probably in any other. We have life on these terms. The organic world develops under pressure from within and from without. Rain brings the perils of rain, fire brings the perils of fire, power brings the perils of power.

The great laws go our way, but they will break us or rend us if we fail to keep step with them. Unmixed good is a dream; unmixed happiness is a dream; perfection is a dream; heaven and hell are both dreams of our mixed and struggling lives, the one the outcome of our aspirations for the good, the other the outcome of our fear of evil.

The trees in the woods, the plants in the fields encounter hostile forces the year through; storms crash or overthrow them; visible and invisible enemies prey upon them; yet the fields are clothed in verdure, and hills and plains mantled with superb forests. Nature's haphazard planting and sowing, her wasteful weeding, and man, the same! Heaven or hell waiting by every doorstep, boundless, beginningless, unspeakable, immeasurable, what wonder that we seek a short cut through this wilderness and appeal to the supernatural?

When I look forth upon the world and see how, regardless of man and his well-being, the operations of Nature go on—how the winds and the storms wreck him or destroy him, how the drought or the floods bring to naught his industries, how not the least force in heaven or earth turns aside for him or makes any exception to him; in short, how all forms of life are perpetually ground between the upper and the nether millstones of the contending and clashing natural material forces—I ask myself: "Is there nothing then under the sun or beyond the sun that has a stake in our well-being? Is life purely a game of chance, and is it all luck that we are here in a world so richly endowed to meet all our requirements?" Serene Reason answers: "No, it is not luck as in a lottery. It is the good fortune of the whole. It was inherent in the constitution of the whole, and it continues because of its adaptability; life is here because it fits itself into the scheme of things; it is flexible and compromising." We find the world good to be in because we are adapted to it, and not it to us. The vegetable growth upon the rocks where the sea is forever pounding is a type of life; the waves favor its development. Life takes advantage of turbulence as well as of quietude, of drought as well as of floods, of deserts as well as of marshes, of the sea bottom as well as of the mountain tops. Both animal and vegetable life trim their sails to the forces that beat upon them. The image of the sail is a good one. Life avails itself of the half-contrary winds; it captures and imprisons their push in its sails; by yielding a little it makes headway in the teeth of the gale; it gives and takes; without struggle, without opposition, life would not be life. The sands of the shore do not struggle with the waves, nor the waves with the sands; the buffeting ends where it began. But trees struggle with the wind, fish struggle with the flood, man struggles with his environment; all draw energy from the forces that oppose them. Life gains as it spends; its waste is an investment. Not so with purely material bodies. They are like the clock, they must be perpetually wound from without. A living body is a clock perpetually self-wound from within.

The faith and composure of the naturalist or naturist are proof against the worst that Nature can do. He sees the cosmic forces only; he sees nothing directly mindful of man but man himself; he sees the intelligence and beneficence of the universe flowering in man; he sees life as a mysterious issue of the warring elements; he sees human consciousness and our sense of right and wrong, of truth and justice, as arising in the evolutionary sequence and turning and sitting in judgment upon all things; he sees that there can be no life without pain and death; that there can be no harmony without discord; that opposites go hand in hand; that good and evil are inextricably mingled; that the sun and blue sky are still there behind the clouds unmindful of them; that all is right with the world if we extend our vision deep enough; that the ways of Nature are the ways of God if we do not make God in our own image and make our comfort and well-being the prime object of Nature. Our comfort and well-being are provided for in the constitution of the world, but we may say that they are not guaranteed; they are dependent upon many things, but the chances are upon our side. He that would save his life shall lose it, lose it in forgetting that the universe is not a close corporation or a patented article, and that it exists for other ends than our own. But he who can lose his life in the larger life of the whole shall save it in a deeper, truer sense.

An Outlook upon Life

I HAVE HAD A HAPPY LIFE, and there is not much of it I would change if I could live it over again. I think I was born under happy stars, with a keen sense of wonder, which has never left me, and which only becomes jaded a little now and then, and with no exaggerated notion of my own deserts. I have shared the common lot, and have found it good enough for me. Unlucky is the man who is born with great expectations, and who finds nothing in life quite up to the mark.

One of the best things a man can bring into the world with him is natural humility of spirit. About the next best thing he can bring, and they usually go together, is an appreciative spirit—a loving and susceptible heart. If he is going to be a reformer and stir up things, and slay the dragons, he needs other qualities more. But if he is going to get the most out of life in a worthy way, if he is going to enjoy the grand spectacle of the world from first to last, then he needs his life pitched in a low key and well attuned to common universal things. The strained, the loud, the far-fetched, the extravagant, the frenzied—how lucky we are to escape them, and to be born with dispositions that cause us to flee from them!

I would gladly chant a paean for the world as I find it. What a mighty interesting place to live in! If I had my life to live over again, and had my choice of celestial abodes, I am sure I should take this planet, and I should choose these men and women for my friends and companions. This great rolling sphere with its sky, its stars, its sunrises and sunsets, and with its outlook into infinity—what could be more desirable? What more satisfying? Garlanded by the seasons, embosomed in sidereal influences, thrilling with life, with a heart of fire and a garment of azure seas, and fruitful continents—one might ransack the heavens in vain for a better or a more picturesque abode. As Emerson says, it is "well worth the heart and pith of great men to subdue and enjoy it."

From *Leaf and Tendril,* 1908.

O to share the great, sunny, joyous life of the earth! to be as happy as the birds are! as contented as the cattle on the hills! as the leaves of the trees that dance and rustle in the wind! as the waters that murmur and sparkle to the sea! To be able to see that the sin and sorrow and suffering of the world are a necessary part of the natural course of things, a phase of the law of growth and development that runs through the universe, bitter in its personal application, but illuminating when we look upon life as a whole! Without death and decay, how could life go on? Without what we call sin (which is another name for imperfection) and the struggle consequent upon it, how could our development proceed? I know the waste, the delay, the suffering in the history of the race are appalling, but they only repeat the waste, the delay, the conflict through which the earth itself has gone and is still going, and which finally issues in peace and tranquillity. Look at the grass, the flowers, the sweet serenity and repose of the fields — at what a price it has all been bought, of what a warring of the elements, of what overturnings and pulverizings and shiftings of land and sea, and slow grindings of the mills of the gods of the fore-world it is all the outcome!

The agony of Russia at the present time [1904] — the fire and sword, the snapping of social and political ties, the chaos and destruction that seem imminent — what is it but a geologic upheaval, the price that must be paid for law and order on a permanent basis? We deplore the waste and the suffering, but these things never can be eliminated from the processes of evolution. As individuals we can mitigate them; as races and nations we have to endure them. Waste, pain, delay — the gods smile at these things; so that the game goes on, that is enough. How many thousand centuries of darkness and horror lie between the man of today and the low animal ancestor from which he sprang! Who can picture the sufferings and the defeats! But here we are, and all that terrible past is forgotten — is, as it were, the soil under our feet.

Our fathers were cheered and sustained by a faith in special providences — that there was a Supreme Power that specially interested itself in man and his doings, and that had throughout the course of history turned the adverse currents in his favor. It is certain that all things have worked together for the final good of the race as a whole, otherwise it would have disappeared from the face of the earth. But Providence does things by wholesale. It is like the rain that falls upon the sea and the land equally, upon the just and the unjust, where it is needed and where it is not needed; and the evolution of the life of the globe, including the life of man, has gone on and still goes on, because, in the conflict of forces, the influences that favored life and forwarded it have in the end triumphed.

Our good fortune is not that there are or may be special providences and dispensations, as our fathers believed, by which we may escape this or that evil, but our good fortune is that we have our part and lot in the total scheme of things, that we share in the slow optimistic tendency of the universe, that we have life and health and wholeness on the same terms as the trees, the flowers, the grass, the animals have, and pay the same price for our well-being, in struggle and effort, that they pay. That is our good fortune. There is nothing accidental or exceptional about it. It is not by the favor or disfavor of some god that things go well or ill with us, but it is by the authority of the whole universe, by the consent and cooperation of every force above us and beneath us. The natural forces crush and destroy man when he transgresses them, as they destroy or neutralize one another. He is a part of the system of things, and has a stake in every wind that blows and cloud that sails. It is to his final interest, whether he sees it or not, that water should always do the work of water, and fire do the work of fire, and frost do the work of frost, and gravity do the work of gravity, though they destroy him ("Though he slay me, yet will I trust him"), rather than that they should ever fail. In fact, he has his life and keeps it only because the natural forces and elements are always true to themselves, and are no respecters of persons.

We should not be here blustering around and sitting in judgment upon the ways of the Eternal, had not the ways of the Eternal been without variableness, or shadow of turning. If we or our fortunes go down prematurely beneath the currents, it is because the currents are vital, and do never and can never cease nor turn aside. The weakest force must give way, and the rotten timber break before the sound. We may fancy that there might be a better universe, but we cannot conceive of a better, because our minds are the outcome of things as they are, and all our ideas of value are based upon the lessons we learn in this world.

Nature is as regardless of a planet or a sun as of a bubble upon the river, has one no more at heart than the other. How many suns have gone out? How many planets have perished? If the earth should collide with some heavenly body today and all its life be extinguished, would it not be just like spendthrift Nature? She has infinite worlds left, and out of old she makes new. You cannot lose or destroy heat or force, nor add to them, though you seem to do so. Nature wins in every game because she bets on both sides. If her suns or systems fail, it is, after all, her laws that succeed. A burnt-out sun vindicates the constancy of her forces.

As individuals we suffer defeat, injustice, pain, sorrow, premature death; multitudes perish to fertilize the soil that is to grow the bread of other multitudes; thousands but make a bridge of their dead bodies over which other thousands are to pass safely to some land of promise. The feeble, the idiotic, the deformed seem to suffer injustice at the hands of their maker; there is no redress, no court of appeal for them; the verdict of natural law cannot be reversed. When the current of life shrinks in its channel, there are causes for it, and if these causes ceased to operate, the universe would go to pieces; but the individual whose measure, by reason of these causes, is only half-full pays the price of the sins or the shortcomings of others; his misfortune but vindicates the law upon which our lives are all strung as beads upon a thread.

In an orchard of apple trees some of the fruit is wormy, some scabbed, some dwarfed, from one cause and another; but Nature approves of the worm, and of the fungus that makes the scab, and of the aphid that makes the dwarf, just as sincerely as she approves of the perfect fruit. She holds the stakes of both sides; she wins, whoever loses. An insect stings a leaf or a stem, and instantly all the forces and fluids that were building the leaf turn to building a home for the young of the insect; the leaf is forgotten, and only the needs of the insect remembered, and we thus have the oak gall and the hickory gall and other like abnormalities. The cancer that is slowly eating a man up—it too is the result of a vital process just as much as is the life it is destroying. Contagion, infection, pestilence illustrate the laws of life. One thing devours or destroys another—the parasite destroys its host, the rust destroys the wheat or the oats, the vermin destroy the poultry, and so forth; still the game of life goes on, and the best wins, if not today, then tomorrow, or in ten thousand years. In the meantime, struggle, pain, defeat, death come in; we suffer, we sorrow, we appeal to the gods. But the gods smile and keep aloof, and the world goes blundering on because there are no other conditions of progress. Evil follows good as its shadow; it is inseparable from the constitution of things. It shades the picture, it affords the contrast, it gives the impetus. The good, the better, the best—these are defined to us, and made to entice us by their opposites. We never fully attain them because our standards rise as we rise; what satisfied us yesterday will not satisfy us to-day. Peace, satisfaction, true repose, come only through effort, and then not for long. I love to recall Whitman's words, and to think how true they are both for nations and for individuals:

> Now understand me well—
> It is provided in the essence of things, that from any fruition of
> success, no matter what, shall come forth something to
> make a greater struggle necessary.

II

Life means such different things to different men and to different generations of men; its values shift from age to age and from country to country. Think what it meant to our Puritan forefathers, the early settlers of New England—freedom of religious opinion, and to worship God in their own way. This was the paramount interest and value of life. To secure this, they were ready to make any sacrifice—friends, home, property, country—and to brave hardship and dangers to the end of their lives. In those days the religious idea pressed heavily upon the minds of men, and the main concern of life related to the other world. We in our time can hardly realize the absolute tyranny of religious prepossessions that the minds of our fathers were under, and that the minds of men were under through all the Middle Ages.

Huxley in his old age said: "It is a great many years since at the outset of my career I had to think seriously what life had to offer that was worth having. I came to the conclusion that the chief good for me was freedom to learn, think, and say what I pleased, when I pleased." This was the old Puritan spirit cropping out again, in quite a different field, and concerned with the truth as it is related to this world, quite irrespective of its possible bearing upon the next.

The value of life to Huxley lay in the opportunity to give free play to that truth-loving mind of his, no matter where the quest led him. If it led him into battle, as it was bound to do, so much the better. He was "ever a fighter." The love of Truth was his paramount passion, but he loved her all the more if he saw her life jeopardized and he could make a gallant charge for her rescue.

To have a mind eager to know the great truths and broad enough to take them in, and not get lost in the maze of apparent contradictions, is undoubtedly the highest good. This, I take it, is what our fathers meant in their way by saying the chief end of man was to serve God and glorify him forever. This formula is not suited to the temper of the modern scientific mind because of the theological savor that clings to it. Theological values have shrunken enormously in our time; but let the modern mind express the idea in its own terms, and it fully agrees. To love the Truth and possess it forever is the supreme good.

Of course, Pilate's question of old comes up, What is truth? since one man's truth may be another man's falsehood. But not in the scientific realm, in the realm of verifiable objective truth. What is one man's truth here must be all men's truth. What is one man's truth in the business affairs of life in trade, in banking, in mechanics, in agriculture, in law—must be all men's truth. It would seem as if what is one man's truth in so vital a matter as religion ought to be all men's truth. But it is not. Religion is such an intensely personal and subjective matter that no two men stand at just the same angle with reference to any one proposition, at least to the evidence of the truth of that proposition. The question of the soul's immortality seems such a vital question to some—while others are quite indifferent to it. One man says, I must have proof. I cannot rest in the idea that death ends all. Another says, What matters it? I am not sure I want endless existence. Ingersoll felt this way. Then if death does end all, we shall not lie in our graves lamenting our fate. If it does not, so much the better.

But is any form of religious belief such a vital matter after all? What noble and beautiful lives have been lived by people of just opposite religious creeds. A man's creed, in our day at least, seems to affect his life little more than the clothes he wears. The church has lost its power, its promises have lost their lure, its threats have lost their terror. It is a question why church attendance has so fallen off. In earlier times people attended church from a sense of duty; now the masses go only when there is a promise of pleasure, and that is less and less often.

Errors of religious belief are not serious. If they were, chaos would have come long ago. Each age repudiates or modifies the creed of the preceding, trims it or renews it as a man trims his orchard, lopping off the dead branches, or grafting new ones on, or resetting it entirely. All denominations are grafting on more liberal and more charitable views. The stock of religious ideas is undoubtedly improving—less personal, perhaps, but more broadly intellectual—generalizations from more universal facts.

In morality, what is one man's truth ought to be all men's truth, because morality is a matter of conduct toward our fellows. We may fail to keep our promises to our gods and nothing comes of it, but if we forget our promissory notes, something does come of it, and, as like as not, that something takes the form of the sheriff.

The scientific mind, like Huxley's, looks with amazement upon the credulity of the theological mind, upon its low standard of evidence.

There are currents and currents in life. A river is one kind of current, the Gulf Stream is another. The currents in the affairs of men are more like the latter—obscure in their origin, vague and shifting in their boundaries, and mysterious in their endings, and the result of large cosmic forces. There are movements in the history of men's minds that are local and temporary, like that, say, of the Crusaders, or of Witchcraft, and there are others that are like ocean currents, a trend of the universal mind. The rise and growth of rationalism seems of this kind, the scientific spirit, the desire to prove all things, and to hold fast to that which is good. It is the conditions of proof that have become strenuous and exacting. The standard of the good has not gone up so much as the standard of evidence. We prove a thing now not by an appeal to a text of some book, or to any ecclesiastical court, but by an appeal to reason. An appeal to conscience is not conclusive, because conscience is more or less the creature of the hour, or of custom, or of training, but reason emancipates us from all false or secondary considerations, and enables us to see the thing as it is, in and of itself.

III

I have drifted into deeper waters than I intended to when I set out. I meant to have kept nearer the shore. I have had, I say, a happy life. When I was a young man (twenty-five), I wrote a little poem called "Waiting," which has had quite a history, and the burden of which is, "My own shall come to me." What my constitution demands, the friends, the helps, the fulfillments, the opportunities, I shall find somewhere, some time. It was a statement of the old doctrine of the elective affinities. Those who are born to strife and contention find strife and contention ready at their hand; those who are born for gentleness and love find gentleness and love drawn to them. The naturally suspicious and distrustful find the world in conspiracy against them; the unkind, the hard-hearted, see themselves in their fellows about them. The tone in which we speak to the world, the world speaks to us. Give your best and you will get the best in return. Give in heaping measure and in heaping measure it shall be returned. We all get our due sooner or later, in one form or another. "Be not weary in well doing"; the reward will surely come, if not in worldly goods, then in inward satisfaction, grace of spirit, peace of mind.

All the best things of my life have come to me unsought, but I hope not unearned. That would contradict the principle of equity I have been illustrating. A man does not, in the long run, get wages he has not earned. What I mean is that most of the good things of my life—friends, travel, opportunity—have been unexpected. I do not feel that fortune has driven sharp bargains with me. I am not a disappointed man. Blessed is he who expects little, but works as if he expected much. Sufficient unto the day is the good thereof. I have invested myself in the present moment, in the things near at hand, in the things that all may have on equal terms. If one sets one's heart on the exceptional, the far-off—on riches, on fame, on power—the chances are he will be disappointed; he will waste his time seeking a short cut to these things. There is no short cut. For anything worth having one must pay the price, and the price is always work, patience, love, self-sacrifice—no paper currency, no promises to pay, but the gold of real service.

I am not decrying ambition, the aiming high; only there is no use aiming unless you are loaded, and it is the loading, and the kind of material to be used, that one is first to be solicitous about.

"Serene I fold my hands and wait"; but if I have waited one day, I have hustled the next. If I have had faith that my own would come to me, I have tried to make sure that it was my own, and not that of another. Waiting with me has been mainly a cheerful acquiescence in the order of the universe as I found it—a faith in the essential veracity of things. I have waited for the sun to rise and for the seasons to come; I have waited for a chance to put in my oar. Which way do the currents of my being set? What do I love that is worthy and of good report? I will extend myself in this direction; I will annex this territory. I will not wait to see if this or that pays, if this or that notion draws the multitude. I will wait only till I can see my way clearly. In the meantime I will be clearing my eyes and training them to know the real values of life when they see them.

Waiting for someone else to do your work, for what you have not earned to come to you, is to murder time. Waiting for something to turn up is equally poor policy, unless you have already set the currents going that will cause a particular something to turn up. The farmer waits for his harvest after he has sown the seed. The sailor waits for a breeze after he has spread his sail. Much of life is taken up in waiting—fruitful waiting.

I never have sought wealth; I have been too much absorbed in enjoying the world about me. I had no talent for business anyhow—for the cutthroat competition that modern business for the most part is—and probably could not have attained wealth had I desired it. I dare not aver that I had really rather be cheated than to cheat, but I am quite sure I could never knowingly overreach a man, and what chance of success could such a tenderfoot have in the conscienceless struggle for money that goes on in the business world? I am a fairly successful farmer and fruit-grower. I love the soil, I love to see the crops grow and mature, but the marketing of them, the turning of them into money, grinds my soul because of the sense of strife and competition that pervades the air of the market-place. If one could afford to give one's fruit away, after he had grown it to perfection, to people who would be sure to appreciate it, that would be worthwhile, and would leave no wounds. But that is what I have in a sense done with my intellectual products. I have not written one book for money (yes, one, and that was a failure); I have written them for love, and the modest sum they have brought me has left no sting.

I look upon this craze for wealth that possesses nearly all classes in our time as one of the most lamentable spectacles the world has ever seen. The old prayer, "Give me neither poverty nor riches," is the only sane one. The grand mistake we make is in supposing that because a little money is a good thing, unlimited means is the sum of all good, or that our happiness will keep pace with the increase of our possessions. But such is not the case, because the number of things we can really make our own is limited. We cannot drink the ocean be we ever so thirsty. A cup of water from the spring is all we need. A friend of mine once said that if he outlived his wife, he should put upon her tombstone, "Died of Things"—killed by the multitude of her possessions. The number of people who are thus killed is no doubt very great. When Thoreau found that the specimens and curiosities that had accumulated upon his mantel-piece needed dusting, he pitched them out of the window.

The massing of a great fortune is a perilous enterprise. The giving away of a great fortune is equally a perilous enterprise, not to the man who gives it—it ought to be salutary to him—but to his beneficiaries.

Very many of the great fortunes of our time have been accumulated by a process like that of turning all the streams into your private reservoir: they have caused a great many people somewhere to be short of water, and have taken away the power of many busy, peaceful wheels. The ideal condition is an even distribution of wealth. When you try to give away your monstrous fortune, to open your dam, then danger begins, because you cannot return the waters to their natural channels. You must make new channels, and you may do more harm than good. It never can go now where it would have gone. The wealth is in a measure redistributed, without enriching those from whom it originally came. Few millionaires could face the questions: Have you rendered a service to your fellows in proportion to your wealth? Have you earned your fortune, or have you grabbed it? Is it an addition to the wealth of the world, or a subtraction from the wealth which others have earned? The wealth that comes to a man through his efforts in furthering the work of the world and promoting the good of all is the only worthy wealth.

Beyond the point of a moderate competency, wealth is a burden. A man may possess a competency; great wealth possesses him. He is the victim. It fills him with unrest; it destroys or perverts his natural relations to his fellows; it corrupts his simplicity; it thrusts the false values of life before him; it gives him power which it is dangerous to exercise; it leads to self-indulgence; it hardens the heart; it fosters a false pride. To give it away is perilous; to keep it is to invite care and vexation of spirit. For a rich man to lead the simple life is about as hard as for a camel to go through the needle's eye. How many things stand between him and the simple open air of our common humanity! Marcus Aurelius thought a man might be happy even in a palace; but it takes a Marcus Aurelius — a man whose simplicity of character is incorruptible — to be so. Yet I have no disposition to rail at wealth as such, though the penalties and dangers that attend it are very obvious. I never expect to see it go out of fashion. Its unequal distribution in all times, no doubt, results from natural causes.

Sooner or later things find their proper level, and the proper level of some things is on top. In the jostle and strife of this world the strong men, the master minds, are bound to be on top. This is inevitable; the very laws of matter are on their side.

Not socialism, or any other "ism," can permanently equalize the fortunes of men. The strong will dominate, the weak must succumb. "For whosoever hath, to him shall be given, and he shall have more abundance: but whosoever hath not, from him shall be taken away even that he hath." Power draws power; inefficiency loses even that which it hath. To abolish poverty, to abolish wealth, we must first abolish the natural inequality among mankind. It is as if some men had longer arms than others and could reach the fruit on the tree of opportunity beyond the grasp of their competitors. Shall we cut off their arms? No, we can only shame them out of making hogs of themselves and of laying up greater stores than they can possibly use. In our day and country, the golden fruit on the tree has been so abundant that the long-armed men have degenerated into wealth-maniacs, and have resorted to all manner of unfair means; they have trampled down the shorter-armed men, and gained an advantage on their prostrate bodies. That is where the injustice comes in. Some of our monstrous trusts and combines, for instance, have killed competition by foul and underhanded means; they have crowded or thrust their competitors entirely away from the tree, or else have mounted up on their shoulders. They have resorted to the methods of the robber and assassin.

I am bound to praise the simple life, because I have lived it and found it good. When I depart from it, evil results follow. I love a small house, plain clothes, simple living. Many persons know the luxury of a skin bath—a plunge in the pool or the wave unhampered by clothing. That is the simple life—direct and immediate contact with things, life with the false wrappings torn away—the fine house, the fine equipage, the expensive habits, all cut off. How free one feels, how good the elements taste, how close one gets to them, how they fit one's body and one's soul! To see the fire that warms you, or better yet, to cut the wood that feeds the fire that warms you; to see the spring where the water bubbles up that slakes your thirst, and to dip your pail into it; to see the beams that are the stay of your four walls, and the timbers that uphold the roof that shelters you; to be in direct and personal contact with the sources of your material life; to want no extras, no shields; to find the universal elements enough; to find the air and the water exhilarating; to be refreshed by a morning walk or an evening saunter; to find a quest of wild berries more satisfying than a gift of tropic fruit; to be thrilled by the stars at night; to be elated over a bird's nest, or over a wild-flower in spring—these are some of the rewards of the simple life.

Part Eight

Autobiography

Wild Life about My Cabin

FRIENDS HAVE OFTEN ASKED me why I turned my back upon the Hudson and retreated into the wilderness. Well, I do not call it a retreat; I call it a withdrawal, a retirement, the taking up of a new position to renew the attack, it may be, more vigorously than ever. It is not always easy to give reasons. There are reasons within reasons, and often no reasons at all that we are aware of.

To a countryman like myself, not born to a great river or an extensive water-view, these things, I think, grow wearisome after a time. He becomes surfeited with a beauty that is alien to him. He longs for something more homely, private, and secluded. Scenery may be too fine or too grand and imposing for one's daily and hourly view. It tires after a while. It demands a mood that comes to you only at intervals. Hence it is never wise to build your house on the most ambitious spot in the landscape. Rather seek out a more humble and secluded nook or corner, which you can fill and warm with your domestic and home instincts and affections. In some things the half is often more satisfying than the whole—a glimpse of the Hudson River between hills or through openings in the trees wears better with me than a long expanse of it constantly spread out before me. One day I had an errand to a farmhouse nestled in a little valley or basin at the foot of a mountain. The earth put out protecting arms all about it—a low hill with an orchard on one side, a sloping pasture on another, and the mountain, with the skirts of its mantling forests, close at hand in the rear. How my heart warmed toward it! I had been so long perched high upon the banks of a great river, in sight of all the world, exposed to every wind that blows, with a horizon-line that sweeps over half a county, that, quite unconsciously to myself, I was pining for a nook to sit down in. I was hungry for the private and the circumscribed; I knew it when I saw this sheltered farmstead. I

From *Far and Near*, 1904.

had long been restless and dissatisfied—a vague kind of homesickness; now I knew the remedy. Hence when, not long afterward, I was offered a tract of wild land, barely a mile from home, that contained a secluded nook and a few acres of level, fertile land shut off from the vain and noisy world of railroads, steamboats, and yachts by a wooded, precipitous mountain, I quickly closed the bargain, and built me a rustic house there, which I call "Slabsides," because its outer walls are covered with slabs. I might have given it a prettier name, but not one more fit, or more in keeping with the mood that brought me thither.

A slab is the first cut from the log, and the bark goes with it. It is like the first cut from the loaf, which we call the crust, and which the children reject, but which we older ones often prefer. I wanted to take a fresh cut of life—something that had the bark on, or, if you please, that was like a well-browned and hardened crust. After three years I am satisfied with the experiment. Life has a different flavor here. It is reduced to simpler terms; its complex equations all disappear. The exact value of x may still elude me, but I can press it hard; I have shorn it of many of its disguises and entanglements.

When I went into the woods, the robins went with me, or rather they followed close. As soon as a space of ground was cleared and the garden planted, they were on hand to pick up the worms and insects, and to superintend the planting of the cherry-trees: three pairs the first summer, and more than double that number the second. In the third, their early morning chorus was almost as marked a feature as it is about the old farm homesteads. The robin is no hermit: he likes company; he likes the busy scenes of the farm and the village; he likes to carol to listening ears, and to build his nest as near your dwelling as he can. Only at rare intervals do I find a real sylvan robin, one that nests in the woods, usually by still waters, remote from human habitation. In such places his morning and evening carol is a welcome surprise to the fisherman or camper-out. It is like a dooryard flower found blooming in the wilderness.

With the robins came the song sparrows and social sparrows, or chippies, also. The latter nested in the bushes near my cabin, and the song sparrows in the bank above the ditch that drains my land. I notice that Chippy finds just as many horsehairs to weave into her nest here in my horseless domain as she does when she builds in the open country. Her partiality for the long hairs from the manes and tails of horses and cattle is so great that she is often known as the hair-bird. What would she do in a country where there were neither cows nor horses? Yet these hairs are not good nesting-material. They are slippery, refractory things, and occasionally cause a tragedy in the nest by getting looped around the legs or the neck of the young or of the parent bird. They probably give a smooth finish to the interior, dear to the heart of Chippy.

The first year of my cabin life a pair of robins attempted to build a nest upon the round timber that forms the plate under my porch roof. But it was a poor place to build in. It took nearly a week's time and caused the birds a great waste of labor to find this out. The coarse material they brought for the foundation would not bed well upon the rounded surface of the timber, and every vagrant breeze that came along swept it off. My porch was kept littered with twigs and weed-stalks for days, till finally the birds abandoned the undertaking. The next season a wiser or more experienced pair made the attempt again, and succeeded. They placed the nest against the rafter where it joins the plate; they used mud from the start to level up with and to hold the first twigs and straws, and had soon completed a firm, shapely structure. When the young were about ready to fly, it was interesting to note that there was apparently an older and a younger, as in most families. One bird was more advanced than any of the others. Had the parent birds intentionally stimulated it with extra quantities of food, so as to be able to launch their offspring into the world one at a time? At any rate, one of the birds was ready to leave the nest a day and a half before any of the others. I happened to be looking at it when the first impulse to get outside the nest seemed to seize it. Its parents were encouraging it with calls and assurances from some rocks a few yards away. It answered their calls in vigorous, strident tones. Then it climbed over the edge of the nest upon the plate, took a few steps forward, then a few more, till it was a yard from the nest and near the end of the timber, and could look off into free space. Its parents apparently shouted, "Come on!" But its courage was not quite equal to the leap; it looked around, and seeing how far it was from home, scampered back to the nest, and climbed into it like a frightened child. It had made its first journey into the world, but the home tie had brought it quickly back.

A few hours afterward it journeyed to the end of the plate again, and then turned and rushed back. The third time its heart was braver, its wings stronger, and leaping into the air with a shout, it flew easily to some rocks a dozen or more yards away. Each of the young in succession, at intervals of nearly a day, left the nest in this manner. There would be the first journey of a few feet along the plate, the first sudden panic at being so far from home, the rush back, a second and perhaps a third attempt, and then the irrevocable leap into the air, and a clamorous flight to a near by bush or rock. Young birds never go back when they have once taken flight. The first free flap of the wing severs forever the ties that bind them to home.

The chickadees we have always with us. They are like the evergreens among the trees and plants. Winter has no terrors for them. They are properly wood-birds, but the groves and orchards know them also. Did they come near my cabin for better protection, or did they chance to find a little cavity in a tree there that suited them? Branch-builders and ground-builders are easily accommodated, but the chickadee must find a cavity, and a small one at that. The woodpeckers make a cavity when a suitable trunk or branch is found, but the chickadee, with its small, sharp beak, rarely does so; it usually smooths and deepens one already formed. This a pair did a few yards from my cabin. The opening was into the heart of a little sassafras, about four feet from the ground. Day after day the birds took turns in deepening and enlarging the cavity: a soft, gentle hammering for a few moments in the heart of the little tree, and then the appearance of the worker at the opening, with the chips in his, or her, beak. They changed off every little while, one working while the other gathered food. Absolute equality of the sexes, both in plumage and in duties, seems to prevail among these birds, as among a few other species. During the preparations for housekeeping the birds were hourly seen and heard, but as soon as the first egg was laid, all this was changed. They suddenly became very shy and quiet. Had it not been for the new egg that was added each day, one would have concluded that they had abandoned the place. There was a precious secret now that must be well kept. After incubation began, it was only by watching that I could get a glimpse of one of the birds as it came quickly to feed or to relieve the other.

One day a lot of Vassar girls came to visit me, and I led them out to the little sassafras to see the chickadees' nest. The sitting bird kept her place as head after head, with its nodding plumes and millinery, appeared above the opening to her chamber, and a pair of inquisitive eyes peered down upon her. But I saw that she was getting ready to play her little trick to frighten them away. Presently I heard a faint explosion at the bottom of the cavity, when the peeping girl jerked her head quickly back, with the exclamation, "Why, it spit at me!" The trick of the bird on such occasions is apparently to draw in its breath till its form perceptibly swells, and then give forth a quick, explosive sound like an escaping jet of steam. One involuntarily

John Burroughs inside Slabsides. Courtesy of the American Museum of
Natural History.

closes his eyes and jerks back his head. The girls, to their great amusement, provoked the bird into this pretty outburst of her impatience two or three times. But as the ruse failed of its effect, the bird did not keep it up, but let the laughing faces gaze till they were satisfied.

There is only one other bird known to me that resorts to the same trick to scare away intruders, and that is the great crested flycatcher. As your head appears before the entrance to the cavity in which the mother bird is sitting, a sudden burst of escaping steam seems directed at your face, and your backward movement leaves the way open for the bird to escape, which she quickly does.

The chickadee is a prolific bird, laying from six to eight eggs, and it seems to have few natural enemies. I think it is seldom molested by squirrels or black snakes or weasels or crows or owls. The entrance to the nest is usually so small that none of these creatures can come at them. Yet the number of chickadees in any given territory seems small. What keeps them in check? Probably the rigors of winter and a limited food-supply. The ant-eaters, fruit-eaters, and seed-eaters mostly migrate. Our all-the-year-round birds, like the chickadees, woodpeckers, jays, and nuthatches, live mostly on nuts and the eggs and larvae of tree-insects, and hence their larder is a restricted one; hence, also, these birds rear only one brood in a season. A hairy wood-pecker passed the winter in the woods near me by subsisting on a certain small white grub which he found in the bark of some dead hemlock-trees. He "worked" these trees—four of them—as the slang is, "for all they were worth." The grub was under the outer shell of bark—and the bird literally skinned the trees in getting at his favorite morsel. He worked from the top downward, hammering or prying off this shell, and leaving the trunk of the tree with a red, denuded look. Bushels of the fragments of the bark covered the ground at the foot of the tree in spring, and the trunk looked as if it had been flayed—as it had.

The big chimney of my cabin of course attracted the chimney swifts, and as it was not used in summer, two pairs built their nests in it, and we had the muffled thunder of their wings at all hours of the day and night. One night, when one of the broods was nearly fledged, the nest that held them fell down into the fireplace. Such a din of screeching and chattering as they instantly set up! Neither my dog nor I could sleep. They yelled in chorus, stopping at the end of every half-minute as if upon signal. Now they were all screeching at the top of their voices, then a sudden, dead silence ensued. Then the din began again, to terminate at the instant as before. If they had been long practicing together, they could not have succeeded better. I never before heard the cry of birds so accurately timed. After a while I got up and put them back up the chimney, and stopped up the throat of the flue with newspapers. The next day one of the parent birds, in bringing food to them, came down the chimney with such force that it passed through the papers and brought up in the fireplace. On capturing it I saw that its throat was distended with food as a chipmunk's cheek with corn, or a boy's pocket with chestnuts. I opened its mandibles, when it ejected a wad of insects as large as a bean. Most of them were much macerated, but there were two house-flies yet alive and but little the worse for their close confinement. They stretched themselves, and walked about upon my hand, enjoying a breath of fresh air once more. It was nearly two hours before the swift again ventured into the chimney with food.

These birds do not perch, nor alight upon buildings or the ground. They are apparently upon the wing all day. They outride the storms. I have in my mind a cheering picture of three of them I saw facing a heavy thunder-shower one afternoon. The wind was blowing a gale, the clouds were rolling in black, portentous billows out of the west, the peals of thunder were shaking the heavens, and the big drops were just beginning to come down, when, on looking up, I saw three swifts high in air, working their way slowly, straight into the teeth of the storm. They were not hurried or disturbed; they held themselves firmly and steadily; indeed, they were fairly at anchor in the air till the rage of the elements should have subsided. I do not know that any other of our land birds outride the storms in this way.

The phoebe-birds also soon found me out in my retreat, and a pair of them deliberated a long while about building on a little shelf in one of my gables. But, much to my regret, they finally decided in favor of a niche in the face of a ledge of rocks not far from my spring. The place was well screened by bushes and well guarded against the approach of snakes or four-footed prowlers, and the birds prospered well and reared two broods. They have now occupied the same nest three years in succession. This is unusual: Phoebe prefers a new nest each season, but in this case there is no room for another, and, the site being a choice one, she slightly repairs and refurnishes her nest each spring, leaving the new houses for her more ambitious neighbors.

Of wood-warblers my territory affords many specimens. One spring a solitary Nashville warbler lingered near my cabin for a week. I heard his bright, ringing song at all hours of the day. The next spring there were two or more, and they nested in my pea-bushes. The black-and-white creeping warblers are perhaps the most abundant. A pair of them built a nest in a steep moss- and lichen-covered hillside, beside a high gray rock. Our path to Julian's Rock led just above it. It was an ideal spot and an ideal nest, but it came to grief. Some small creature sucked the eggs. On removing the nest I found an earth-stained egg beneath it. Evidently the egg had ripened before its receptacle was ready, and the mother, for good luck, had placed it in the foundation.

One day, as I sat at my table writing, I had a call from the worm-eating warbler. It came into the open door, flitted about inquisitively, and then, startled by the apparition at the table, dashed against the window-pane and fell down stunned. I picked it up, and it lay with closed eyes panting in my hand. I carried it into the open air. In a moment or two it opened its eyes, looked about, and then closed them and fell to panting again. Soon it looked up at me once more and about the room, and seemed to say: "Where am I? What has happened to me?" Presently the panting ceased, the bird's breathing became more normal, it gradually got its bearings, and, at a motion of my hand, darted away. This is an abundant warbler in my vicinity, and nested this year near by. I have discovered that it has an air-song—the song of ecstasy—like that of the oven-bird. I had long suspected it, as I frequently heard a fine burst of melody that was new to me. One June day I was fortunate enough to see the bird delivering its song in the air above the low trees. As with the oven-bird, its favorite hour is the early twilight, though I hear the song occasionally at other hours. The bird darts upward fifty feet or more, about half the height that the oven-bird attains, and gives forth a series of rapid, ringing musical notes, which quickly glide into the long, sparrowlike trill that forms its ordinary workaday song. While this part is being uttered, the singer is on its downward flight into the woods. The flight-song of the oven-bird is louder and more striking, and is not so shy and furtive a performance. The latter I hear many times every June twilight, and I frequently see the singer reach his climax a hundred feet or more in the air, and then mark his arrowlike flight downward. I have heard this song also in the middle of the night near my cabin. At such times it stands out on the stillness like a bursting rocket on the background of the night.

One or two mornings in April, at a very early hour, I am quite sure to hear the hermit thrush singing in the bushes near my window. How quickly I am transported to the Delectable Mountains and to the mossy solitudes of the northern woods! The winter wren also pauses briefly in his northern journey, and surprises and delights my ear with his sudden lyrical burst of melody. Such a dapper, fidgety, gesticulating, bobbing-up-and-down-and-out-and-in little bird, and yet full of such sweet, wild melody! To get him at his best, one needs to hear him in a dim, northern hemlock wood, where his voice reverberates as in a great hall; just as one should hear the veery in a beech and birch wood, beside a purling trout brook, when the evening shades are falling. It then becomes to you the voice of some particular spirit of the place and the hour. The veery does not inhabit the woods immediately about my cabin, but in the summer twilight he frequently comes up from the valley below and sings along the borders of my territory. How welcome his simple flutelike strain! The wood thrush is the leading chorister in the woods about me. He does not voice the wildness, but seems to give a touch of something half-rural, half-urban, such is the power of association in bird-songs. In the evening twilight I often sit on the highest point of the rocky rim of the great granite bowl that holds my three acres of prairie soil, and see the shadows deepen, and listen to the bird voices that rise up from the forest below me. The songs of many wood thrushes make a sort of golden warp in the texture of sounds that is being woven about me. Now the flight-song of the oven-bird holds the ear, then the fainter one of the worm-eating warbler lures it. The carol of the robin, the vesper hymn of the tanager, the flute of the veery, are all on the air. Finally, as the shadows deepen and the stars begin to come out, the whip-poor-will suddenly strikes up. What a rude intrusion upon the serenity and harmony of the hour! A cry without music, insistent, reiterated, loud, penetrating, and yet the ear welcomes it also; the night and the solitude are so vast that they can stand it; and when, an hour later, as the night enters into full possession, the bird comes and serenades me under my window or upon my doorstep, my heart warms toward it. Its cry is a love-call, and there is something of the ardor and persistence of love in it, and when the female responds, and comes and hovers near, there is an interchange of subdued, caressing tones between the two birds that it is a delight to hear. During my first summer here one bird used to strike up every night from a high ledge of rocks in front of my door. At just such a moment in the twilight he would begin, the first to break the stillness. Then the others would follow, till the solitude was vocal with their calls. They are rarely heard later than ten o'clock. Then at daybreak they take up the tale again, whipping poor Will till one pities him. One April morning between three and four o'clock, hearing one strike up near my window, I began counting its calls. My neighbor had told me he had heard one call over two hundred times without a break, which seemed to me a big story. But I have a much bigger one to tell. This bird actually laid upon the back of poor Will one thousand and eighty-eight blows, with only a barely perceptible pause here and there, as if to catch its breath. Then it stopped about half a minute and began again, uttering this time three hundred and ninety calls, when it paused, flew a little farther away, took up the tale once more, and continued till I fell asleep.

By day the whip-poor-will apparently sits motionless upon the ground. A few times in my walks through the woods I have started one up from almost under my feet. On such occasions the bird's movements suggest those of a bat; its wings make no noise, and it wavers about in an uncertain manner, and quickly drops to the ground again. One June day we flushed an old one with her two young, but there was no indecision or hesitation in the manner of the mother bird this time. The young were more than half-fledged, and they scampered away a few yards and suddenly squatted upon the ground, where their protective coloring rendered them almost invisible. Then the anxious parent put forth all her arts to absorb our attention and lure us away from her offspring. She flitted before us from side to side, with spread wings and tail, now falling upon the ground, where she would remain a moment as if quite disabled, then perching upon an old stump or low branch with drooping, quivering wings, and imploring us by every gesture to take her and spare her young. My companion had his camera with him, but the bird would not remain long enough in one position for him to get her picture.

The whip-poor-will builds no nest but lays her two blunt, speckled eggs upon the dry leaves, where the plumage of the sitting bird blends perfectly with her surroundings. The eye, only a few feet away, has to search long and carefully to make her out. Every gray and brown and black tint of dry leaf and lichen, and bit of bark or broken twig, is copied in her plumage. In a day or two, after the young are hatched, the mother begins to move about with them through the woods.

When I want the wild of a little different flavor and quality from that immediately about my cabin, I go a mile through the woods to Black Creek, here called the Chateauguay, and put my canoe into a long, smooth, silent stretch of water that winds through a heavily timbered marsh till it leads into Black Pond, an oval sheet of water half a mile or more across. Here I get the moist, spongy, tranquil, luxurious side of Nature. Here she stands or sits knee-deep in water, and wreathes herself with pond-lilies in summer, and bedecks herself with scarlet maples in autumn. She is an Indian maiden, dark, subtle, dreaming, with glances now and then that thrill the wild blood in one's veins. The Chateauguay here is a stream without banks and with a just perceptible current. It is a waterway through a timbered marsh. The level floor of the woods ends in an irregular line where the level surface of the water begins. As one glides along in his boat, he sees various rank aquatic growths slowly waving in the shadowy depths beneath him. The larger trees on each side unite their branches above his head, so that at times he seems to be entering an arboreal cave out of which glides the stream. In the more open places the woods mirror themselves in the glassy surface till one seems floating between two worlds, clouds and sky and trees below him matching those around and above him. A bird flits from shore to shore, and one sees it duplicated against the sky in the under-world.

What vistas open! What banks of drooping foliage, what grain and arch of gnarled branches lure the eye as one drifts or silently paddles along! The stream has absorbed the shadows so long that it is itself like a liquid shadow. Its bed is lined with various dark vegetable growths, as with the skin of some huge, shaggy animal, the fur of which slowly stirs in the languid current. I go here in early spring, after the ice has broken up, to get a glimpse of the first wild ducks and to play the sportsman without a gun. I am sure I would not exchange the quiet surprise and pleasure I feel, as, on rounding some point or curve in the stream, two or more ducks spring suddenly out from some little cove or indentation in the shore, and with an alarum *quack, quack,* launch into the air and quickly gain the free spaces above the treetops, for the satisfaction of the gunner who sees their dead bodies fall before his murderous fire. He has only a dead duck, which, the chances are, he will not find very toothsome at this season, while I have a live duck with whistling wings cleaving the air northward, where, in some lake or river of Maine or Canada, in late summer, I may meet him again with his brood. It is so easy, too, to bag the game with your eye, while your gun may leave you only a feather or two floating upon the water. The duck has wit, and its wit is as quick as, or quicker than, the sportsman's gun. One day in spring I saw a gunner cut down a duck when it had gained an altitude of thirty or forty feet above the stream. At the report it stopped suddenly, turned a somersault, and fell with a splash into the water. It fell like a brick, and disappeared like one; only a feather and a few bubbles marked the spot where it struck. Had it sunk? No; it had dived. It was probably winged, and in the moment it occupied in falling to the water it had decided what to do. It would go beneath the hunter, since it could not escape above him; it could fly in the water with only one wing, with its feet to aid it. The gunner instantly set up a diligent search in all directions, up and down along the shores, peering long and intently into the depths, thrusting his oar into the weeds and driftwood at the edge of the water, but no duck or sign of duck could he find. It was as if the wounded bird had taken to the mimic heaven that looked so sunny and real down there, and gone on to Canada by that route. What astonished me was that the duck should have kept its presence of mind under such trying circumstances, and not have lost a fraction of a second of time in deciding on a course of action. The duck, I am convinced, has more sagacity than any other of our commoner fowl.

The day I see the first ducks I am pretty sure to come upon the first flock of blackbirds — rusty grackles — resting awhile on their northward journey amid the reeds, alders, and spice-bush beside the stream. They allow me to approach till I can see their yellow eyes and the brilliant iris on the necks and heads of the males. Many of them are vocal, and their united voices make a volume of sound that is analogous to a bundle of slivers. Sputtering, splintering, rasping, rending, their notes chafe and excite the ear. They suggest thorns and briars of sound, and yet are most welcome. What voice that rises from our woods or beside our waters in April is not tempered or attuned to the ear? Just as I like to chew the crinkleroot and the twigs of the spice-bush at this time, or at any time, for that matter, so I like to treat my ear to these more aspirated and astringent bird voices. Is it Thoreau who says they are like pepper and salt to this sense? In all the blackbirds we hear the voice of April not yet quite articulate; there is a suggestion of catarrh and influenza still in the air-passages. I should, perhaps, except the red-shouldered starling, whose clear and liquid *gur-ga-lee* or *o-ka-lee* above the full water-courses makes a different impression. The cowbird also has a clear note, but it seems to be wrenched or pumped up with much effort.

In May I go to Black Creek to hear the warbler and the water-thrushes. It is the only locality where I have ever heard the two water-thrushes, or accentors, singing at the same time — the New York and the large-billed. The latter is much more abundant and much the finer songster. How he does make these watery solitudes ring with his sudden, brilliant burst of song! But the more northern species pleases the ear also with his quieter and less-hurried strain. I drift in my boat and let the ear attend to the one, then to the other, while the eye takes note of their quick, nervous movements and darting flight. The smaller species probably does not nest along this stream, but the large-billed breeds here abundantly. The last nest I found was in the roots of an upturned tree, with the water immediately beneath it. I had asked a neighboring farm-boy if he knew of any birds' nests.

"Yes," he said; and he named over the nests of robins, high-holes, sparrows, and others, and then that of a "tip-up."

At this last I pricked up my ears, so to speak. I had not seen a tip-up's nest in many a day.

"Where?" I inquired.

"In the roots of a tree in the woods," said Charley.

"Not the nest of the 'tip-up,' or sandpiper," said I. "It builds on the ground in the open country near streams."

"Anyhow, it tipped," replied the boy.

He directed me to the spot, and I found, as I expected to find, the nest of the water-thrush. When the Vassar girls came again, I conducted them to the spot, and they took turns in walking a small tree trunk above the water, and gazing upon a nest brimming with the downy backs of young birds.

When I am listening to the water-thrushes, I am also noting with both eye and ear the warblers and vireos. There comes a week in May when the speckled Canada warblers are in the ascendant. They feed in the low bushes near the water's edge, and are very brisk and animated in voice and movement. The eye easily notes their slate-blue backs and yellow breasts with their broad band of black spots, and the ear quickly discriminates their not less-marked and emphatic song.

In late summer I go to the Chateauguay, and to the lake out of which it flows, for white pond-lilies, and to feast my eye on the masses of purple loosestrife and the more brilliant but more hidden and retired cardinal-flower that bloom upon its banks. One cannot praise the pond-lily; his best words mar it, like the insects that eat its petals: but he can contemplate it as it opens in the morning sun and distills such perfume, such purity, such snow of petal and such gold of anther, from the dark water and still darker ooze. How feminine it seems beside its coarser and more robust congeners; how shy, how pliant, how fine in texture and starlike in form!

The loosestrife is a foreign plant, but it has made itself thoroughly at home here, and its masses of royal purple make the woods look civil and festive. The cardinal burns with a more intense fire, and fairly lights up the little dark nooks where it glasses itself in the still water. One must pause and look at it. Its intensity, its pure scarlet, the dark background upon which it is projected, its image in the still darker water, and its general air of retirement and seclusion, all arrest and delight the eye. It is a heart-throb of color on the bosom of the dark solitude.

The rarest and wildest animal that my neighborhood boasts of is the otter. Every winter we see the tracks of one or more of them upon the snow along Black Creek. But the eye that has seen the animal itself in recent years I cannot find. It probably makes its excursions along the creek by night.

Follow its track—as large as that of a fair-sized dog—over the ice, and you will find that it ends at every open pool and rapid, and begins again upon the ice beyond. Sometimes it makes little excursions up the bank, its body often dragging in the snow like a log. My son followed the track one day far up the mountain-side, where the absence of the snow caused him to lose it. I like to think of so wild and shy a creature holding its own within sound of the locomotive's whistle.

The fox passes my door in winter, and probably in summer too, as do also the 'possum and the coon. The latter tears down my sweet corn in the garden, and the rabbit eats off my raspberry-bushes and nibbles my first strawberries, while the woodchucks eat my celery and beans and peas. Chipmunks carry off the corn I put out for the chickens, and weasels eat the chickens themselves.

Many times during the season I have in my solitude a visit from a bald eagle. There is a dead tree near the summit, where he often perches, and which we call the "old eagle-tree." It is a pine, killed years ago by a thunderbolt—the bolt of Jove—and now the bird of Jove hovers about it or sits upon it. I have little doubt that what attracted me to this spot attracts him—the seclusion, the savageness, the elemental grandeur. Sometimes, as I look out of my window early in the morning, I see the eagle upon his perch, preening his plumage, or waiting for the rising sun to gild the mountain-tops. When the smoke begins to rise from my chimney, or he sees me going to the spring for water, he concludes it is time for him to be off. But he need not fear the crack of the rifle here; nothing more deadly than field-glasses shall be pointed at him while I am about. Often in the course of the day I see him circling above my domain, or winging his way toward the mountains. His home is apparently in the Shawangunk Range, twenty or more miles distant, and I fancy he stops or lingers above me on his way to the river. The days on which I see him are not quite the same as the other days. I think my thoughts soar a little higher all the rest of the morning: I have had a visit from a messenger of Jove. The lift or range of those great wings has passed into my thought.

I once heard a collector get up in a scientific body and tell how many eggs of the bald eagle he had clutched that season, how many from this nest, how many from that, and how one of the eagles had deported itself after he had killed its mate. I felt ashamed for him. He had only proved himself a superior human weasel. The man with the rifle and the man with the collector's craze are fast reducing the number of eagles in the country. Twenty years ago I used to see a dozen or more along the river in the spring when the ice was breaking up, where I now see only one or two, or none at all. In the present case, what would it profit me could I find and plunder my eagle's nest, or strip his skin from his dead carcass? Should I know him better? I do not want to know him that way. I want rather to feel the inspiration of his presence and noble bearing. I want my interest and sympathy to go with him in his continental voyaging up and down, and in his long, elevated flights to and from his eyrie upon the remote, solitary cliffs. He draws great lines across the sky; he sees the forests like a carpet beneath him, he sees the hills and valleys as folds and wrinkles in a many-colored tapestry; he sees the river as a silver belt connecting remote horizons. We climb mountain-peaks to get a glimpse of the spectacle that is hourly spread out beneath him. Dignity, elevation, repose are his. I would have my thoughts take as wide a sweep. I would be as far removed from the petty cares and turmoils of this noisy and blustering world.

From *My Boyhood*

YOU ASK ME to give you some account of my life—how it was with me, and now in my seventy-sixth year I find myself in the mood to do so. You know enough about me to know that it will not be an exciting narrative or of any great historical value. It is mainly the life of a country man and a rather obscure man of letters, lived in eventful times indeed, but largely lived apart from the men and events that have given character to the last three-quarters of a century. Like tens of thousands of others, I have been a spectator of, rather than a participator in, the activities—political, commercial, sociological, scientific—of the times in which I have lived. My life, like your own, has been along the by-paths, rather than along the great public highways. I have known but few great men and have played no part in any great public events, not even in the Civil War, which I lived through and in which my duty plainly called me to take part. I am a man who recoils from noise and strife, even from fair competition, and who likes to see his days "linked each to each" by some quiet, congenial occupation.

The first seventeen years of my life were spent on the farm where I was born (1837–1854); the next ten years I was a teacher in rural district schools (1854– 1864); then I was for ten years a government clerk in Washington (1864–1873); then in the summer of 1873, while a national bank examiner and bank receiver, I purchased the small fruit farm on the Hudson where you were brought up and where I have since lived, cultivating the land for marketable fruit and the fields and woods for nature literature, as you well know. I have gotten out of my footpaths a few times and traversed some of the great highways of travel—have been twice to Europe, going only as far as Paris (1871 and 1882)—the first time sent to London by the Government with three other men to convey $50,000,000 of bonds to be refunded; the second time going with my family on my own account. I was a member of the Harriman expedition to Alaska in the summer of 1899, going as far as Plover Bay on the extreme N. E. part of Siberia. I was the companion of

President Roosevelt on a trip to Yellowstone Park in the spring of 1903. In the winter and spring of 1909 I went to California with two women friends and extended the journey to the Hawaiian Islands, returning home in June. In 1911 I again crossed the continent to California. I have camped and tramped in Maine and in Canada, and have spent part of a winter in Bermuda and in Jamaica. This is an outline of my travels. . . .

. . . My books are, in a way, a record of my life—that part of it that came to flower and fruit in my mind. You could reconstruct my days pretty well from these volumes. A writer who gleans his literary harvest in the fields and woods reaps mainly where he has sown himself. He is a husbandman whose crop springs from the seed of his own heart.

My life has been a fortunate one; I was born under a lucky star. It seems as if both wind and tide had favoured me. I have suffered no great losses, or defeats, or illness, or accidents, and have undergone no great struggles or privations; I have had no grouch, I have not wanted the earth. I am pessimistic by night, but by day I am a confirmed optimist, and it is the days that have stamped my life. I have found this planet a good corner of the universe to live in and I am not in a hurry to exchange it for any other. I hope the joy of living may be as keen with you, my dear boy, as it has been with me and that you may have life on as easy terms as I have. With this foreword I will begin the record in more detail.

I have spoken of my good luck. It began in my having been born on a farm, of parents in the prime of their days, and in humble circumstance. I deem it good luck too that my birth fell in April, a month in which so many other things find it good to begin life. Father probably tapped the sugar bush about this time or a little earlier; the bluebird and the robin and song sparrow may have arrived that very day. New calves were bleating in the barn and young lambs under the shed. There were earth-stained snow drifts on the hillside, and along the stone walls, and through the forests that covered the mountains the coat of snow showed unbroken. The fields were generally bare and the frost was leaving the ground. The stress of winter was over and the warmth of spring began to be felt in the air. I had come into a household of five children, two girls and three boys, the oldest ten years and the youngest two. One had died in infancy, making me the seventh child. Mother was twenty-nine and father thirty-five, a medium-sized, freckled, red-haired man, showing very plainly the Celtic or Welsh strain in his blood, as did mother, who was a Kelly and of Irish extraction on the paternal side. I had come into a family of neither wealth nor poverty as those things were looked upon in those days, but a family dedicated to hard work winter and summer in paying for and improving a large farm, in a country of wide open valleys and long, broad-backed hills and gentle flowing mountain lines; very old geologically, but only one generation from the stump in the history of the settlement. Indeed, the stumps lingered in many of the fields late into my boyhood, and one of my tasks in the dry mid-spring weather was to burn these stumps—an occupation I always enjoyed because the adventure of it made play of the work.

The climate was severe in winter, the mercury often dropping to 30° below, though we then had no thermometer to measure it, and the summers, at an altitude of two thousand feet, cool and salubrious. The soil was fairly good, though encumbered with the laminated rock and stones of the Catskill formation, which the old ice sheet had broken and shouldered and transported about. About every five or six acres had loose stones and rock enough to put a rock-bottomed wall around it and still leave enough in and on the soil to worry the ploughman and the mower. All the farms in that section reposing in the valleys and bending up and over the broad-backed hills are checker-boards of stone walls, and the right-angled fields, in their many colours of green and brown and yellow and red, give a striking map-like appearance to the landscape. Good crops of grain, such as rye, oats, buckwheat, and yellow corn, are grown, but grass is the most natural product. It is a grazing country and the dairy cow thrives there, and her products are the chief source of income of the farms.

I had come into a home where all the elements were sweet, the water and the air as good as there is in the world, and where the conditions of life were of a temper to discipline both mind and body. The settlers of my part of the Catskills were largely from Connecticut and Long Island, coming in after or near the close of the Revolution, and with a good mixture of Scotch emigrants.

My great-grandfather, Ephraim Burroughs, came, with his family of eight or ten children, from near Danbury, Conn., and settled in the town of Stamford shortly after the Revolution. He died there in 1818. My grandfather, Eden, came into the town of Roxbury, then a part of Ulster County.

I had come into a land flowing with milk, if not with honey. The maple syrup may very well take the place of the honey. The sugar-maple was the dominant tree in the woods and the maple sugar the principal sweetening used in the family. Maple, beech, and birch wood kept us warm in winter, and pine and hemlock timber made from trees that grew in the deeper valleys formed the roofs and the walls of the houses. The breath of kine early mingled with my own breath. From my earliest memory the cow was the

chief factor on the farm and her products the main source of the family income; around her revolved the haying and the harvesting. It was for her
that we toiled from early July until late August, gathering the hay into the
barns or into the stacks, mowing and raking it by hand. That was the day of
the scythe and the good mower, of the cradle and the good cradler, of the
pitchfork and the good pitcher. . . .

The farm work to which I was early called upon to lend a hand, as I have
said, revolved around the dairy cow. Her paths were in the fields and
woods, her sonorous voice was upon the hills, her fragrant breath was upon
every breeze. She was the centre of our industries. To keep her in good condition, well pastured in summer and well housed and fed in winter, and the
whole dairy up to its highest point of efficiency—to this end the farmer directed his efforts. It was an exacting occupation. . . .

⁕   ⁕   ⁕

In milking we all took a hand when we had reached the age of about ten
years, Mother and my sisters usually doing their share. At first we milked
the cows in the road in front of the house, setting the pails of milk on the
stone work; later we milked them in a yard in the orchard behind the
house, and of late years the milking is done in the stable. Mother said that
when they first came upon the farm, as she sat milking a cow in the road
one evening, she saw a large black animal come out of the woods out where
the clover meadow now is, and cross the road and disappear in the woods
on the other side. Bears sometimes carried off the farmers' hogs in those
days, boldly invading the pens to do so. My father kept about thirty cows of
the Durham breed; now the dairy herds are made up of Jerseys or Holsteins.
Then the product that went to market was butter; now it is milk. Then the
butter was made on the farm by the farmer's wife or the hired girl; now it is
made in the creameries by men. My mother made most of the butter for
nearly forty years, packing thousands of tubs and firkins of it in that time.
The milk was set in tin pans on a rack in the milk house for the cream to
rise, and as soon as the milk clabbered it was skimmed.

About three o'clock in the afternoon during the warm weather, Mother
would begin skimming the milk, carrying it pan by pan to the big cream
pan, where with a quick movement of a case knife the cream was separated
from the sides of the pan, the pan tilted on the edge of the cream pan, and
the heavy mantle of cream, in folds or flakes, slid off into the receptacle,
and the thick milk emptied into pails to be carried to the swill barrel for the
hogs. I used to help Mother at times by handing her the pans of milk from

the rack and emptying the pails. Then came the washing of the pans at the trough, at which I also often aided her by standing the pans up to dry and sun on the big bench. Rows of drying tin pans were always a noticeable feature about farmhouses in those days, also the churning machine attached to the milk house and the sound of the wheel, propelled by the "old churner"—either a big dog or a wether sheep. Every summer morning by eight o'clock the old sheep or the old dog was brought and tied to his task upon the big wheel. Sheep were usually more unwilling churners than were the dogs. They rarely acquired any sense of duty or obedience as a dog did. This endless walking and getting nowhere very soon called forth vigorous protests. The churner would pull back, brace himself, choke, and stop the machine: one churner threw himself off and was choked to death before he was discovered. I remember when the old hetchel from the day of flax dressing, fastened to a board, did duty behind the old churner, spurring him up with its score or more of sharp teeth when he settled back to stop the machine. "Run and start the old sheep," was a command we heard less often after that. He could not long hold out against the pressure of that phalanx of sharp points upon his broad rear end.

The churn dog was less obdurate and perverse, but he would sometimes hide away as the hour of churning approached, and we would have to hustle around to find him. But we had one dog that seemed to take pleasure in the task and would go quickly to the wheel when told to and finish his task without being tied. In the absence of both dog and sheep, I have a few times taken their place on the wheel. In winter and early spring there was less cream to churn, and we did it by hand, two of us lifting the dasher together. Heavy work for even big boys, and when the stuff was reluctant and the butter would not come sometimes until the end of an hour, the task tried our mettle. Sometimes it would not gather well after it had come, then some deft handling of the dasher was necessary.

I never tired of seeing Mother lift the great masses of golden butter from the churn with her ladle and pile them up in the big butter bowl, with the drops of buttermilk standing upon them as if they were sweating from the ordeal they had been put through. Then the working and the washing of it to free it from the milk and the final packing into tub or firkin, its fresh odour in the air—what a picture it was! How much of the virtue of the farm went each year into those firkins! Literally the cream of the land. Ah, the alchemy of Life, that in the bee can transform one product of those wild rough fields into honey, and in the cow can transform another product into milk!

The spring butter was packed into fifty-pound tubs to be shipped to market as fast as made. The packing into one-hundred-pound firkins to be held over till November did not begin till the cows were turned out to pasture in May. To have made forty tubs by that time and sold them for eighteen or twenty cents a pound was considered very satisfactory. Then to make forty or fifty firkins during the summer and fall and to get as good a price for it made the farmer's heart glad. When Father first came on the farm, in 1827, butter brought only twelve or fourteen cents per pound, but the price steadily crept up till in my time it sold from seventeen to eighteen and a half. The firkin butter was usually sold to a local butter buyer named Dowie. He usually appeared in early fall, always on horseback, having notified Father in advance. At the breakfast table Father would say, "Dowie is coming to try the butter today."

"I hope he will not try that firkin I packed that hot week in July," Mother would say. But very likely that was the one among others he would ask for. His long, half-round steel butter probe or tryer was thrust down the centre of the firkin to the bottom, given a turn or two, and withdrawn, its tapering cavity filled with a sample of every inch of butter in the firkin. Dowie would pass it rapidly to and from under his nose, maybe sometimes tasting it, then push the tryer back into the hole, then withdrawing it, leaving its core of butter where it found it. If the butter suited him, and it rarely failed to do so, he would make his offer and ride away to the next dairy.

The butter had always to be delivered at a date agreed upon, on the Hudson River at Catskill. This usually took place in November. It was the event of the fall: two loads of butter, of twenty or more firkins each, to be transported fifty miles in a lumber wagon, each round trip taking about four days. The firkins had to be headed up and gotten ready. This job in my time usually fell to Hiram. He would begin the day before Father was to start and have a load headed and placed in the wagon on time, with straw between the firkins so they would not rub. How many times I have heard those loads start off over the frozen ground in the morning before it was light! Sometimes a neighbor's wagon would go slowly jolting by just after or just before Father had started, but on the same errand. Father usually took a bag of oats for his horses and a box of food for himself so as to avoid all needless expenses. The first night would usually find him in Steel's tavern in Greene County, halfway to Catskill. The next afternoon would find him at his journey's end and by night unloaded at the steamboat wharf, his groceries and other purchases made, and ready for an early start homeward in the morning. On the fourth night we would be on the lookout for his return.

Mother would be sitting, sewing by the light of her tallow dip, with one ear bent toward the road. She usually caught the sound of his wagon first. "There comes your father," she would say, and Hiram or Wilson would quickly get and light the old tin lantern and stand ready on the stonework to receive him and help put out the team. By the time he was in the house his supper would be on the table—a cold pork stew, I remember, used to delight him on such occasions, and a cup of green tea. After supper, his pipe, and the story of his trip told, with a list of family purchases, and then to bed. In a few days the second trip would be made.

As his boys grew old enough he gave each of them in turn a trip with him to Catskill. It was a great event in the life of each of us. When it came my turn, I was probably eleven or twelve years old and the coming event loomed big on my horizon. I was actually to see my first steamboat, the Hudson River, and maybe the steam cars. For several days in advance I hunted the woods for game to stock the provision box so as to keep down the expense. I killed my first partridge and probably a wild pigeon or two and gray squirrels. Perched high on that springboard beside Father, my feet hardly touching the tops of the firkins, at the rate of about two miles an hour over rough roads in chilly November weather, I made my first considerable journey into the world. I crossed the Catskill Mountains and got that surprising panoramic view of the land beyond from the top.

At Cairo, where it seems we passed the second night, I disgraced myself in the morning, when Father, after praising me to some bystanders, told me to get up in the wagon and drive the load out in the road. In my earnest effort to do so I ran foul of one side of the big door, and came near smashing things. Father was humiliated and I was dreadfully mortified.

With the wonders of Catskill I was duly impressed, but one of my most vivid remembrances is a passage at arms (verbal) at the steamboat between Father and old Dowie. The latter had questioned the correctness of the weight of the empty firkin which was to be deducted as tare from the total weight. Hot words followed. Father said, "Strip it, strip it." Dowie said, "I will," and in a moment there stood on the scales the naked firkin of butter, sweating drops of salt water. Which won, I do not know. I remember only that peace soon reigned and Dowie continued to buy our butter.

One other incident of that trip still sticks in my mind. I was walking along a street just at dusk, when I saw a drove of cattle coming. The drover, seeing me, called out, "Here, boy, turn those cows up that street!" This was in my line, I was at home with cows, and I turned the drove up in fine style. As the man came along, he said, "Well done," and placed six big copper cents in my hand. Never was my palm more unexpectedly and more agreeably tickled. The feel of it is with me yet! . . .

*[*]   *[*]   *[*]

The work on the farm in those days varied little from year to year. In winter the care of the cattle, the cutting of the wood, and the thrashing of the oats and rye filled the time. From the age of ten or twelve till we were grown up, we went to school only in winter, doing the chores morning and evening, and engaging in general work every other Saturday, which was a holiday. Often my older brothers would have to leave school by three o'clock to get home to put up the cows in my father's absence.

Those school days, how they come back to me! — the long walk across lots, through the snow-choked fields and woods, our narrow path so often obliterated by a fresh fall of snow; the cutting winds, the bitter cold, the snow squeaking beneath our frozen cowhide boots, our trousers' legs often tied down with tow strings to keep the snow from pushing them up above our boot tops; the wide open white landscape with its faint black lines of stone wall when we had passed the woods and began to dip down into West Settlement valley; the Smith boys and Bouton boys and Dart boys, afar off, threading the fields on their way to school, their forms etched on the white hillsides, one of the bigger boys, Ria Bouton, who had many chores to do, morning after morning running the whole distance so as not to be late; the red schoolhouse in the distance by the roadside with the dark spot in its centre made by the open door of the entry way; the creek in the valley, often choked with anchor ice, which our path crossed and into which I one morning slumped, reaching the school house with my clothes freezing upon me and the water gurgling in my boots; the boys and girls there, Jay Gould among them, two-thirds of them now dead and the living scattered from the Hudson to the Pacific; the teachers now all dead; the studies, the games, the wrestlings, the baseball — all these things and more pass before me as I recall those long-gone days. Two years ago I hunted up one of those schoolmates in California whom I had not seen for over sixty years. She was my senior by seven or eight years, and I had a boy's remembrance of her fresh sweet face, her kindly eyes and gentle manners. I was greeted by a woman of eighty-two, with dimmed sight and dulled hearing, but instantly I recognized some vestiges of the charm and sweetness of my elder schoolmate of so long ago. No cloud was on her mind or memory and for an hour we again lived among the old people and scenes. . . .

⸙⸙ ⸙⸙ ⸙⸙

The first considerable work in spring was sugar-making, always a happy time for me. Usually the last half of March, when rills from the melting snow began to come through the fields, the veins of the sugar maples began to thrill with the spring warmth. There was a general awakening about the farm at this time—the cackling of the hens, the bleating of young lambs and calves, and the wistful lowing of the cows. Earlier in the month the "sap spiles" had been overhauled, resharpened, and new ones made, usually from basswood. In my time the sap gouge was used instead of the auger, and the manner of tapping was crude and wasteful. A slanting gash three or four inches long and a half inch or more deep was cut, and an inch below the lower end of this the gouge was driven in to make the place for the spile, a piece of wood two inches wide, shaped to the gouge, and a foot or more in length. It gave the tree a double and unnecessary wound. The bigger the gash the more the sap, seemed to be the theory, as if the tree was a barrel filled with liquid, whereas a small wound made by a half-inch bit does the work just as well and is far less injurious to the tree. . . .

⸙⸙ ⸙⸙ ⸙⸙

When there came a bright morning, wind northwest and warm enough to begin to thaw by eight o'clock, the sugar-making utensils—pans, kettles, spiles, hogsheads were loaded upon the sled and taken to the woods, and by ten o'clock the trees began to feel the cruel ax and gouge once more. It usually fell to my part to carry the pans and spiles for one of the tappers, Hiram or Father, and to arrange the pans on a level foundation of sticks or stones, in position. Father often used to haggle the tree a good deal in tapping. "By Fagus," he would say, "how awkward I am!" The rapid tinkle of those first drops of sap in the tin pan, how well I remember it! Probably the note of the first song sparrow or first bluebird, or the spring call of the nuthatch, sounded in unison. Usually only patches of snow lingered here and there in the woods and the earth-stained remnants of old drifts on the sides of the hills and along the stone walls. Those lucid warm March days in the naked maple woods under the blue sky, with the first drops of sap ringing in the pans, had a charm that does not fade from my mind. After the trees were all tapped, two hundred and fifty of them, the big kettles were again set up in the old stone arch, and the hogsheads in which to store the sap placed in position. By four o'clock many of the pans—milk pans from the dairy—would be full, and the gathering with neck yoke and pails began.

When I was fourteen or fifteen, I took a hand in this part of the work. It used to tax my strength to carry the two twelve-quart pails full through the rough places and up the steep banks in the woods and then lift them up and alternately empty them into the hogsheads without displacing the neck yoke. But I could do it. Now all this work is done by the aid of a team and a pipe fastened on a sled. Before I was old enough to gather sap, it fell to me to go to the barns and put in hay for the cows and help stable them. The next morning the boiling of the sap would begin, with Hiram in charge. The big deep iron kettles were slow evaporators compared with the broad shallow sheet-iron pans now in use. Profundity cannot keep up with shallowness in sugar-making, the more superficial your evaporator, within limits, the more rapid your progress. It took the farmers nearly a hundred years to find this out, or at least to act upon it.

At the end of a couple of days of hard boiling, Hiram would "syrup off," having reduced two hundred pails of sap to five or six of syrup. The syruping-off often occurred after dark. When the liquid dropped from a dipper which was dipped into it and, held up in the cool air, formed into stiff thin masses, it had reached the stage of syrup. How we minded our steps over the rough path, in the semi-darkness of the old tin lantern, in carrying those precious pails of syrup to the house, where the final process of "sugaring off" was to be completed by Mother and Jane! . . .

᙭ᛞ ᙭ᛞ ᙭ᛞ

My boyhood days in the spring sugar bush were my most enjoyable on the farm. How I came to know each one of those two hundred and fifty trees— what a distinct sense of individuality seemed to adhere to most of them, as much so as to each cow in a dairy! I knew at which trees I would be pretty sure to find a full pan and at which ones a less amount. One huge tree always gave a cream-pan full—a double measure—while the others were filling an ordinary pan. This was known as "the old cream-pan tree." Its place has long been vacant; about half the others are still standing, but with the decrepitude of age appearing in their tops; a new generation of maples has taken the place of the vanished veterans.

While tending the kettles there beside the old arch in the bright, warm March or April days, with my brother, or while he had gone to dinner, looking down the long valley and off over the curving backs of the distant mountain ranges, what dreams I used to have, what vague longings, and, I may say, what happy anticipations! I am sure I gathered more than sap and sugar in those youthful days amid the maples. When I visit the old home now, I have to walk up to the sugar bush and stand around the old "boiling place," trying to transport myself back into the magic atmosphere of that boyhood time. The man has his dreams too, but to his eyes the world is not steeped in romance as it is to the eyes of youth.

One springtime in the sugar season my cousin, Gib Kelly, a boy of my own age, visited me, staying two or three days. (He died last fall.) When he went away, I was minding the kettles in the woods, and as I saw him crossing the bare fields in the March sunshine, his steps bent toward the distant mountains, I still remember what a sense of loss came over me, his comradeship had so brightened my enjoyment of the beautiful days. He seemed to take my whole world with him, and on that and the following day I went about my duties in the sap bush in a wistful and pensive mood I had never before felt. I early showed the capacity for comradeship. A boy friend could throw the witchery of romance over everything. Oh, the enchanted days with my youthful mates! . . .

. . . From the first day in early July till the end of August we lived for the hayfield. No respite except on rainy days and Sundays, and no change except from one meadow to another. No eight-hour days then, rather twelve and fourteen, including the milking. No horse rakes, no mowing machines or hay tedders or loading or pitching devices then. The scythe, the hand rake, the pitchfork in the callused hands of men and boys did the work, occasionally the women even taking a turn with the rake or in mowing away. . . .

At this season the cows were brought to the yard by or before five, breakfast was at six, lunch in the field at ten, dinner at twelve and supper at five, with milking and hay drawing and heaping up till sundown. Those midforenoon lunches of mother's good rye bread and butter, with crullers or gingerbread, and in August a fresh green cucumber and a sweating jug of water fresh from the spring—sweating, not as we did, because it was hot, but because it was cold, partaken under an ash or a maple tree—how sweet and fragrant the memory of it all is to me!

Till I reached my teens it was my task to spread hay and to rake after; later I took my turn with the mowers and pitchers. I never loaded, hence I never pitched over the big beam. How father watched the weather! The rain that makes the grass ruins the hay. If the morning did not promise a good hay day our scythes would be ground but hung back in their places. When a thunderstorm was gathering in the west and much hay was ready for hauling, how it quickened our steps and our strokes! It was the sound of the guns of the approaching foe. In one hour we would do, or try to do, the work of two. How the wagon would rattle over the road, how the men would mop their faces, and how I, while hurrying, would secretly exult that now I would have an hour to finish my crossbow or to work on my pond in the pasture lot!

Those late summer afternoons after the shower—what man who has spent his youth on the farm does not recall them! The high-piled thunderheads of the retreating storm above the eastern mountains, the moist fresh smell of the hay and the fields, the red puddles in the road, the robins singing from the tree tops, the washed and cooler air, and the welcomed feeling of relaxation which they brought. . . .

⚜ ⚜ ⚜

Father and Mother had a pretty hard struggle to pay for the farm and to clothe and feed and school us all. We lived off the products of the farm to an extent that people do not think of doing nowadays. Not only was our food largely home grown but our clothes also were home grown and home spun. In my early youth our house linen and our summer shirts and trousers were made from flax that grew on the farm. Those pioneer shirts, how vividly I remember them! They dated from the stump, and bits of the stump in the shape of "shives" were inwoven in their texture and made the wearer of them an unwilling penitent for weeks, or until use and the washboard had subdued them. Peas in your shoes are no worse than "shives" on your shirt. But those tow shirts stood by you. If you lost your hold in climbing a tree and caught on a limb, your shirt or your linen trousers would hold you. The stuff from which they were made had a history behind it—pulled up by the roots, rooted on the ground, broken with a crackle, flogged with a swingle, and drawn through a hetchel, and out of all this ordeal came the flax.

How clearly I remember Father working with it in the bright, sharp March days, breaking it, then swingling it with a long wooden swordlike tool over the end of an upright board fixed at the base in a heavy block. This was to separate the brittle fragments of the bark from the fibres of the flax. Then in large handfuls he drew it through the hetchel an instrument with a score or more long sharp iron teeth, set in a board, row behind row. This combed out the tow and other worthless material. It was a mighty good discipline for the flax; it straightened out its fibres and made it as clear and straight as a girl's tresses. Out of the tow we twisted bag strings, flail strings, and other strings. With the worthless portions we made huge bonfires. The flax, Mother would mass upon her distaff and spin into threads.

The last I saw of the old crackle, fifty or more years ago, it served as a hen roost under the shed, and the savage old hetchel was doing duty behind the old churner when he sulked and pulled back so as to stop the churning machine. It was hetcheling wool then instead of flax. The flax was spun on a quill which ran by the foot, and the quills or spools holding the thread were used in a shuttle when the cloth was woven. The old loom stood in the hogpen chamber, and there Mother wove her linen, her rag carpets, and her woollen goods. I have "quilled" for her many a time—that is, run the yarn off the reel into spools for use in the shuttle.

Father had a flock of sheep which yielded wool enough for our stockings, mittens, comforts, and underwear, and woollen sheets and comforts for the beds. I have some of those home-made woolen sheets and bed covers now at Slabsides.

Before the sheep were sheared in June they were driven two miles to the creek to be washed. Washing-sheep-day was an event on the farm. It was no small task to get the sheep off the mountain, drive them to the deep pool behind old Jonas More's grist mill, pen them up there, and drag them one by one into the water and make good clean Baptists of them! But sheep are no fighters, they struggle for a moment and then passively submit to the baptism. My older brothers usually did the washing and I the herding. When the shearing was done, a few days later the poor creatures were put through another ordeal, to which after a brief struggle they quickly resigned themselves. Father did the shearing, while I at times held the animal's legs. Father was not an adept hand with the shears, and the poor beast usually had to part with many a bit of her hide along with her fleece. It used to make me wince as much as it did the sheep to see the crests of those little wrinkles in her skin clipped off. I used to wonder how the sheep knew one another and how the lambs knew their mothers when shorn of their fleeces. But they did. . . .

※ ※ ※

I was in many respects an odd one in my father's family. I was like a graft from some other tree. And this is always a disadvantage to a man—not to be the logical outcome of what went before him, not to be backed up by his family and inheritance—to be of the nature of a sport. It seems as if I had more intellectual capital than I was entitled to and robbed some of the rest of the family, while I had a full measure of the family weaknesses. I can remember how abashed I used to be as a child when strangers or relatives, visiting us for the first time, after looking the rest of the children over, would ask, pointing to me, "That is not your boy—whose is he?" I have no idea that I looked different from the others, because I can see the family stamp upon my face very plainly until this day. My face resembles Hiram's more than any of the others, and I have a deeper attachment for him than for any of the rest of my brothers. Hiram was a dreamer too, and he had his own idealism which expressed itself in love of bees, of which he kept many hives at one time, and of fancy stock, sheep, pigs, poultry, and a desire to see other lands. His bees and fancy stock never paid him, but he always expected they would the next year. But they yielded him honey and wool of a certain intangible, satisfying kind. . . .

Hiram always had to have some sort of a plaything. Though no hunter and an indifferent marksman, he had during his life several fancy rifles. . . . Another plaything of his was a kettle drum with which he amused himself in the summer twilight for many seasons. Then he got a bass drum, which Curtis learned to play, and a very warlike sound often went up from the peaceful old homestead. When I was married and came driving home one October twilight with my wife, the martial music began as soon as we hove in sight of the house. . . .

. . . I tell you all these things about Hiram because I am a chip out of the same block and see myself in him. His vain regrets, his ineffectual resolutions, his day-dreams, and his playthings—do I not know them all?—only nature in some way dealt a little more liberally with me and made many of my dreams come true. The dear brother!—he stood next to Father and Mother to me. How many times he broke the path for me through the winter snows on the long way to school! How faithful he was to write to me and to visit me wherever I was, after I left home! How he longed to follow my example and break away from the old place but could never quite screw his courage up to the sticking point! He never read one of my books, but he rejoiced in all the good fortune that was mine. Once when I was away at school and fell short of money, Hiram sent me a small sum when Father could not or would not send. In later life he got it paid back manyfold—and what a satisfaction it was to me thus to repay him! . . .

⚜ ⚜ ⚜

. . . I have told elsewhere what a revelation to me was my first glimpse of one of the warblers, the black-throated blue-back, indicating as it did a world of bird life of which I had never dreamed, the bird life in the inner heart of the woods. My brothers and other boys were with me, but they did not see the new bird. The first time I saw the veery, or Wilson's thrush, also stands out in my memory. It alighted in the road before us on the edge of the woods. "A brown thrasher," said Bill Chase. It was not the thrasher, but it was a new bird to me, and the picture of it is in my mind as if made only yesterday. Natural History was a subject unknown to me in my boyhood, and such a thing as nature study in the schools was of course unheard of. Our natural history we got unconsciously in the sport at noon time, or on our way to and from school or in our Sunday excursions to the streams and woods. We learned much about the ways of foxes and woodchucks and coons and skunks and squirrels by hunting them. The partridge too, and the crows, hawks, and owls, and the song birds of the field and orchard, all enter into the farm boy's life. I early became familiar with the songs and habits of all the common birds, and with field mice and the frogs, toads, lizards, and snakes. Also with the wild bees and wasps. One season I made a collection of bumble-bee honey, studying the habits of five or six different kinds and rifling their nests. I kept my store of bumble-bee honey in the attic where I had a small box full of the comb and a large phial filled with the honey. How well I came to know the different dispositions of the various kinds—the small red-vested that made its nest in a hole in the ground; the small black-vested, the large black-vested, the yellow-necked, the black-banded, etc., that made their nests in old mice nests in the meadow or in the barn and other places.

I used to watch and woo the little piping frogs in the spring marshes when I had driven the cows to pasture at night, till they would sit in my open hand and pipe. I used to creep on my hands and knees through the woods to see the partridge in the act of drumming. I used to watch the mud wasps building their nests in the old attic and noted their complaining cry while in the act of pressing on the mud. I noted the same complaining cry from the bees when working on the flower of the purple-flowering raspberry, what we called "scotch caps." . . .

✳ ✳ ✳

. . . I was born at Roxbury, N.Y., April 3, 1837. . . . I was the son of a farmer, who was the son of a farmer, who was again the son of a farmer. There are no professional or commercial men in my line for several generations, my blood has the flavour of the soil in it; it is rural to the last drop. I can find no city dwellers in the line of my descent in this country. The Burroughs tribe, as far back as I can find any account of them, were mainly country-men and tillers of the soil. The Rev. George Burroughs, who was hung as a witch at Salem, Mass., in 1694, may have been of the family, though I can find no proof of it. I wanted to believe that he was, and in 1898 I made a visit to Salem and to Gallows Hill to see the spot where he, the last victim of the witchcraft craze, ended his life. . . .

✳ ✳ ✳

My maternal grandfather, Edmund Kelly was Irish, though born in this country about 1765. It is from his Irish strain that I get many of my Celtic characteristics, my decidedly feminine temperament. I always felt that I was more a Kelly than a Burroughs. Grandfather Kelly was a small man, with a big head and marked Irish features. He entered the Continental army when a mere lad in some menial capacity, but before the end he carried a musket in the ranks. He was with Washington at Valley Forge and had many sto-ries to tell of their hardships. He was upward of seventy-five years old when I first remember him — a little man in a blue coat with brass buttons.

He and Granny used to come to our house once or twice a year for a week or two at a time. Their permanent home was with Uncle Martin Kelly in Red Kill, eight miles away. I remember him as a great angler. How many times in the May or June mornings, as soon as he had had his breakfast, have I seen him digging worms and getting ready to go a-fishing up Mont-gomery Hollow or over in Meeker's Hollow, or over in West Settlement! You could always be sure he would bring home a nice string of trout. Oc-casionally I was permitted to go with him. How nimbly he would walk, even when he was over eighty, and how skillfully he would take the trout! I was an angler myself before I was ten, but Grandfather would take trout from places in the stream where I would not think it worthwhile to cast my hook. But I never fished when I went with him, I carried the fish and watched him. The pull home, often two or three miles, tried my young legs, but Grandfather would show very little fatigue, and I know he did not have the ravenous hunger I always had when I went fishing, so much so that I used to think there was in this respect something peculiar about going fishing. One hour along the trout streams would develop more hunger in me than half a day hoeing corn or working on the road—a peculiarly fierce, all-absorbing desire for food, so that a piece of rye bread and butter was the most delicious thing in the world. I remember that one June day my cousin and I, when we were about seven or eight years old, set out for Meeker's Hollow for trout. It was a pull of over two miles and over a pretty hard hill. Our courage held out until we reached the creek, but we were too hungry to fish; we turned homeward and fed upon the wild strawberries in the pastures and meadows we passed through, and they kept us alive until we reached home. Oh, that youthful hunger beside the trout stream, was there ever anything else like it in the world!

Waiting

Serene, I fold my hands and wait,
    Nor care for wind, nor tide, nor sea;
Rave no more 'gainst Time or Fate,
    For lo! my own shall come to me.

I stay my haste, I make delays,
    For what avails this eager pace?
I stand amid the eternal ways,
    And what is mine shall know my face.

Asleep, awake, by night or day,
    The friends I seek are seeking me
No wind can drive my bark astray,
    Nor change the tide of destiny.

What matter if I stand alone
    I wait with joy the coming years
My heart shall reap where it hath sown,
    And garner up its fruit of tears.

The waters know their own, and draw
    The brook that springs in yonder heights,
So flows the good with equal law
    Unto the soul of pure delights.

The stars come nightly to the sky
    The tidal wave comes to the sea;
Nor time, nor space, nor deep, nor high,
    Can keep my own away from me.

First published in *Knickerbocker Magazine,* March 1863. See Burroughs's discussion of this poem in "An Outlook upon Life" in this volume.

A John Burroughs Bibliography

THE STANDARD EDITION of the works of John Burroughs is the Riverby edition, published by Houghton Mifflin. For details on the variants of the Riverby and other editions, see William Perkins, *Indexes to the Writings of John Burroughs* (New York: John Burroughs Association, 1995).

For more extensive bibliographic information, see Perry Westbrook, *John Burroughs* (New York: Twayne, 1974); Edward Renehan, *John Burroughs, an American Naturalist* (Post Mills, Vt.: Chelsea Green, 1992; Hensonville, N.Y.: Black Dome, 1997); Edward Kanze, *The World of John Burroughs* (San Francisco: Sierra Club Books, 1999); and Frank Bergon's bibliographic notes at the end of *A Sharp Lookout* (Washington, D.C.: Smithsonian, 1987).

For primary source materials, the largest collections of Burroughs's writings are at Vassar College Library (which has Burroughs's journals), the Berg Collection of the New York Public Library, and the Huntington Library.

Works by John Burroughs

Works are listed in the order of their initial publication.

Notes on Walt Whitman as Poet and Person. New York: American News, 1867.
Wake-Robin. New York: Hurd and Houghton, 1871.
Winter Sunshine. New York: Hurd and Houghton, 1875.
Birds and Poets. New York: Houghton Mifflin, 1877.
Locusts and Wild Honey. Boston: Houghton, Osgood, 1879.
Pepacton. Boston: Houghton Mifflin, 1881.
Fresh Fields. Boston: Houghton Mifflin, 1884.
Signs and Seasons. Boston: Houghton Mifflin, 1886.
Indoor Studies. Boston: Houghton Mifflin, 1889.
Riverby. Boston: Houghton Mifflin, 1894.
Whitman: A Study. Boston: Houghton Mifflin, 1896.

The Light of Day. Boston: Houghton Mifflin, 1900.
"Narrative of the Expedition." In *Harriman Alaska Expedition,* edited by
    C. Hart Merriam. Vol. 1. New York: Doubleday, Page, 1901.
John James Audubon. Boston: Small, Maynard, 1902.
Literary Values and Other Papers. Boston: Houghton Mifflin, 1902.
Far and Near. Boston: Houghton Mifflin, 1904.
Ways of Nature. Boston: Houghton Mifflin, 1905.
Bird and Bough. Boston: Houghton Mifflin, 1906.
Camping with President Roosevelt. Boston: Houghton Mifflin, 1906. Reprinted
    in 1907 as *Camping and Tramping with Roosevelt,* with added chapter.
Leaf and Tendril. Boston: Houghton Mifflin, 1908.
Time and Change. Boston: Houghton Mifflin, 1912.
The Summit of the Years. Boston: Houghton Mifflin, 1913.
The Breath of Life. Boston: Houghton Mifflin, 1915.
Under the Apple Trees. Boston: Houghton Mifflin, 1916.
Field and Study. Boston: Houghton Mifflin, 1919.
Accepting the Universe. Boston: Houghton Mifflin, 1920.
Under the Maples. Boston: Houghton Mifflin, 1921.
The Last Harvest. Boston: Houghton Mifflin, 1922.
My Boyhood, with a Conclusion by His Son, Julian Burroughs. Garden City,
    N.Y.: Doubleday, Page, 1922.

Edited Collections and Reprint Editions
of Burroughs's Writings

Barrus, Clara, ed. *The Heart of Burroughs' Journals.* Boston: Houghton Mifflin,
    1928.
Bergon, Frank, ed. *A Sharp Lookout: Selected Nature Essays of John Burroughs.*
    Washington, D.C., and London: The Smithsonian Institution Press,
    1987.
Burroughs, John. *Accepting the Universe: Essays in Naturalism.* Commemora-
    tive edition. Edited by George W. Lugg. Boston: Houghton Mifflin,
    1920. Reprinted, Moore Haven, Fl.: Rainbow Books, 1987.
Burroughs, John. *In the Catskills: Selections from the Writings of John Burroughs.*
    West Park, N.Y.: Riverby Books, 1988. Reprint of 1910 Houghton
    Mifflin edition, copyright by Elizabeth Burroughs Kelley.
*John Burroughs at Troutbeck: Being Extracts from His Writings Published and
    Unpublished.* Introduction by Vachel Lindsay. Troutbeck Leaflets, no. 10,
    compiled by J. E. Springarn. Amenia, N.Y.: Troutbeck, 1926.

Dans, Charles F., ed. *Harvest of a Quiet Eye: The Natural World of John Burroughs.* Introduction by Edwin Way Teale. Madison, Wis.: Tamarack, 1976.

Fleck, Richard, ed. *Deep Woods: John Burroughs.* Syracuse, N.Y.: Syracuse Univ. Press, 1998.

Kelley, Elizabeth Burroughs, ed. *With John Burroughs in Field and Wood.* With illustrations by Elizabeth Burroughs Kelley. South Brunswick, N.J., and New York: A. S. Barnes, 1969.

Kligerman, Jack, ed. *The Birds of John Burroughs: A Great Naturalist's Meditations and Essays on Bird Watching.* Woodstock, N.Y.: Overlook, 1988.

McKibben, Bill, ed. *Birch Browsings.* New York: Penguin, 1993.

Renehan, Edward J., Jr., ed. *A River View and Other Hudson Valley Essays by John Burroughs.* Croton-on-Hudson, N.Y.: North River, 1981.

Wiley, Farida A., ed. *John Burroughs' America: Selections From the Writings of the Hudson River Naturalist.* Introduction by the editor, foreword by Julian Burroughs. New York: Devin Adair, 1951.

Books and Articles about John Burroughs

Askins, Justin. "'Thankfully, the Center Cannot Hold': John Burroughs." *North Dakota Quarterly* 59 (spring 1991): 45–61.

Barrus, Clara. *John Burroughs, Boy and Man.* New York: Doubleday, Page, 1920.

———. *The Life and Letters of John Burroughs.* 2 vols. Boston: Houghton Mifflin, 1925.

———. *Our Friend John Burroughs.* Boston: Houghton Mifflin, 1914.

———. *Whitman and Burroughs: Comrades.* Boston: Houghton Mifflin, 1931.

Black, Ralph. "John Burroughs." In *American Nature Writers,* vol. 1, edited by John Elder, 121–38. New York: Charles Scribner's Sons, 1996.

Brauer, Norman. *There to Breathe the Beauty: The Camping Trips of John Burroughs, Henry Ford, Thomas Edison, and Harvey Firestone.* Dalton, Penn.: Norman Brauer, 1995.

DeLoach, R. H. *Rambles With John Burroughs.* Boston: Gorham, 1912.

Garland, Hamlin. *Afternoon Neighbors.* New York: Macmillan, 1934.

———. *Roadside Meetings.* New York: Macmillan, 1930.

Goetzman, William H., and Kay Sloan. *Looking Far North: The Harriman Expedition to Alaska, 1899.* Princeton, N.J.: Princeton Univ. Press, 1982.

Frisbee, Lucy. *John Burroughs: Boy of Field and Stream.* "Childhood of Famous Americans" series. Indianapolis: Bobbs-Merrill, 1964.

Haring, H. A., ed. *The Slabsides Book of John Burroughs.* Boston: Houghton Mifflin, 1931.

Hubbard, Elbert [Fra Elbertus, pseudonym]. *Old John Burroughs.* East Aurora, N.Y.: Roycroft Bookshop, 1901.

Johnson, Clifton, ed. *John Burroughs Talks.* Boston: Houghton Mifflin, 1922.

Kanze, Edward. *The World of John Burroughs.* New York: Harry N. Abrams, 1991. Reprint, San Francisco: Sierra Club Books, 1999.

Kelley, Elizabeth Burroughs. *John Burroughs, Naturalist: The Story of His Work and Family by His Granddaughter.* 1959. Reprint, West Park, N.Y.: Riverby Books, 1986.

———. *John Burroughs' Slabsides.* Rhinebeck, N.Y.: Moran, 1974. Reprint, West Park, N.Y.: Riverby Books, 1987.

Kennedy, William Sloane. *The Real John Burroughs.* New York: Funk and Wagnalls, 1924.

McKibben, Bill. "The Call of the Not So Wild." *New York Review of Books,* 14 May 1992: 32–33.

Osborne, Clifford H. *The Religion of John Burroughs.* Boston: Houghton Mifflin, 1930.

Perkins, William. *Indexes to the Writings of John Burroughs.* New York: John Burroughs Association, 1995.

Renehan, Edward J., Jr. *John Burroughs, An American Naturalist.* Post Mills, Vt.: Chelsea-Green, 1992. Paperback edition, Hensonville, N.Y.: Black Dome, 1997.

Sharp, Dallas Lore. *The Boys' Life of John Burroughs.* New York: Century, 1928.

———. 1974. *The Seer of Slabsides.* 1921. Reprint, Boston: Houghton Mifflin, 1974.

Walker, Charlotte Zoë. "John Burroughs." In *Encyclopedia of the Essay,* edited by Tracy Chevalier, 130–32. London and Chicago: Fitzroy Dearborn, 1997.

———. ed. *Sharp Eyes: John Burroughs and American Nature Writing.* Syracuse, N.Y.: Syracuse Univ. Press, 2000.

Westbrook, Perry. *John Burroughs.* New York: Twayne, 1974.